Experiments and Competition Policy

Over the last decade, economists have been making much greater use of experimental methods in their research. The award of the Nobel Prize in 2002 to Vernon Smith confirmed that the use of such methods is now seen as an important and credible part of the economist's toolkit. In *Experiments and Competition Policy*, leading scholars in the field of experimental economics survey the use of experimental methods and show how they can help us understand the behavior of firms in relation to various forms of competition policy. Chapters are organized in terms of the main fields of competition policy — collusion, abusive practices and mergers — and there is also a separate section dealing with auctions and procurement. Written in a clear and nontechnical style, this volume is an excellent introduction to what the increasingly important field of experimental economics can bring to the theory and practice of competition policy.

JEROEN HINLOOPEN is Professor of Economics at the University of Amsterdam and at the Catholic University of Leuven. He is also Research Fellow of the Tinbergen Institute, a member of the editorial board of the *Review of Industrial Organization*, an ENCORE fellow and a fellow of the Amsterdam Centre for Law and Economics.

HANS-THEO NORMANN is Professor of Economics at Royal Holloway College, University of London. He is also Senior Research Fellow at the Max Planck Institute for Research on Collective Goods in Bonn and a fellow at ENCORE.

Experiments and Competition Policy

EDITED BY

JEROEN HINLOOPEN

AND

HANS-THEO NORMANN

CAMBRIDGE
UNIVERSITY PRESS

CAMBRIDGE
UNIVERSITY PRESS

University Printing House, Cambridge CB2 8BS, United Kingdom

One Liberty Plaza, 20th Floor, New York, NY 10006, USA

477 Williamstown Road, Port Melbourne, VIC 3207, Australia

4843/24, 2nd Floor, Ansari Road, Daryaganj, Delhi - 110002, India

79 Anson Road, #06-04/06, Singapore 079906

Cambridge University Press is part of the University of Cambridge.

It furthers the University's mission by disseminating knowledge in the pursuit of education, learning and research at the highest international levels of excellence.

www.cambridge.org
Information on this title: www.cambridge.org/9780521493420

© Cambridge University Press 2009

First published 2009

A catalogue record for this publication is available from the British Library

Library of Congress Cataloging in Publication data
Experiments and competition policy / [edited by] Jeroen Hinloopen,
Hans-Theo Normann.
    p.   cm.
    Includes index.
    ISBN 978-0-521-49342-0 (hardback)
    1. Competition. 2. Economics–Experiments. 3. Industrial policy.
    I. Hinloopen, Jeroen. II. Normann, Hans-Theo. III. Title.
    HD41.E97 2009
    338.8'2–dc22   2008050652

ISBN 978-0-521-49342-0 Hardback

Contents

Figures

Tables

Contributors

KLAUS ABBINK — Center for Research in Experimental Economics and Political Decision-making (CREED), Amsterdam School of Economics, University of Amsterdam

JORDI BRANDTS — Institut d'Anàlisi Econòmica, CSIC Barcelona

ERIC VAN DAMME — CentER for Economic Research and Tilburg Law and Economics Centre, Tilburg University

DIRK ENGELMANN — Department of Economics, Royal Holloway College, University of London

LORENZ GÖTTE — Federal Reserve Bank of Boston

VERONIKA GRIMM — Department of Economics University of Erlangen-Nuremberg

MARCO HAAN — Department of Economics and Econometrics, University of Groningen

JEROEN HINLOOPEN — Amsterdam School of Economics, University of Amsterdam

STEFFEN HUCK — Department of Economics and ELSE, University College London

PIERRE LAROUCHE — Law Faculty and Tilburg Law and Economics Centre, Tilburg University

FRIEDERIKE MENGEL — Department of Economics, Maastricht University

WIELAND MÜLLER — CentER for Economic Research and Tilburg Law and Economics Centre, Tilburg University

HANS-THEO NORMANN	Department of Economics, Royal Holloway College, University of London
THEO OFFERMAN	Center for Research in Experimental Economics and Political Decision-making (CREED), Amsterdam School of Economics, University of Amsterdam
SANDER ONDERSTAL	Center for Research in Experimental Economics and Political Decision-making (CREED), Amsterdam School of Economics, University of Amsterdam
GIOVANNI PONTI	Departamento de Fundamentos del Análisis Económico, Universidad de Alicante
JAN POTTERS	CentER for Economic Research and Tilburg Law and Economics Centre, Tilburg University
BRADLEY RUFFLE	Department of Economics, Ben-Gurion University of the Negev
ARMIN SCHMUTZLER	Socioeconomic Institute, University of Zurich
LAMBERT SCHOONBEEK	Department of Economics and Econometrics, University of Groningen
LARI ARTHUR VIIANTO	Departamento de Fundamentos del Análisis Económico, Universidad de Alicante
BARBARA WINKEL	Faculty of Economics and Business, University of Sydney

1 | Introduction

JEROEN HINLOOPEN AND
HANS-THEO NORMANN

This book comprises original research in the field of experimental economics and competition policies. All chapters have in common that they address specific competition issues, policy problems and institutions from the point of view of experimental economics. The chapters of the book cover basically all areas of competition policy making: collusive practices, abusive practices, mergers and we also include auctions. The aim of the book is to assess the scope and the specific contribution of laboratory experiments for competition law and policy. Where appropriate, the articles also cover the relevant legal and game-theoretic background.

The chapters have been specifically written for this book and are not available elsewhere. With one exception, all chapters have been presented at a workshop in Hilversum (Netherlands) in 2005. The workshop and this book are an initiative of the Dutch Economics Network for Competition and Regulation (ENCORE).

Competition issues have a long tradition in experimental economics. In one of the first economics experiments, Chamberlin (1948) already addressed questions central to competition policy. (See also Roth, 1993, on early contributions in experimental economics.) Chamberlin found that in his experimental markets (involving the sale of a fictitious good between many sellers and many buyers) negotiated prices failed to converge to the competitive equilibrium as most of the markets had an average price below the equilibrium. He noted "failure, upon reflection of the problem, to find any reason" why markets should converge to the competitive equilibrium. Yet, Nobel laureate Vernon Smith's (1962, 1964) experimental work on double auctions provided strong evidence that markets will be competitive. He changed Chamberlin's experimental design in some significant details and found reliable convergence to the competitive equilibrium. Later research confirmed this result in "at least a thousand market sessions" (Holt, 1995).

1

Smith's work led the way to detailed experimental analyses of various market "trading institutions". This research answers, for example, the following questions. Does it make a difference whether sellers' prices are fixed once posted or whether they remain flexible? To what extent does the number of sellers and buyers affect market outcomes? Does it matter if buyers are allowed to make price bids as opposed to sellers setting the price? What happens if sellers are quantity rather than price setters? This research gave rise to a large number of trading institutions that can be analyzed in the laboratory. Holt (1995) lists fourteen different types, and since then many new institutions have been developed, in particular various auction formats.

The design of these market trading institutions was often motivated by real-world (field) markets. For example, Smith (1962) mentions that his double-auction markets are similar to the stock exchange, and Holt (1995) points out the resemblance of another trading institution (the posted-offer market) to retail and mail-order markets. Outstanding along this line of research are the papers by Hong and Plott (1982) and Grether and Plott (1984) where the experiments mimic markets in actual antitrust cases rather closely and realistically in terms trading rules, numbers of firms and customers, and cost and demand parameters. A more recent contribution is by Deck and Wilson (2008).

Other researchers put less emphasis on realism of the trading institution and designed their experiments according to the requirements and assumptions of the theoretical model they wanted to test instead. A prominent early example is the work of Siegel and Fouraker (1960) and Fouraker and Siegel (1963). The research reported in these two books analyzes, to a large extent, standard economic textbook models like bilateral monopoly and Cournot oligopoly. Arguably few markets, if any, resemble a simple textbook Cournot duopoly with linear demand and cost. Nevertheless, Fouraker and Siegel's meticulous work shows that experimental tests of economic theories can provide interesting insights and can have implications for competition policy even though they may not resemble any markets in the field at all. For one thing, these experiments can indicate whether the theory underlying the experiments reliably predicts the results. If so, we can see this as support of the theory and the policy conclusions derived from it. Perhaps more importantly, the experimental data can also inform us about treatment effects where the theory is silent. For example, Fouraker and Siegel (1963) varied the information feedback to participants and found strong effects resulting from them. However, the Nash equilibrium prediction is unaffected by the changed information feedback. In such a case, the experiment goes beyond the theory and may indeed give rise to a newly modified theoretical approach.

Even if there is a long and pronounced tradition for addressing competition policy questions with experimental methods, the emphasis on policy questions in this book may provoke questions about the applicability of experiments. Can simple laboratory experiments, conducted with inexperienced student participants who get paid only relatively little money, be useful and informative regarding intricate policy questions? These objections are to be taken very seriously. There is, however, evidence strengthening the case for experiments. For example, an investigation about subject-pool effects by Ball and Cech (1996) showed that there are almost no systematic differences between student and non-student subject pools. Similarly, most experimental results prevail (at least qualitatively) when the monetary stakes are much higher (e.g. Slonim and Roth, 1998). As for the simplicity of the laboratory setup, it could be that this may also be an advantage. If some theoretical argument fails to have predictive power in the simple experimental markets, can we expect it to work well in more difficult and complex field environments? Could it be that, compared to the pure incentive structure of the experiment, the additional elements of the richer field environment cause further deviations from the prediction by blurring the incentives? These are important questions, and studying both the simple experimental environment and the complex environments in the field can lead to significant insights. The experimental evidence should probably best be seen as complementary to field studies. (See also Plott, 1982, 1989 who lists — and refutes — the most common objections against laboratory methods.)

The chapters in this book are organized in terms of main fields of competition policy: collusion, abusive practices and mergers. We also include a separate part on auctions and procurement.

Part I is on collusion and starts with an informative survey by Marco Haan, Lambert Schoonbeek and Barbara Winkel on collusion experiments. They study a broad range of issues and make a case in favor of specific and realistically designed experiments in the tradition of Hong and Plott (1982) and Grether and Plott (1984). They also identify a number of topics in the area that have hitherto not been explored. The second chapter in this section is an intriguing and innovative experiment by Klaus Abbink and Jordi Brandts. They study the classic problem of whether price agreements are more stable in phases of high or low demand. Contrary to game-theoretic predictions but in line with the "conventional wisdom" in the informal industrial organization literature, they find that shrinking, not growing, markets facilitate collusion. Dirk Engelmann and Hans-Theo Normann report on an experiment on the collusive effects of price ceilings. Despite numerous design features chosen to facilitate coordination via the price ceiling, they find no evidence that price ceilings matter. Finally Jan Potters reviews experimental results on how market transparency affects prices and the likelihood of a price conspiracy. The chapter carefully distinguishes between transparency on past, current and future conduct. One interesting conclusion is that a high degree of market transparency may be a consequence rather than a cause of collusion.

Part II contains two chapters on abusive practices. The chapter by Eric van Damme, Pierre Larouche and Wieland Müller covers the entire range of abusive practices. In a very comprehensive study, they review the EU Case Law and Commission decision practice under article 82 and relate this to existing experimental literature. Bradley Ruffle's chapter covers the research relating to buyer power (sometimes also labeled "countervailing power"). This issue has recently attracted a lot of attention among policy makers as the level of bargaining of power of the buyers in the inputs markets has reached unprecedented heights in several industries.

Part III contains the research chapter on mergers. Lorenz Götte and Armin Schmutzler survey the existing merger experiments. They draw some very positive conclusions about the insights from merger experiments but they also note the lack of a clear research agenda and identify problems regarding the external validity of experiments. Steffen Huck provides new data on the "merger paradox", which says that mergers will often not be profitable. Even though he lets participants play in a market with a Stackelberg leader–follower structure where the paradox should be resolved and where mergers should pay off, the merged firms jointly still do not earn more than before the merger.

The final part, Part IV, is on auctions. It contains a chapter by Theo Offerman and Sander Onderstal. In auctions, collusion, abusive practices and also mergers can be relevant. Therefore, the section on auctions is separate from the other chapters of the book. The authors review a large number of auction formats with respect to their performance in terms of generating revenues and overall economic efficiency. The chapter by Veronika Grimm, Friederike Mengel, Giovanni Ponti and Lari Arthur Viianto is on procurement auctions. Using laboratory data, they show how the auctions format affects incentives for cost-reducing investments.

In the concluding Chapter 12, we discuss more specifically the use of experimental economics for the enforcement of competition policies. We give some examples and report on laboratory data partly generated with executives of the Dutch competition authority as participants.

References

Ball, S.B. and Cech, P.A. (1996), Subject Pool Choice and Treatment Effects in Economic Laboratory Research, in: R.M. Isaac (ed.), *Research in Experimental Economics* Volume VI, JAI Press, Greenwich, 239–292.

Deck, C.A. and Wilson, B. (2008), Experimental Gasoline Markets, *Journal of Economic Behavior and Organization*, 67(1), 134–149.

Chamberlin, E.H. (1948), An experimental imperfect market, *Journal of Political Economy* 56(2), 95–108.

Fouraker, Lawrence E. and Siegel, Sidney (1963), *Bargaining Behavior*, New York: McGraw-Hill.

Grether, David M. and Plott, Charles R. (1984), The Effects of Market Practices in Oligopolistic Markets: An Experimental Examination of the Ethyl Case, *Economic Inquiry* 22, 479–507.

Holt, Charles A. (1995), Industrial Organization: A Survey of Laboratory Research, in J. Kagel and A. Roth (eds.), *Handbook of Experimental Economics*, Princeton: Princeton University Press, 349–443.

Hong, James T. and Plott, Charles R. (1982), Rate Filing Policies for Inland Water Transportation: An Experimental Approach, *Bell Journal of Economics* 13, 1–19.

Plott, Charles R. (1982), Industrial Organization Theory and Experimental Economics, *Journal of Economic Literature* 20, 1485–1527.

(1989), An Updated Review of Industrial Organization Applications of Experimental Methods, in R. Schmalensee and R. Willig (eds.), *Handbook of Industrial Organization* Volume II, Elsevier Science Publishers B.V., 1111–1176.

Roth, Alvin E. (1993), On the Early History of Experimental Economics, *Journal of the History of Economic Thought* 15, 184–209.

Siegel, Sidney and Fouraker, Lawrence E. (1960), *Bargaining and Group Decisions Making*, New York: McGraw-Hill.
Slonim, Robert and Roth, Alvin E. (1998), Learning in High Stakes Ultimatum Games: An Experiment in the Slovak Republic, *Econometrica* 66, 569–596.
Smith, Vernon L. (1962), An Experimental Study of Competitive Market Behavior, *Journal of Political Economy* 70:2, 111–137.
    (1964), The effect of market organization on competitive equilibrium, *Quarterly Journal of Economics* 78: 181–201.

PART I

2 | Experimental results on collusion

MARCO A. HAAN, LAMBERT SCHOONBEEK
AND BARBARA M. WINKEL*

We review the experimental literature on collusion, focusing in particular on the role of information. We confront the results with the theoretical literature and discuss the policy implications. The main insights from the experimental literature are the following. In the standard environment, firms have little success in achieving collusion. The only mildly collusive results are achieved when just two firms are active. Evidence on the effect of increasing the amount of available information on the likelihood of collusion is mixed. Voluntary information sharing has some collusive effect, even though collusion is not the main reason that firms choose to do so. The availability of the history of an industry's past prices seems to have some effect on the ability to collude.

1. Introduction

Collusion is a major issue in competition policy. One important objective of competition authorities is to prevent firms that are supposed to compete against each other from achieving prices that are higher than the prices that would result from free and fair competition. Another important objective is to track down and punish those firms that do engage in price- or quantity-fixing agreements.

It is not easy to achieve these goals, especially in a world in which competition authorities have only limited funds at their disposal, and need to make choices with respect to the firms and industries they investigate. Many important yet difficult questions have to be answered. When exactly are prices too high? Is collusion always detrimental, or are there circumstances in which it can actually be beneficial? How can one establish that an industry engages in collusion? Under what circumstances is collusion more likely to occur? Which market structures and which market institutions are susceptible to

* The authors thank Eric van Damme, Jeroen Hinloopen and Hans-Theo Normann for useful comments and discussion.

collusion, and therefore deserve closer scrutiny from antitrust authorities? Many related questions readily spring to mind.

In trying to answer these questions, policy makers can draw upon a large and growing body of economic research. Economic theory provides a framework to understand what collusion entails exactly, why it is harmful, and which market data are consistent with price fixing. The framework is that of repeated games, pioneered by Friedman (1971) and described in more detail in e.g. Tirole (1988) or Motta (2004). Empirical economics provides tools that are helpful in evaluating whether certain markets are collusive. Experimental economics provides further insights into which institutional settings are most susceptible to collusion. In this chapter, we survey those insights. Our aim is thus to give an overview of the experimental results on collusion. In doing so, we try to emphasize how these experimental methods and results can be of help to policy makers.

We are not the first to survey at least some of the experimental literature on collusion. Holt (1995) is an excellent survey of experimental work in the field of industrial organization in general, and also gives an extensive discussion of collusion. Wellford (2002) is a more recent survey of similar issues. Huck *et al.* (2004) provide a useful overview of experimental studies with repeated oligopolies that have Cournot competition as a stage game, and that study the effect of the number of firms on cartel stability. Our focus is not so much on the experimental details of the papers that we survey. Rather, we emphasize the relevance for our understanding of real-world markets. As a final caveat, we do not do full justice to all papers that we discuss, in the sense that we do not always give a full description of the main research questions that these papers address, and do not always evaluate the papers in the light of their original research questions. Rather we only discuss the aspects of these experiments that can teach us something about collusion.

Arguably, there are two broad categories of experimental work regarding collusion. On the one hand, we have the experiments that are primarily inspired by theory, and that mainly aim to test that theory. On the other hand, we have experiments that are more loosely related to theoretical work, and that mainly aim to identify the factors that facilitate or hinder collusion in the real world. Needless to say, the latter category is of particular interest to policy makers. Nevertheless, the first category is also relevant, as it aims to test the theory that ultimately underlies competition policy towards collusion. We therefore survey both categories.

In the next section we first give a short introduction into the theory of collusion. As noted, the insights obtained in theoretical work have been a major source of inspiration for experimental work. Therefore, a short discussion of that theory is indispensable. We will especially discuss the theoretical work that has relevance for either experiments or policy. Section 3 gives some general background to experiments in this field. Section 4 addresses the question of to what extent firms in experiments are able to collude. For that purpose, we survey the experiments that are as close to the standard theory as possible. The remainder of the chapter studies institutional environments that may hinder or facilitate collusion. Factors concerning the amount of information that market participants have and that is typically provided by trade associations are discussed in Section 5.

Our chapter ends with a conclusion, in which we sketch the main lessons that can be drawn from experiments, and their relevance for real markets. One should however be careful in drawing general real-world lessons from experiments in collusion. A situation in which inexperienced students have to make decisions in a matter of seconds is fundamentally different from one in which multinationals can spend months pondering the strategic decisions to be made. Still, experiments are potentially able to tell more about antitrust policy towards collusion than they have done so far. Many experiments are primarily designed to test the existing theory rather than to test how collusion may occur in the real world, and how an antitrust authority may be able to curb collusion. We will discuss how experiments may further aid to shape policy in this important area.

2. A short overview of the standard theory

The typical textbook treatment of oligopoly behavior starts with static competition models. In such models firms meet only once. The non-cooperative Nash equilibrium has each firm setting a price or quantity that maximizes its profits, given the action taken by its competitors. Profits of each firm would be higher if the firms could agree to either restrict output, or set a higher price. Yet, in a one-shot game such an agreement is impossible to make. Every firm would have an incentive to defect from the agreement. Doing so would increase profits, at the expense of the other firms. Moreover, a defection cannot have any future repercussions, as there simply is no future in a one-shot model.

In a seminal paper, Friedman (1971) introduced a dynamic model. In his paper, firms play a supergame which consists of a simple static stage game that is repeated an infinite number of times. This changes the picture entirely. In the noncooperative subgame-perfect equilibrium of a repeated game, firms *are* able to achieve profits that are higher than the Nash profits in a one-shot game, provided that the discount factor is high enough. Even the cooperative equilibrium of the one-shot game can be achieved as the noncooperative equilibrium of a repeated game. In other words, in a repeated game, firms may be able to maximize their joint profits. Moreover, they may be able to do so without any of the firms having an incentive to defect and increase its profits. A firm that defects now faces the possibility of adverse effects in the future, as this will likely cause a breakdown of the cartel. Hence, a firm will only defect if the short-term benefits of doing so outweigh the long-term costs caused by the breakdown of the cartel. Importantly, firms can even do so without making an explicit agreement. In the literature, this is referred to as *tacit collusion*, contrary to *overt collusion*, where an explicit agreement is made.

The simplest possible version of this model is as follows. Suppose that we have n identical firms that form a cartel. The Nash equilibrium profits of the stage game are denoted Π^N. Per-period profits of each firm in the cartel are denoted Π^k, with $\Pi^k > \Pi^N$. Defecting from the agreement yields a one-time profit of $\Pi^d > \Pi^k$. Suppose that the firms have the implicit understanding that, as soon as one of them defects from the cartel agreement, they will play the one-shot equilibrium forever after. This is a *grim trigger strategy*. In each period, every firm then faces a tradeoff. By sticking to the cartel agreement, it can earn Π^k in every period. By cheating, it will earn Π^d in this period, but only Π^N in every future period. When the discount factor is denoted by δ, each firm will thus stick to the agreement if and only if

$$\Pi^k + \delta\Pi^k + \delta^2\Pi^k + \delta^3\Pi^k + \delta^4\Pi^k + \cdots$$
$$\geq \Pi^d + \delta\Pi^N + \delta^2\Pi^N + \delta^3\Pi^N + \delta^4\Pi^N + \cdots$$

After some rearranging, this condition can be written as

$$\delta \geq (\Pi^d - \Pi^k)/(\Pi^d - \Pi^N) \tag{1}$$

If (1) is satisfied, the cartel is said to be stable. If the condition is not satisfied, every firm knows in advance that nobody will adhere to the agreement, which in turn implies that such an agreement will never be made.

This model of collusion is simple and attractive, and also readily yields interesting comparative-statics results (see Tirole, 1988 or Motta, 2004). First, it can be shown that an increase in the number of firms makes it less likely that collusion will occur. An increase in the number of firms will usually imply a decrease in per-firm cartel profits Π^k that is larger than the decrease in Nash profits of the stage game Π^N. As Π^d will often increase, the right-hand side of (1) will be larger. Hence there is a smaller range of the discount factor, δ, for which collusion is stable. Also, when firms meet less often, or can observe each other's behavior less often, collusion becomes less likely. The effective defection profits Π^d will then be higher as a defection goes undetected for a longer time. Again, this implies a smaller range of δ for which (1) holds. See Ivaldi *et al.* (2003) for more comparative-statics results that are beyond the scope of this chapter.

However, the collusion model has one major drawback, which is the multiplicity of equilibria. Note that in the discussion above we have not pinned down Π^k in any manner. Indeed, the theory only states that *any* agreement that yields cartel profits $\Pi^k > \Pi^N$ can be sustained as a Nash equilibrium of the repeated game, provided that (1) is satisfied. But the multiplicity of equilibria is even worse. So far, we have assumed grim trigger strategies. But also the punishment phase is not uniquely determined. Abreu (1986) shows that other forms of punishment may yield cartel stability for a larger range of the minimum discount factor. He focuses on *stick and carrot strategies*, where firms earn a negative profit in the period after the deviation, and return to collusive behavior in the subsequent period.

To reflect the multiplicity of equilibria, we will refer in the remainder of this chapter to a *collusive outcome* as *any* outcome of the market process in which realized profits are higher than the Nash equilibrium profits of the stage game. We will refer to *perfect collusion* as a situation in which firms manage to maximize their joint profits. We thus focus on an economic rather than a legal definition of collusion. For example, legal action often also requires that there is some explicit agreement between firms. Following the economic literature, we merely require that "prices are higher than some competitive benchmark" (Motta, 2004: 138), and hence that profits are also higher than the benchmark.

One crucial assumption in the theory set out above is that the game is repeated an infinite number of times. As soon as the number of periods is finite and known in advance, the entire logic breaks down. Firms then know that in the final period they will all defect from any collusive agreement they could possibly have, as there is no future left in that period. Backward induction implies that they will also defect in the penultimate period, knowing that they will play the Nash equilibrium of the stage game in the final period. Carrying through this logic implies that collusion can never be stable, and firms play the static Nash equilibrium in every single period. This argument dates back to Selten (1978), albeit in a slightly different context. In the next section, we will discuss how experiments deal with this problem.

As argued above, the model is often interpreted as one of tacit collusion, i.e. a situation in which firms do not have to formally agree on some collusive arrangement. But that interpretation becomes hard to swallow with such a multiplicity of equilibria. It seems that in practice firms at least need to communicate in order to make some agreement about which of the infinitely many equilibria they are going to play.

This issue becomes even more relevant when firms are asymmetric with respect to e.g. their cost function, their individual demand or their discount factor. In the real world, this is obviously the case. In an idealized world where firms are perfectly symmetric and demand is known, there may be an infinite number of equilibria, but there is one obvious focal equilibrium, which is the one that maximizes joint profits of the firms. If firms are asymmetric, such a focal equilibrium does not exist. Hence, coordination then becomes even more difficult. For a theoretical exposition of collusion among asymmetric firms, see e.g. Harrington (1989).

The basic model assumes that firms can readily observe the price or quantity their competitors set, and can react accordingly. In reality, this will often not be the case. Stigler (1964) already argued that if firms cannot observe each other's actions, collusion is less likely, as there is scope for secret price cuts. Green and Porter (1984) assume that there is uncertainty regarding total market demand. A simplified version of their model, which is due to Tirole (1988), is as follows.

Suppose that in each period demand can be either high or low. Each firm can only observe its own demand. It cannot observe the price set by its competitor, and neither can it observe total market demand. Suppose that in a given period a firm observes that its own sales are low. This may be due to low market demand, but it may also be due to the other firm cheating on the cartel agreement by setting a low price. Hence, when a firm's sales are low, it is clearly not a good idea to play the Nash equilibrium of the one-shot game in all future periods. Such a reaction would imply a fierce punishment, whereas it may well be the case that no one has cheated. Green and Porter show that under certain conditions the best strategy is a punishment phase that lasts for a finite number of periods. After that punishment phase, firms go back to the collusive agreement. Such a strategy yields the optimal tradeoff between taking into account the possibility of low market demand on the one hand, and on the other hand preventing defections from the collusive agreement. In such a framework, collusion becomes more difficult to sustain than in the standard case. Defection will be very tempting in a high-demand period, as the defection profits are evaluated for a high state of demand, whereas future cartel profits will be evaluated as the average for low- and high-demand states. Thus, compared to a case of constant demand, defection profits will increase relative to cartel profits, making defection more attractive.

Summarizing, the main results from the theory are as follows:

- When firms meet repeatedly, collusive outcomes can be sustained in a subgame-perfect equilibrium.
- Collusion becomes more difficult as the number of firms increases, as firms meet less often, or as firms observe each other's behavior less often.
- Many collusive outcomes can be sustained in equilibrium, and different punishment strategies can be part of an equilibrium. Hence, especially when firms cannot communicate, it may be hard for them to coordinate on some collusive outcome.
- Asymmetric firms will find it harder to coordinate on a collusive outcome.
- When firms cannot fully observe each other's actions, collusion may still be feasible, but is less likely to occur.

3. Some experimental issues

It is not always straightforward how to implement theories regarding collusion in economic experiments. Many choices need to be made, regarding e.g. the trading institution, the mode of competition, and the way the demand side of the market is implemented. Implementing the possibility of collusion in an experiment inevitably requires one to make choices regarding the set-up of that experiment. In this section, we highlight and discuss some possible choices.

Note that the theory describes a situation in which the same group of firms play a repeated game for an infinite number of periods. For that reason, we mostly restrict attention to experiments that use the same group composition for the entire duration of the experiment, rather than, say, reshuffling groups after each trading period. Of course it is impossible to play an infinitely repeated game in the laboratory. It can be shown, however, that this is analytically equivalent to having a fixed probability of the experiment ending after each period, with the discount factor equal to the probability of continuation. Experiments therefore often use such a fixed probability of continuation after each period, provided that a certain minimum number of periods has been played. On the other hand, there is probably relatively little harm in using a fixed horizon in collusion experiments, provided that that horizon is sufficiently long. Indeed, Selten and Stoecker (1986) note that the observed behavior in a treatment with a long finite horizon is very similar to behavior observed in an infinitely repeated game, apart from an end-game effect.

After determining the number of periods and group composition, an important issue is how to implement the actual market. A first crucial choice is whether to use real buyers, or to implement a simulated market using some implicit demand function. With real buyers, the next choice is the trading institution to use. With a demand function, the next choice is the mode of competition to use.

First, consider the trading institution. Holt (1995; section 5) gives an exhaustive description of all possibilities. For our purposes, the following institutions deserve attention. Consider a market in which both buyers and sellers are active. In a *posted-offer auction*, each seller independently selects a price, and buyers are called on in random order to make purchase decisions. In a *posted-bid auction*, each buyer selects a price, and sellers are called on in random order to make selling decisions. In a *double auction* buyers and sellers are treated symmetrically, in the sense that both can actively post and accept prices. The choice of trading institution can have a crucial influence on the outcome of the experiment. For example, Smith (1981) compares these institutions using a monopolist seller. In the last session of each of his experiments, he calculates the *monopoly effectiveness index*, defined as the difference between the actual profit and the competitive profit, divided by the difference between the theoretical monopoly profit and the competitive profit. Thus, when a monopoly can perfectly exploit its monopoly power, the index will be equal to one. When the monopolist only manages to set a price equal to marginal costs, the index equals zero. Smith (1981) finds that with a posted-offer monopoly the average value of the index in his experiments is 1. With a posted-bid monopoly it is only 0.15, whereas it equals 0.36 with a double-auction monopoly. These results suggest that the results of collusion experiments with active buyers should be treated with particular care. If an oligopoly is not able to reach the perfectly collusive outcome, then this may not say too much about the possibility of collusion when in that particular trading institution even a monopoly is not able to achieve the monopoly outcome.

The second factor to consider is the mode of competition. Some experimentalists prefer the use of Cournot models, whereas others prefer Bertrand models. Bertrand competition can be studied using homogeneous products. In that case, competition has a winner-take-all character: the firm that sets the lowest price will capture the entire market. Alternatively, Bertrand competition can be studied with heterogeneous products. If that is the case, firms that do not set the lowest price may still earn positive profits. In many experiments, subjects are not given the explicit demand, cost and profit function. Rather, they face a payoff table that gives their payoffs for all possible choices of themselves and their competitors. Such a payoff table may consist of many possible choices, but there are also cases in which subjects can choose between only three options; for example, a high, an intermediate or a low price.

The choice between using Bertrand or Cournot competition is a contentious issue. Holt (1995), for example, argues against the use of Cournot competition, since it implies the use of a rather mechanical market-clearing assumption. In most market contexts, price setting seems a much more natural assumption and for that reason, industrial organization economists prefer the use of price rather than quantity competition to study such markets. Of course, following Kreps and Scheinkman (1983) one could defend the use of Cournot competition with the argument that if firms first choose capacities and then set prices, the outcome will be the Cournot equilibrium.

Unfortunately, the experimental evidence for the Kreps–Scheinkman defense is weak. Davis (1999) considers triopoly markets. There are two treatments: the first is a posted-offer market; the second is a posted-offer market with advance production. Without advance production, prices decline slowly toward the competitive level, where prices equal marginal costs. With advance production, prices are somewhat higher and quantities somewhat lower. However, there is no convergence to Cournot levels. Muren (2000) also considers triopolies with advance production. In sessions with inexperienced participants quantities are higher than the Cournot level. In sessions with experienced participants outcomes are close to the Cournot level. Anderhub *et al.* (2003) look at duopoly markets with heterogeneous goods where sellers first choose a capacity, then a price. Chosen capacities are fixed for five periods. In the first ten periods, quantities are exogenously fixed. In contrast to Davis (1999) and Muren (2000), capacity constraints are not strict: sellers can sell more at a cost. Subjects set prices at or close to the equilibrium level most of the time, given the capacity choices. Capacity choices are clustered around the competitive level, and to a lesser extent around the Cournot level, with the average between the two. So, Anderhub *et al.* (2003) also do not find that capacity-then-price competition leads to Cournot outcomes. Thus, as the Kreps–Scheinkman defense of Cournot competition finds little support in the laboratory, it seems indeed preferable to conduct experiments with price rather than quantity setting.

Experiments regarding collusion also differ in more subtle ways, for example with respect to the amount of information that firms receive regarding the market environment, and with respect to the possibilities to communicate. The effect that information has on the extent of collusion is an issue that we address in Section 5 of this chapter[1].

---

[1] As mentioned in the introduction, the effects of communication are studied in Potters (this volume).

4. Experimental tests of the standard theory

In this section, we first try to answer the question as to whether firms in experiments manage to collude in the first place. In other words, we consider experiments with a set-up that is as close as possible to the canonical theoretical model outlined in Section 2: firms meet each other repeatedly, and no communication is possible. Are firms in such experiments able to collude? That is, are they able to achieve profits that are consistently above the Nash equilibrium profits of the stage game? And if so, are they able to reach the price that maximizes their joint profits?

Huck *et al.* (2004) survey the evidence for Cournot models. All the experiments they consider have no communication. After each round, firms only receive aggregate information about the behavior of other firms. There is complete information about their own payoff function, and firms are symmetric. Huck *et al.* (2004) find that, in studies with two firms, total output falls short of the Cournot prediction by some 7% on average. Hence, industries with two firms manage to collude to some extent; total quantity is lower than in the Cournot model and profits are higher. Yet, these firms come nowhere near perfect collusion, in which joint industry profits are maximized. With a linear demand function, which is commonly used in experiments, perfect collusion would imply that total output falls short of the Cournot prediction by 25%.

With more than two firms the effect disappears entirely. On average, total output in markets with more than two firms slightly exceeds the Cournot prediction. Tentatively, this effect seems to become slightly stronger as the number of firms increases, but this is barely significant. Hence, there seems to be a discontinuity when moving from two to three firms. In experiments, industries with two firms have at least some success in achieving collusion. Industries with more than two firms are not successful in doing so at all. In fact, this result was already found in the seminal experiments by Fouraker and Siegel (1963). They find industry outputs often below the Cournot level with a duopoly, but above the Cournot level in about two-thirds of the cases with a triopoly.

So far, we have only discussed aggregate outcomes. Individual differences between markets can be huge. Nevertheless, from his reading of the literature, Holt (1995) notes that "with Cournot duopolies, outcomes fall on both sides of the Cournot prediction, and some cases of near collusion occur [...] with more than two sellers, outcomes are often more competitive than the Cournot prediction" (p. 404). He also concludes that increasing the number of sellers results in more competitive behavior. But with more than three sellers, there "seems to be little or no evidence for a pure-numbers effect that is measured by changing the number of sellers in a way that does not alter the incentive structure" (p. 409).

In experiments with Bertrand pricing, results are similar to those with Cournot competition. From her review of the experimental literature, Wellford (2002) concludes that price-setting duopolies are sometimes able to achieve collusive outcomes, but that there is often fierce competition. With more than two firms, competitive outcomes are again the norm.

Some papers have tried to gain more insights into how exactly firms in experiments behave. Mason and Phillips (2002) investigate whether trigger strategies can explain observed behavior in infinitely repeated experimental Cournot duopolies with perfect information. Using a comparative-statics approach, they conclude that observed behavior is generally consistent with the use of such strategies. They also find evidence that observed behavior is better explained by grim trigger strategies than by stick and carrot strategies (see Section 2). Selten *et al.* (1997), however, seem to contradict this. They elicit strategies from experienced players in a two-player Cournot game using the strategy method, in which subjects have to specify in advance how they will react to different possible choices of their opponents. The authors find that players use strategies that are similar to the tit for tat strategies in Axelrod (1984).

It is an interesting question why in an experiment, at least with Cournot competition, two firms are able to collude, whereas three firms are never able to do so. Holt (1995) gives an intriguing interpretation. The difference may be due to the inability of triopolists to punish one noncooperative rival without harming the other. The standard model predicts that, after a defection from some implicit cartel agreement, firms will punish other firms forever by effectively abandoning the cartel. Yet, such punishment is crude and might be ill-directed. In the case of two firms, the punishment is still relatively straightforward. When one firm defects, the other reacts by setting a much higher quantity in all future periods. This indeed hurts the other firm. But now consider a set-up in which more firms are active. Suppose again that one firm defects. When one of the other firms reacts by increasing its quantity, it will not only punish the defector, but will also adversely affect the other firms. It is likely that subjects in experiments will be much more reluctant to carry out such a punishment. First, they often cannot observe which firm exactly did the defection. Second, even if they could observe this, they would not be able to single out this firm for punishment. Indeed, much of the experimental literature suggests that subjects are driven by some sense of fairness, over and above the objectives that are routinely assumed by economists. And once firms are reluctant to punish a defection from some collusive agreement, it becomes much more attractive to defect in the first place. This in turn makes it much less likely that cartels will be formed.

One may question, however, whether firms in the real world are also driven by a sense of fairness. Indeed, subjects in experiments may be reluctant to punish cartel defection when this also hurts innocent firms. But it is likely that firms in the real world will be much less reluctant to punish in that manner. One may argue that in reality firms will be much less concerned about the well-being of their competitors than firms in experiments are. If that is indeed the case, then real-world industries with more than two firms are more likely to collude than industries in experiments with more than two firms. As a result, the discontinuity in the success of collusion when moving from two to three firms may just be an artifact of experimental work.

Summarizing, economic experiments that test the standard *tacit* collusion model find the following. Industries with two firms are able to collude to some extent. But they are not able to achieve perfect collusion by far: on average, total output is still much closer to Cournot equilibrium output than it is to monopoly output. Industries with more than two firms are not able to collude at all. However, this may be an artifact of experiments. A plausible explanation is that firms are reluctant to implicitly punish firms that did not defect from the collusive outcome. Arguably, real-world firms are much less reluctant to do so. In Section 6 of this chapter, we will give a more extensive discussion on what collusion experiments can teach us about the real world.

It is important to note that in all the experiments considered so far, firms were not able to communicate. Hence, these were all tests of truly tacit collusion. As we argued in Section 2, one may indeed expect that firms will find it hard to collude in such a world. The model allows for a wide range of possible equilibria and without an exchange of information and communication it may be hard to coordinate on one of these. Therefore, in Section 5 we study the role of information in experiments. Interestingly, in a survey paper on competition policy enforcement against collusion, Kühn (2001) focuses on these exact same issues.

5. The role of information

In the experiments described in the previous section, firms know their own payoff functions, and they know that firms are symmetric, so they can also infer their competitor's payoff function. In this section we review the literature that studies the effects of changing the information regime. Such effects are important: if more information indeed facilitates collusion then institutions such as trade associations, which collect and disseminate information among their members, can be deemed a facilitating practice. More generally, policy makers may then need to devise specific policies as to which information competing firms can share with their competitors or their consumers, and which information they cannot share. For a full discussion on such issues, see Kühn (2001).

In this section, we consider information regarding the state of the world. We first study experiments in which the availability of that information is exogenously given. We then consider experiments in which firms decide for themselves whether to share private information with the competitors.[2] Finally, we report on experiments which analyze the impact the history of an industry has.

In our discussion we will not so much focus on the extent to which firms in experiments are successful in colluding. Rather, we will stress the comparative statics of collusion. In other words, we will study the extent to which changing some aspect of the environment in which firms operate has an effect on their ability to collude. We will focus on recent work.

---

[2] A recent strand of the theoretical literature suggests that information regarding past actions and profits of competitors may induce firms to imitate the firm that has achieved the highest profits in the past. If true, this would yield the perfectly competitive outcome in the long run, with prices equal to marginal costs. The chapter by Potters in this volume reviews experiments testing this hypothesis.

5.1. Information about the state of the world

Dolbear *et al.* (1968) are among the first to study the role of information in experiments regarding collusion. They implement what effectively boils down to a Bertrand model with differentiated products, in markets with two, four, or sixteen firms. It turns out that information about the rivals' payoff function does not have a significant effect on average price and profit levels. This information increases the variability across markets, but reduces the variability within a market. Also, the number of firms adversely affects the extent of collusion in this experiment.

Mason and Phillips (1997) study the effect of uncertainty about the rival's cost function in a Cournot duopoly with homogeneous products. For each firm, marginal costs can be either high or low. With incomplete information, firms only know their own marginal costs. With complete information they also know the costs of their competitor. With incomplete information, outputs in the experiment are close to Cournot levels. In asymmetric markets, where both firms have different marginal costs, the same is true with complete information. But in symmetric markets with complete information, outputs are significantly lower. This suggests that information about one's competitor facilitates collusion — but only if firms are symmetric. Also, information about one's competitor reduces the variability within a market. Mason and Phillips argue that their results justify a rule-of-reason approach towards information sharing. If information sharing takes place between firms with symmetric costs, then anti-trust authorities should be concerned. If firms have asymmetric costs, there is less need to worry. Of course, it is hard to see how such a policy could be implemented. Mason and Phillips note that their incomplete information set-up is related to Green and Porter (1984), which we discussed in Section 2. For the results in Green and Porter, however, it is crucial that the rival's payoff function may fluctuate in every period. In this experiment, the rival's payoff function is fixed.

Feinberg and Snyder (2002) is more closely related to Green and Porter (1984). They conduct an experiment with symmetric price-setting duopolists. Importantly, firms can only choose among three prices: a collusive price, an undercutting price and a punishment price. Obviously, prices are not labeled as such in the experiment. If demand is given and known in each period, the results show some convergence to the collusive outcome. A second treatment introduces negative demand shocks in 10–15% of all periods. A demand shock leads to low payoffs irrespective of the rival's choice, and is revealed immediately after it occurs. Competitors' prices are no longer revealed after each period. In this treatment, the temptation to collude in the experiment remains unaffected. If the demand shock is not revealed after it has occurred, there is a sharp decline in collusion. Thus, uncertainty about both rivals' actions *and* demand turns out to dramatically impede collusion. This is particularly interesting as the set-up has no effect on the theoretical ability to collude; parameters are chosen such that collusion is always an equilibrium. This suggests that the anti-collusive effect of demand uncertainty and the possibility of secret price cuts is stronger than suggested by Green and Porter (1984). Other aspects of behavior are in line with the theory. Punishments are mostly used one period after the rival has chosen an undercutting price, and after such a punishment period firms mostly revert to the collusive price.

Summarizing, evidence on the effect of information regarding the competitor's type on the ability to collude is mixed. More information regarding the competitor's type does make a given market more stable, but also less predictable. Demand shocks have no effect on the ability to collude — provided that the demand shock is revealed afterwards.

5.2. The decision to share information

In the experiments described above, the possible sharing of information is merely something that is imposed by the experimenter. Some experimental papers investigate whether voluntary information sharing might facilitate collusion. A body of theoretical research studies whether such arrangements are desirable. Typically, papers in this area study one-shot duopoly models in which firms first decide whether to exchange information about uncertain demand or cost conditions, and then compete on the output market. The predictions of this literature are ambiguous. Vives (1984) shows that with quantity competition, demand uncertainty and substitute products, the equilibrium has firms concealing information from their rivals. Based on such results, Clarke (1983) argues that information-sharing arrangements must be considered as direct evidence of collusive behavior.

Cason (1994) studies a one-period price-setting duopoly with differentiated products. There may be uncertainty regarding either demand or marginal costs, which is equal for both firms. Only firm 1 receives accurate information, and has to decide in advance whether to share this with its rival. In most cases, prices in the experiment are close to Nash equilibrium levels. Only with cost uncertainty and complementary goods, some collusive pricing is observed if firm 1 chooses to share information. Hence, the experiments provide only weak support for the claim that information sharing between firms enhances the possibility of collusive behavior.

However, that picture may change entirely if we study this issue in the framework of a repeated game. Cason and Mason (1999) do exactly that. In their experiment, a duopoly sells homogeneous products and competes in quantities. Demand is unknown. In each period, each firm first decides whether it will share information with its rival. Then, each firm receives some signal about true demand. Demand can be high, medium or low. If *both* firms have chosen to share information, then combining the two signals allows one to infer the true state of demand. Without information sharing, each firm remains only imperfectly informed about true demand. Finally, firms compete. At the end of each period, firms are informed about their own payoff as well as the rival's output choice and payoff. The set-up is such that in the theoretical equilibrium of a one-shot game each firm chooses to conceal information.

In the experiment, firms often share information. In cases where they do, they reduce output significantly below the Cournot output in situations with high demand, and even more so in situations with low demand. This is in line with the predictions of Rotemberg and Saloner (1986) who argue that in states with low demand, collusion is more effective. In the experiment, the perfectly collusive output is not attained. In cases where firms choose not to share information, output in low-demand states is significantly *larger* than the Cournot output. Apparently, firms then conceal information to punish non-collusive behavior of rivals in previous periods. In a second experiment, Cason and Mason (1999) drastically reduce the difference between the perfectly collusive and Cournot payoffs. This implies that information sharing can no longer be explained by collusive motivations. Firms still share information at the same rate as they do in the original experiment. It seems that the decision to share information is not a deliberate attempt to facilitate collusion. Risk aversion seems to be the most plausible explanation. Information sharing only has a moderate collusive effect in states of low demand but might be valuable for firms as it reduces uncertainty. Hence, Cason and Mason argue, anti-trust authorities should not worry about information-sharing arrangements such as trade associations.

One may argue about these conclusions. First, information sharing indeed only has moderately collusive effects in the experiment. But outputs are still significantly below Cournot outputs, so there *is* collusion. Second, although collusion may not be the main *reason* that firms share information, it is still an important *effect* of it. Third, this experiment may not be the most appropriate way to evaluate the effects of trade associations. Suppose that firms *unilaterally* benefit from revealing information to their competitors. In that case, they will simply choose to do so, and do not need a trade association. But there may be cases in which disclosing information is a prisoner's dilemma: each individual firm does not have an incentive to disclose, but all firms would be better off if they could all commit to do so. The relevant policy question then becomes not whether firms should be allowed to disclose information, but rather whether they should be allowed to use a trade association to commit to exchange information.

Summarizing, in a repeated game the voluntary sharing of information has a collusive effect, even though collusion is not the main reason that firms choose to share information.

5.3. Does history matter?

There may be another device available through which firms can coordinate on a collusive outcome. The history of an industry may have an influence on the feasibility of collusion. Firms that have colluded in the past may also be more successful in achieving collusion in the future. Firms that have never colluded may find it hard to start colluding. Indeed, one may argue that in the Netherlands, one likely reason that the construction sector was so successful in achieving collusion was that they were simply allowed to collude in the past, and that the institutions and mindsets that facilitate collusive practices were still in place (see e.g. Commissie Vos, 2002). If history is important, and an industry has colluded in the past, then it may be particularly difficult to break down such a cartel once and for all.

Also from a theoretical perspective, past experience may affect the future ability to collude. In Section 2 we argued that the multiplicity of equilibria may make it difficult for firms to coordinate on some collusive equilibrium, especially when there is no focal point. Whatever has happened in the past may provide exactly such a focal point. Theoretical work by Kreps and Spence (1985) also suggests that market history might have a large impact on the ability of firms to reach a collusive outcome.

Phillips *et al.* (1987; as cited by Holcomb and Nelson, 1997) provide experimental evidence for this suggestion by examining repeated quantity-setting and repeated price-setting duopolies. The former are more conducive to collusion than the latter. Players start out in one treatment, and are later switched to the other. It turns out that players that start out in a more conducive environment are also more successful in achieving collusion in the less conducive environment. Similarly, players that start out in the less conducive environment are also less successful in achieving collusion in the more conducive environment. So, indeed, history does matter in the ability to collude.

Holcomb and Nelson (1997) qualify this result by looking at the role of information (or monitoring, as they call it) in a repeated duopoly. They have a symmetric Cournot set-up with differentiated products. First, at least twenty periods were played under complete information, where after each period a firm learns the choice made by its rival. During the first five periods, firms are also allowed to communicate by means of written messages. After the periods with complete information, the experiment is put on hold and the firms are told that they will enter a new environment with incomplete information. With incomplete information, firms also receive information about their competitor's choice after each period — known to them with 50% probability this information is not the true choice but rather some randomly chosen number. After a sequence of at least twenty periods with imperfect information, the experiment is put on hold again and returns to the environment with complete information.

In seventeen out of twenty markets, the firms reach the perfectly collusive outcome during the first twenty periods with complete information. After incomplete information is introduced output significantly increases towards the Cournot output in sixteen of these markets, with the one remaining market sticking to the perfectly collusive outcome. When firms switch back to the complete information environment, all pairs again set collusive output levels.

The lessons that can be drawn from this experiment are numerous. First, at one level it appears that here history does not matter for the ability to collude. A switch to incomplete information destroys collusion, while the switch back to complete information reinstates it just as easily. This is exactly what Holcomb and Nelson claim. But on the other hand, one could argue that the possibility to communicate at the beginning of the game is crucial to achieve collusion — as firms in very similar experiments that are not allowed to communicate fall short in achieving full collusion by far. In fact the effect of communication is so strong that, even after a spell of non-collusion, firms are still able to get back to the fully collusive outcome that results from that early communication. Hence, in that sense, history matters a great deal.

6. Conclusions and policy implications

The main insights we gain from the experimental literature on collusion are the following. First, in an environment in which firms are unable to communicate, they have little success in achieving collusion. The only mildly collusive results are achieved when only two firms are active. In that case, per-period profits are somewhat higher than in the Nash equilibrium of the stage game. With more than two firms, this is no longer the case. Second, the effect of increasing the amount of available information is mixed. It does, however, have a positive effect on market stability. Third, voluntary information sharing has some collusive effect, even though collusion is not the main reason that firms choose to do so. Fourth, the availability of the history of an industry's past prices seems to have some effect on the ability to collude.

Trade associations are typically involved in the activities relating to results two to four. The results thus suggest that there is no unambiguous experimental evidence that trade associations, where firms are able to exchange information regarding their sales, prices and profits, facilitate collusion. Of course, it is an entirely different story when these trade associations also facilitate communication among firms. As we noted already in our introduction, direct communication between firms has a strong and positive effect on the ability to collude.

Taken at face value, the evidence suggests that collusion, if it occurs at all, is most likely to occur in industries where a limited number of firms is active, where firms are able to communicate with each other, and where there is no scope for secret discounts. Thus, the experimental evidence also suggests that antitrust authorities do not have to worry about tacit collusion. Coordinating the actions of an oligopoly does require explicit communication. With more than two firms, tacit collusion just won't work.

At the same time, we feel that one should be extremely careful in drawing general real-world lessons from experiments in collusion. A situation in which inexperienced students have to make decisions in a matter of seconds is fundamentally different from one in which multinationals can spend months pondering the strategic decisions to be made. Still, even when acknowledging this important caveat, we feel that experiments are potentially able to tell more about antitrust policy towards collusion than they have done so far. Many experiments are primarily designed to test the existing theory. They are conducted by experimentalists that put an emphasis on the importance of control in the laboratory. This emphasis is justified if the aim of an experiment is to test some theoretical results, but much less so if the aim is to test how collusion occurs in the real world, and how an antitrust authority may be able to curb collusion. For that purpose, the situation in the laboratory should resemble the real world as closely as possible, rather than resembling the idealized world assumed by the theory. The ideal experimental set-up would be one with both buyers and sellers that have some possibility to interact with each other. Davis and Holt (1998), for example, is a first step towards that ideal. Also, it may be fruitful to have experiments that are more case-based and are inspired by specific antitrust cases. The classic example of this is Grether and Plott (1984).

From real-world cartels, we also know that it is hard to draw general conclusions (see e.g. the survey by Suslow and Levenstein, 2006). This is also true in experimental work on cartels. In some experimental markets, firms are able to collude, whereas in others they are not, even if these markets are subject to the exact same experimental treatment. Something similar seems to hold in the real world. In real cartels, the challenge for firms is often to find robust cartel agreements that survive external shocks (again, see Suslow and Levenstein, 2006). A particularly robust agreement is one in which firms divide the market along some geographical lines. Also, bargaining over the rents earned by the cartel is an important issue. To our knowledge, there are no experiments that focus on these issues.

To be useful for antitrust policy, economic experiments should study issues that are close to real-world situations, and that theory is not or hardly able to address. Bringing experiments closer to practice could yield some new insights. As an example, experiments show that firms are much more successful in colluding with direct communication than they are without communication. But in the real world, neither of these two extreme cases occurs. A world in which firms are not able to communicate whatsoever is impossible to imagine. But a world in which firms can explicitly and overtly talk about future prices also does not exist, as antitrust authorities do not allow it. Hence, it would be interesting to conduct an experiment in which firms are able to communicate — but not about future conduct. More generally, it seems worthwhile to have experiments with an explicit role for an antitrust authority. Other issues that have not been studied include e. g. firm size asymmetries, the possibility of a geographical division of the market, price leadership and information sharing among buyers.

If experiments about collusion teach us anything, it is that small institutional details can matter a great deal for market outcomes. We feel that this lesson also holds for the real world. Institutional details in a certain industry may determine whether firms in that industry are able to collude successfully. If small institutional details are indeed that important, then that also implies that it is extremely difficult to use experiments in order to evaluate whether real-world industries are susceptible to collusion.

References

Abreu, D. (1986), Extremal equilibria of oligopolistic supergames, *Journal of Economic Theory*, 39, 191–225.

Anderhub, V., W. Güth, U. Kamecke, and H.-T. Normann (2003), Capacity choices and price competition in experimental markets, *Experimental Economics*, 6, 27–52.

Axelrod, R. (1984), *The Evolution of Cooperation*. Basic, NY.

Cason, T. N. (1994), The impact of information sharing opportunities on market outcomes: an experimental study, *Southern Economic Journal*, 61, 18–39.

(1995), Cheap talk price signaling in laboratory markets, *Information Economics and Policy*, 7, 183–204.

Cason, T. N., and C. F. Mason (1999), Information sharing and tacit collusion in laboratory duopoly markets, *Economic Inquiry*, 37, 258–281.

Clarke, R. N. (1983), Collusion and the incentives for risk sharing, *Bell Journal of Economics*, 14, 383–394.

Commissie Vos (2002), *De bouw uit de schaduw, eindrapport enquête bouwnijverheid*. Sdu Uitgevers, Den Haag.

Davis, D. D. (1999), Advance production and Cournot outcomes: an experimental investigation, *Journal of Economic Behavior and Organization*, 40, 59–79.

Davis, D. D., and C. A. Holt (1998), Conspiracies and secret price discounts in laboratory markets, *Economic Journal*, 108, 736–756.

Dolbear, F. T., L. B. Lave, G. Bowman, A. Lieberman, E. C. Prescott, F. H. Rueter, and R. Sherman (1968), Collusion in oligopoly, an experiment on the effect of numbers and information, *Quarterly Journal of Economics*, 82, 240–259.

Feinberg, R. M., and C. Snyder (2002), Collusion with secret price cuts, an experimental investigation, *Economics Bulletin*, 3, 1–11.

Fouraker, L. E., and S. Siegel (1963), *Bargaining Behavior*. McGraw-Hill, NY.

Friedman, J. W. (1971), Non-cooperative equilibrium for supergames, *Review of Economic Studies*, 38, 1–12.

Green, E. J., and R. H. Porter (1984), Noncooperative collusion under imperfect price information, *Econometrica*, 52, 87–100.

Grether, D., and C. Plott (1984), The effects of market practices in oligopolistic markets, An experimental examination of the ethyl case, *Economic Inquiry*, 22, 479–507.

Harrington, J. E. (1989), Collusion among asymmetric firms, *International Journal of Industrial Organization*, 7, 289–307.

Holcomb, J. H., and P. S. Nelson (1997), The role of monitoring in duopoly market outcomes, *Journal of Socio-Economics*, 26, 79–93.

Holt, C. A. (1995), Industrial organization, a survey of laboratory research, in: *The handbook of experimental economics*, eds. J. H. Kagel, and A. E. Roth. Princeton University Press, Princeton, NJ.

Holt, C. A., and D. D. Davis (1990), The effects of non-binding price announcements on posted offer markets, *Economics Letters*, 34, 307–310.

Huck, S., H.-T. Normann, and J. Oechssler (2004), Two are few and four are many, number effects in experimental oligopolies, *Journal of Economic Behavior and Organization*, 53, 435–446.

Ivaldi, M., B. Jullien, P. Rey, P. Seabright, and J. Tirole (2003), The economics of tacit collusion: Report for DG Competition, European Commission.

Kreps, D., and J. Scheinkman (1983), Quantity precommitment and Bertrand competition yield Cournot outcomes, *Bell Journal of Economics*, 14.

Kreps, D., and A. M. Spence (1985), Modelling the role of history in industrial organization and competition, in: *Issues in contemporary microeconomics and welfare*, ed. by G. R. Feiwel, Albany, NY. State University of New York Press.

Kühn, K.-U. (2001), Fighting collusion by regulating communication between firms, *Economic Policy, A European Forum*, 16(32), 167–197.

Mason, C. F., and O. R. Phillips (1997), Information and cost asymmetry in experimental duopoly markets, *Review of Economics and Statistics*, 79, 290–299.

Mason, C. F., and O. R. Phillips (2002), In support of trigger strategies: experimental evidence from two-person noncooperative games, *Journal of Economics and Management Strategy*, 11, 685–716.

Motta, M. (2004), *Competition policy, theory and practice*. Cambridge University Press, Cambridge.

Muren, A. (2000), Quantity precommitment in experimental oligopoly, *Journal of Economic Behavior and Organization*, 41, 147–157.

Phillips, O. R., R. C. Battalio, and J. H. Holcomb (1987), Duopoly behavior with market history, *Working Paper*, University of Wyoming.

Rotemberg, J. J., and G. Saloner (1986), A supergame-theoretic model of price wars during booms, *American Economic Review*, 76, 390–407.

Selten, R. (1978), The chain-store paradox, *Theory and Decision*, 9, 127–59.

Selten, R., M. Mitzkewitz, and G. R. Uhlich (1997), Duopoly strategies programmed by experienced players, *Econometrica*, 65(3), 517–55.

Selten, R., and R. Stoecker (1986), End behavior in finite prisoner's dilemma supergames, *Journal of Economic Behavior and Organization*, 7, 47–70.

Smith, V. L. (1981), An empirical study of decentralized institutions of monopoly restraint, in: *Essays in contemporary fields of economics in honor of E.T. Weiler (1914–1979)*, eds. J. Quirk, and G. Horwich, 83–106, West Lafayette. Purdue University Press.

Stigler, G. J. (1964), A theory of oligopoly, *Journal of Political Economy*, 72, 44–61.

Suslow, V. Y., and M. Levenstein (2006), What determines cartel success?, *Journal of Economic Literature*, 44(1), 43–95.

Tirole, J. (1988), *The Theory of Industrial Organization*. MIT-Press, Cambridge, Mass.

Vives, X. (1984), Duopoly information equilibrium, Cournot and Bertrand, *Journal of Economic Theory*, 34, 71–94.

Wellford, C. (2002), Antitrust, results from the laboratory, in: *Experiments investigating market power*, ed. by C. Holt, and R. Isaac, 1–60. JAI Elsevier, Amsterdam.

3 | Collusion in growing and shrinking markets: empirical evidence from experimental duopolies

KLAUS ABBINK AND JORDI BRANDTS[*]

In this chapter we study collusive behavior in experimental duopolies that compete in prices under dynamic demand conditions. In one treatment the demand grows at a constant rate. In the other treatment the demand declines at another constant rate. The rates are chosen so that the evolution of the demand in one case is just the reverse in time than the one for the other case. We use a box-design demand function so that there are no issues of finding and coordinating on the collusive price. Contrary to game-theoretic reasoning, our results show that collusion is significantly larger when the demand shrinks than when it grows. We conjecture that the prospect of rapidly declining profit opportunities exerts a disciplining effect on firms that facilitates collusion and discourages deviation.

1. Introduction

Game-theoretic analysis of price competition suggests that collusion will arise more easily in growing than in declining markets. Tacitly collusive agreements involve that deviations from the collusive path trigger retaliations by other firms, such that, from that point on, the deviating firm's profits will be lower than if it had stuck to the agreed behavior. When the demand grows steadily the gains from deviating from the collusive agreement are, at any point in time, small in comparison to the future losses from retaliation. Analogously, when the demand keeps shrinking these losses will be relatively small

* We thank Hans-Theo Normann and Bradley Ruffle for helpful comments and suggestions. Financial support from ENCORE, the Spanish Ministerio de Ciencia y Tecnologia (BEC 2003–00412), the Ministerio de Educación y Cultura (PB98–0465), the Barcelona Economics programme CREA, the British Academy and the University of Nottingham is gratefully acknowledged. This research has been carried out while Abbink was a visitor at the Institut d'Anàlisi Econòmica (CSIC), Barcelona. He gratefully acknowledges their hospitality and support.

compared to the short-term gains from deviations. Indeed, when the market is on the verge of collapsing, it will be virtually impossible to motivate firms to maintain the collusive agreement.[1]

This prediction is somewhat at odds with some of the views of the European Commission where demand growth is often interpreted to be a factor that makes collusion more difficult. This discrepancy can be explained by the fact that the above reasoning assumes a constant number of market participants despite market growth, while in markets with growing demand the pro-competitive effect of entry may have to be taken into account. Nevertheless, there do exist markets with high entry barriers in which the intrinsic impact of demand growth is not moderated by entry. In addition, the study of the pure effect of market growth and decline is interesting in its own right given economists' general interest in understanding collusion.

Here it is important to point out that the game-theoretic rationale presented above seems rather intuitive and may, hence, be expected to have some predictive value. However, other possibilities are also reasonable a priori and need to be considered. For instance, one can argue that in an industry with brilliant future demand conditions firms might not punish deviations very severely, since the short-term losses of firms that have been cheated on are small in comparison to the possibilities of earning, in one way or another, good profits in the future. In contrast, in industries with declining demand firms may have the tendency to stick together out of a sense of desparation.

We believe that the relation between demand growth and collusion is a relevant policy issue. In their analysis of the economics of tacit collusion for the European Commission, Ivaldi *et al.* (2003) discuss demand growth as one of the potentially relevant factors for collusion, together with, among others, the number of competitors, the symmetry of market shares and market transparency. In his comprehensive analysis of competition policy, Motta (2004) also refers to the relation between demand evolution and collusion.

To shed some light on this issue we present an experimental comparison of collusion under price competition in duopoly markets with

---

[1] There is an ongoing debate on the relation between collusion and the business cycle. The traditional view is that price-cutting is more likely during recessions (see Vives, 1999, ch. 9). In contrast, Rotemberg and Saloner (1986) present a model in which price wars are typically fought during booms.

growing and shrinking demand. In designing the experiment we took advantage of the possibility yielded by experiments of studying the two cases completely in parallel. The evolution of demand in our growing markets is just the reverse in time of the one for the shrinking markets. Our design choices also make it possible to completely eliminate issues related to the complexity of identifying what (perfectly) collusive behavior consists of. As a result of these choices we have what we believe is a very clean comparison of behavior under the two conditions.

Collusion has been one of the subjects of several experimental studies on price competition, albeit in a static demand framework. Dufwenberg and Gneezy (2000) study the effects of market concentration in a one-shot price competition framework with constant marginal cost and inelastic demand. In equilibrium, prices are at the marginal costs and profits are zero, but if firms manage to establish collusion, substantial profits are possible. In their experiments, price is above marginal cost for the case of two firms but equal to that cost for three and four firms.[2] Thus collusion is a relevant phenomenon in duopolies, but for markets with three firms or more the competitive equilibrium retains its predictive power. Apesteguía *et al.* (2006) study theoretically and experimentally how leniency programs in anti-trust influence pricing as well as the formation and detection of cartels in a simple Bertrand competition environment. The experimental results show that leniency conditions which grant whistle-blowers immunity from fines lead to lower prices than the standard anti-cartel conditions under which all firms in a detected cartel will be punished.

Selten and Apesteguía (2005) experimentally study price competition in a model of spatial competition. The authors can identify collusive behavior in individual markets, and average prices slightly above those chosen in equilibrium. Abbink and Brandts (2008) examine an experimental design in which price competition can lead to positive equilibrium price–cost margins. Their design is based on the theoretical model by Dastidar (1995) in which there are multiple equilibria in pure strategies. Firms operate under decreasing returns to

---

[2] With duopolies, Dufwenberg *et al.* (2007) find that the introduction of price floors (the minimum feasible price is above marginal costs) lead to *lower* average prices compared to the standard Bertrand game. Thus, collusion is weakened when price floors are introduced.

scale and have to serve the whole market. In the experimental results the collusive outcome is, though not an equilibrium, one of the most frequently observed. The result that average prices tend to decrease with the number of firms is mainly due to less collusion in larger oligopolies.

Numerous studies report results on related issues from quantity competition environments. Huck *et al.* (1999, 2004) provide results and a recent survey of work on collusion and competition under repeated quantity competition. Their conclusion is that duopolists sometimes manage to collude, but that in markets with more than three firms, collusion is difficult. With exactly three firms, Offerman *et al.* (2002) observe that market outcomes depend on the information environment: firms collude when they are provided with information on individual quantities, but not individual profits. In many instances, however, total average output even exceeds the Nash prediction.

Holt (1995) discusses some experimental research on so-called plus factors for collusion, but does not refer to any work with demand changing over time. The closest work to ours is by Davis *et al.* (1993), who compare behavior in posted price and double auction settings with a demand that first grows and then shrinks. The side demand is represented by human subjects and, in the tradition of the older market experiment literature, participants only know their own parameter values. This means that sellers are not informed about demand shifts. In the analysis observed prices are compared to the Walrasian one. It turns out that double auction prices tend to be close to the Walrasian one. In contrast, the posted offer prices tend to start, when the demand grows, below the Walrasian price and drift slowly upward; when the demand then declines prices exhibit some inertia and remain high with respect to the Walrasian.

Our work is different in several ways. First, we will have complete information about market conditions, including the time-evolution of demand. This is the case the game-theoretic analysis directly pertains to and it is also the natural one in many instances. Second, we will study the case of demand growth and the one of demand decline in separate treatments. Therefore, we will not have to deal with any possible sequence effects, which are not relevant in our context. Third, we are interested in the case of an indefinite temporal relation between firms and not in the case of a fixed and known number of market rounds. In the design section we will explain how we implemented such an environment. Finally, our demand and cost conditions are extremely simple so as to be able to focus on the issue at hand.[3]

Our results show that, contrary to the game-theoretic intuition, collusion is significantly higher in shrinking than in growing markets. Moreover, it is for all the rounds of the experiment that average market prices for the shrinking demand case are above those for the growing demand case. Overall, prices are more than twice as high under shrinking demand conditions. We conjecture that the prospect of rapidly decreasing profits exerts a disciplining effect on decision makers in the shrinking demand environment. High profits need to be made quickly. In growing markets, on the other hand, cooperation becomes more essential in the future, such that it seems of little harm to experiment with different strategies early on. This may be illusionary, however, as erratic and competitive pricing might be interpreted as aggressive and destroy trust between the firms. This makes it then very difficult to establish trust and cooperation later when it really matters.

Though our experiment was designed with antitrust applications in mind, our results are relevant to a broader range of issues. Competition and cooperation are vital issues in the huge literature on public good and dilemma games. (See Ledyard, 1995 and Camerer, 2003 for surveys of public goods experiments.) Like in our framework, the stage game equilibrium and the pareto-efficient cooperative outcome are at the opposite ends of the strategy space (an important difference, though, is that there is no dominant strategy in our price competition environment). We might expect that outcomes in public good games are also sensitive to dynamics in the stakes.

2. Design and procedures

The background model for both our treatments in duopolistic price competition is a homogenenous good market with exogenously given demand and no costs. In each round the demand is willing to buy any amount of the good at a constant price up to a certain maximum quantity. This kind of "box" demand schedule has previously been used for the study of double auctions by Smith (1982), Holt *et al.* (1986), and more recently by Dufwenberg and Gneezy (2000) for the

---

[3] For other experimental work with dynamic market features see the work of Isaac and Reynolds (1992a and 1992b) on R&D competition.

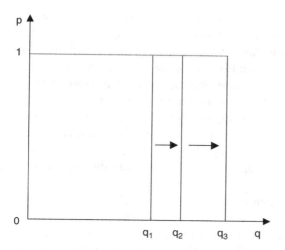

Figure 3.1 The demand schedule

study of Bertrand competition. Figure 3.1 illustrates the demand schedule we used. The diagram depicts the case of a growing market. The demand's willingness-to-pay is normalized to 1. The variables q_t, etc. are the quantities demanded in period t.

2.1. The model and the experimental environment

In our design, firms compete by simultaneously posting a price. The firm that has posted the lower price serves the entire market and realizes a profit of its price times the market demand. If both firms set the same price, then it is assumed that each of the firms serves exactly half of the demand. (Alternatively, a random draw could decide which firm sells the good. This does not alter any of the theoretical arguments.) The strategic analysis of the stage game is straightforward and leads to the well-known Bertrand paradox (Bertrand, 1883). Whatever the price set by the competitor, each firm's best response is to slightly undercut that price. It follows that if there is no smallest money unit, there can be no equilibrium with a positive price, and the unique equilibrium is one in which both firms set a price of zero and hence make zero profit. If a smallest money unit exists (as it typically does in both real life and experimental environments), then another equilibrium exists in which both firms set their price equal to the smallest money unit.

In the context of an infinitely repeated game the equilibrium analysis leaves us with an embarrassment of riches. If players value future payoffs sufficiently high, then virtually every distribution of profits is supported by an equilibrium of the repeated game. In this framework collusion is no longer incompatible with rational play. Firms could, for example, agree to first set always the maximum price, but punish deviations by playing the competitive equilibrium ever after. It is easy to see that such an agreement is self-enforcing. The short-term gain from undercutting the competitor once is far outweighed by the loss from being stuck in the unprofitable equilibrium forever after the cheat.

This is just one example of a retaliation strategy that triggers a collusive equilibrium. Countless others exist; many may involve less harsh retaliation. Notice that the collusive "agreements" we are talking about are only figurative. When collusion is illegal and explicit agreements subject to prosecution, such agreements need to be tacit. The question then arises as to which factors of the economic environment facilitate the emergence of collusive behavior without explicit negotiation. A market that is characterized by strong growth, as depicted in Figure 3.1, looks much more susceptible to the emergence of tacit agreements than a market in which demand is contracting. The reason is that in a growing market, future payoffs, as compared to the current payoff, are higher than in a shrinking market. Thus, the gains from undercutting the competitor now are relatively low compared with the foregone profit that future cooperation would yield. This increases the incentives to sustain collusion, making it more likely to emerge. The experimental environment we create here allows us to put this conjecture to a test.

This environment was presented to participants in a very stylized manner. In each round there was a "prize" which, depending on the treatment, either grew or shrank over time. Subjects knew from the start the way in which the prize would change over time. In each round the two players in a match had to separately choose a percentage consisting of an integer between 0 and 100 inclusive; matches were held constant throughout the experiment. If both players chose the same percentage then each player obtained half the prize multiplied by the (common) percentage. If the chosen percentages were not the same then the player who had chosen the lower percentage obtained the prize multiplied by that percentage, while the player who had chosen the higher percentage obtained nothing. Each round took place in exactly the same way, with a new different prize per round. This way of presenting the situation to participants is simple and facilitates focusing on the evolution of demand. Note that it reflects both the case where the demanded quantity changes over time and the one where the (constant) reservation price changes. In the latter case, which is strategically equivalent, the quantity would be normalized to 1 and the demand's willingness-to-pay would grow or shrink. We could have implemented this by asking subjects for the absolute payoff they demand, where we would have allowed a growing or shrinking upper bound. However, we preferred the framing we used because the competitive and the collusive strategies do not change their appearance throughout the experiment. In this study, we do not focus on the question of whether individuals can identify collusive strategies.

In the instructions, reproduced in Appendix A, participants were told that the experiment consisted of a number of rounds, but it was not specified how many. (The Spanish original is available upon request.) At the time of recruitment, subjects had been told that the experiment would last for about two hours so that they probably expected a good number of rounds. In both treatments we ended the experiment after twenty-seven rounds. In this way the data from both treatments were obtained in the same ex-ante and ex-post length conditions. In the case of increasing demand the growth rate of the prize was 25% from round to round. To generate the exact reverse sequence in prizes for the twenty-seven rounds, in the decreasing demand case prizes shrank at 20% from round to round. We chose these high rates to ensure the saliency of the variation in demand.

Figure 3.2 illustrates the development of the market demand (prize), denominated in the fictitious experimental currency. It can be seen that the growth rates we have chosen indeed lead to a rather extreme range of values. The instructions explained the way in which the prize would evolve over time. In addition, at the beginning of each round the prize for the next round was highlighted on the computer screen. At the end of each round participants received information about the percentage chosen by the other player in the match and about the resulting payoffs for both participants.

The number of rounds was chosen as a trade-off between two conflicting goals. On the one hand we aimed at having a large number of rounds to study collusion in a long-term relationship between two

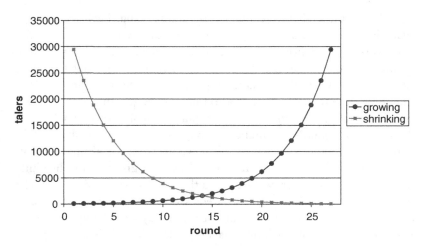

Figure 3.2 Development of the market demand

firms. On the other hand, the exponentially increasing or decreasing prizes meant that the difference between low-payoff and high-payoff rounds would quickly become very large, so large indeed that low-payoff rounds would be worth less than a cent. The choice of twenty-seven rounds balanced these two goals in a reasonable way.

2.2. The conduct of the experiment

The experiment was conducted at the Universitat Autònoma de Barcelona (UAB), Spain. The experiment was computerized, with software developed using the RatImage programming package (Abbink and Sadrieh, 1995).[4] Subjects were recruited by posters placed all over the university campus. Each subject was allowed to participate in only one session, and no subject had participated in experiments similar to the present one. The subjects were undergraduate students from a wide range of disciplines, with slightly more women than men. Almost all participants were Catalan or Spanish.

---

[4] The software was a modified version of the program presented in Abbink and Sadrieh (1996).

At the beginning of a session the written instructions were read aloud. The instructions used a "neutral" language, i.e. we did not refer to "markets" or "prices" and did not explain the underlying market model. We chose this wording solely because the rules of the game seemed easier to understand this way.[5] Especially in the shrinking treatment, where the stakes were high in early rounds, it was vital to be sure that the game was understood right from the beginning.

After all questions were answered, the computer program started play. At the outset of each round, participants were informed about the prize in the current round in *talers* (the fictitious experimental currency). The smallest prize was 89, exponentially increasing to (decreasing from, resp.) 29448 talers. Table 3.1 shows the development of the prize in the two treatments. All prizes, percentages and profits were rounded to integers for convenience.

The same subjects played in the same market throughout the session. To ensure anonymity subjects were not told with whom of the other participants they were paired. The subjects were seated distantly from one another in order to ensure that they could not influence each other's behavior.

The total earnings of subjects from participating in this experiment were equal to the sum of all the profits they made during the experiment. A session lasted for about 45 minutes (this included the time spent to read the instructions). At the end of the experiment, subjects were paid their total earnings anonymously in cash, at a conversion rate of €1 for 1500 talers. Subjects earned between €3.49 and €56.42 with an average of €23.44, which is considerably more than students' regular wages in Barcelona. At the time of the experiment, the exchange rate to other major currencies was approximately US $1.30 and £0.70 to €1.

We conducted one session with each treatment. Subjects interacted with each other within pairs but not across pairs so that each pair can be

---

[5] Evidence for the effects of instruction framing has been very mixed so far. In a tax evasion experiment Baldry (1986) finds far more evasion if the task is presented neutrally as a gambling opportunity. Alm *et al.* (1992), however, do not find any differences. A study by Burnham *et al.* (2000) reports significantly less trustful choices in a reciprocity game when the other player is called "opponent" rather than "partner". On the other hand, Abbink and Hennig-Schmidt (2006) do not find significantly different behavior between a neutrally and a naturally worded version of a bribery experiment.

Table 3.1 *Development of the prizes*

Round	Prize in talers (growing)	Prize in talers (shrinking)	Prize in € (growing)	Prize in € (shrinking)
1	89	29448	0.06	19.63
2	111	23558	0.07	15.71
3	139	18846	0.09	12.56
4	174	15077	0.12	10.05
5	217	12062	0.14	8.04
6	272	9649	0.18	6.43
7	340	7720	0.23	5.15
8	424	6176	0.28	4.12
9	530	4940	0.35	3.29
10	663	3952	0.44	2.63
11	829	3162	0.55	2.11
12	1036	2530	0.69	1.69
13	1295	2024	0.86	1.35
14	1619	1619	1.08	1.08
15	2024	1295	1.35	0.86
16	2530	1036	1.69	0.69
17	3162	829	2.11	0.55
18	3952	663	2.63	0.44
19	4940	530	3.29	0.35
20	6176	424	4.12	0.28
21	7720	340	5.15	0.23
22	9649	272	6.43	0.18
23	12062	217	8.04	0.14
24	15077	174	10.05	0.12
25	18846	139	12.56	0.09
26	23558	111	15.71	0.07
27	29448	89	19.63	0.06

considered as a statistically independent observation. We gathered seven independent observations with growing markets and nine independent observations with shrinking markets. The difference in the number of observations stems from a different show-up rate in the sessions.

Our analysis consists of nonparametric tests performed on these data points. Most analyses comprise comparisons across treatments.

For these we use Fisher's two-sample randomization test, applied to test statistics (e.g. average prices) from the independent observations. This test can be seen as a non-parametric variant of the t-test, with which differences in the mean of two samples can be detected. For a discussion of the power of this test, see Moir (1998). On some occasions we also apply tests to statistics within one sample, e.g. to identify effects in the treatments separately. In this case, we use the nonparametric binomial test.

3. Results

Tables 3.2 and 3.3 show the raw data of our experiment. These consist of an asking price for each subject and each of the twenty-seven rounds of the experiment. Two adjacent columns, separated from the others by a vertical line, represent two players that were matched to the same market. The ordering of the markets as "market 1" through "market 9" is arbitrary, as well as the labeling of the firms as "firm 1" and "firm 2". In our symmetric set-up the two firms play exactly the same role.

In this study we focus on the incidence of collusion. A natural measure of collusion is the degree to which the firms in a market are able to sustain high market prices. Thus we look at this measure first to identify which of the treatments leads to more collusion. Later, we will also look explicitly at the occurrence of perfect collusion, i.e. the coordinated posting of an asking price of 100.

3.1. Market prices and the occurrence of collusion

The two treatments of our experiment allow us to study the effect of the market development on collusive behavior. In particular, we can analyze whether market prices in growing markets are, as game-theoretic reasoning would suggest, higher than in shrinking markets. Table 3.4 indicates that, on average, this is not the case. The table shows average market prices, i.e. the lower of chosen percentages, for the different groups over the twenty-seven rounds of the experiment. In all following tables, the ordering of observations is as in Tables 3.2 and 3.3. Indeed, the average market price is more than twice as high in shrinking as in growing markets. Fisher's two-sample randomization

Table 3.2 *Asking prices in the treatment with growing markets*

rd.	Market 1		Market 2		Market 3		Market 4		Market 5		Market 6		Market 7	
	F1	F2	F1	F2	F1	F2	F1	F2	F1	F2	F1	F2	F1	F2
1	30	50	50	5	40	20	30	50	50	80	78	45	100	10
2	25	30	1	1	19	30	15	35	30	50	11	35	100	20
3	15	10	1	4	25	10	20	75	25	20	30	25	29	100
4	20	10	1	90	15	15	45	20	5	20	10	15	100	100
5	5	20	45	1	20	15	40	15	10	50	1	12	100	100
6	5	20	1	0	5	20	5	20	30	50	13	1	100	100
7	10	20	90	1	25	25	25	1	45	30	6	5	100	100
8	10	20	1	1	50	30	50	10	30	50	2	3	100	100
9	15	10	1	1	11	35	11	15	25	70	1	1	100	100
10	5	15	1	5	40	40	5	12	50	40	4	5	100	100
11	10	15	1	5	45	45	50	6	50	50	3	2	100	100
12	15	10	4	5	50	50	50	7	50	50	1	2	100	100
13	10	15	1	5	55	55	50	8	50	60	0	2	100	100
14	10	10	1	5	60	60	40	100	40	60	3	1	100	100
15	10	10	1	1	65	65	40	50	40	60	41	2	100	100
16	5	10	10	1	70	70	10	100	35	50	29	15	100	100
17	10	5	1	10	75	75	30	45	40	50	60	20	100	100
18	5	5	1	10	80	80	50	30	50	50	100	30	100	100
19	10	4	2	10	85	85	45	90	45	50	1	30	100	100
20	5	10	8	2	90	90	45	35	45	50	1	15	100	100
21	5	50	1	8	95	95	50	70	45	30	2	1	100	100
22	20	4	1	8	99	100	50	18	50	40	1	1	100	100
23	15	20	2	1	100	100	45	17	50	50	1	1	100	100
24	10	15	1	1	99	100	45	9	45	45	1	1	100	100
25	10	4	1	1	100	99	30	10	45	50	1	1	100	100
26	5	5	1	1	99	99	50	9	50	50	1	1	100	100
27	10	5	1	1	100	99	45	19	45	50	1	1	100	100

Note: "F1" and "F2" stand for Firm 1 and Firm 2, respectively.

Table 3.3 *Asking prices in the treatment with shrinking markets*

rd.	Market 1		Market 2		Market 3		Market 4		Market 5		Market 6		Market 7		Market 8		Market 9	
	F1	F2	F1	F2	F1	F2	F1	F2	F1	F2	F1	F2	F1	F2	F1	F2	F1	F2
1	30	75	80	50	100	25	50	10	50	55	100	80	30	100	80	50	50	25
2	45	20	40	50	25	80	10	26	49	50	20	100	50	50	50	50	20	25
3	20	40	40	40	50	50	10	6	45	30	100	100	50	50	50	80	25	10
4	40	60	40	40	75	50	0	5	80	29	100	100	50	50	75	70	10	25
5	45	70	50	40	50	70	30	0	80	80	100	100	50	50	70	70	10	15
6	50	50	40	50	50	45	100	20	80	80	100	100	50	50	70	75	100	15
7	60	60	50	50	40	39	30	30	80	80	100	10	50	50	75	70	15	15
8	58	70	60	80	20	70	40	35	80	80	1	100	50	50	69	75	20	10
9	70	60	80	80	15	70	20	30	80	80	100	100	50	50	70	75	15	50
10	40	65	100	80	50	64	0	30	80	80	100	100	50	50	74	70	20	50
11	50	70	100	100	55	55	30	20	80	80	100	100	50	50	69	73	50	50
12	30	60	100	100	50	60	10	15	80	80	100	100	50	50	65	69	50	50
13	60	75	100	100	48	50	10	15	80	80	100	100	50	50	65	60	100	100
14	70	75	100	100	39	47	10	5	80	80	100	100	50	50	90	64	100	100
15	75	70	100	100	34	25	5	5	80	80	100	100	50	50	90	90	100	100
16	65	70	100	100	25	23	10	20	80	80	100	100	50	50	89	95	100	100
17	70	70	100	100	100	100	20	15	80	80	100	100	50	50	90	90	100	100
18	65	70	100	100	100	100	20	10	80	80	100	100	50	50	89	95	100	100
19	65	80	100	100	100	100	5	30	80	80	100	100	50	50	95	88	100	100
20	80	80	100	100	100	100	20	25	80	80	100	100	100	50	85	95	100	100
21	90	80	100	100	100	100	20	15	80	80	100	100	100	50	90	90	100	100
22	80	90	100	100	100	100	10	15	80	80	100	100	50	100	89	95	100	100
23	90	90	100	100	100	100	10	5	80	80	100	100	100	50	90	95	100	100
24	100	100	100	100	100	100	5	5	80	80	100	100	100	100	89	89	100	100
25	100	100	100	100	100	100	5	5	80	80	100	100	100	100	90	95	100	100
26	100	100	100	100	100	100	5	5	80	80	100	100	100	100	84	90	100	100
27	90	100	100	100	100	100	5	80	80	80	100	100	100	100	90	84	100	100

Note: "F1" and "F2" stand for Firm 1 and Firm 2, respectively.

Table 3.4 *Average market prices*

No.	growing markets	shrinking markets
1	8.96	62.52
2	1.30	82.22
3	59.04	63.30
4	15.41	10.78
5	37.22	74.00
6	6.85	89.30
7	91.07	56.67
8		75.52
9		68.15
Average	31.41	64.72

test rejects the null hypothesis of equal average prices at a one-sided p-value of p=0.018.[6]

This result appears counterintuitive, as it is the opposite of what the theoretical argument would lead us to expect. It seems that the prospect of great future profits in growing markets does not encourage collusion; on the contrary, high prices are much more common in shrinking markets, where we would expect greater incentives to realize a short-term gain by deviating from a collusive agreement. It seems that it is not the promise of growing profit opportunities, but rather the pressure from rapidly declining profits that exerts a disciplining effect on firms. If the prize shrinks at a dramatic rate, high profits need to be made early.

The reverse effect holds for growing markets. Since prizes are relatively small in early rounds, firms feel less pressure to coordinate quickly and can experiment with different strategies. We conjecture that these early deviations from collusion make it difficult to establish cooperation in later rounds, when prizes become very substantial. As a

---

[6] As a general rule two-sided p-values are twice as high. However, ties in different permutations of the sample might lead to slight variations from this rule. We know of no software that computes two-sided p-values for the two-sample randomization test, which is computationally extremely intensive. Since there are no ties in the raw data, we do not believe such variations to have a great impact.

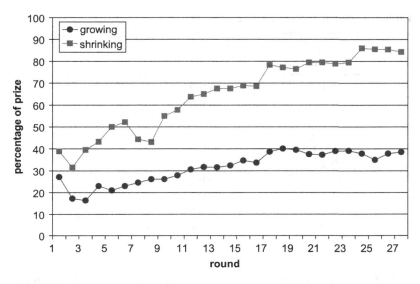

Figure 3.3 Average market price

result, firms in these markets fail to cooperate and realize low prices over the entire experiment.

3.2. Evolution of market prices over time

We now turn our attention to the dynamic aspects of behavior in our setting. Figure 3.3 shows the evolution of average prices, for each round averaged over all markets within a treatment. In both treatments the figure suggests rising prices over time, with this effect being much stronger in shrinking than in growing markets. Further, over the entire duration of play average prices are higher under shrinking than under growing demand conditions. The difference is relatively small in early rounds, but the gap widens with time.

To test for trends statistically, we use the following method. We compute, for each session separately, non-parametric Pearson correlation coefficients between the market price and the round number. Using these as summary statistics, we apply the binomial test to detect a systematic tendency to rising or falling prices. The binomial test rejects the null hypothesis at a one-sided 5% level if all seven observations (which corresponds to a one-sided p-value of 0.0078) for growing

Table 3.5 *Pearson correlation coefficients for*
market prices over time

No.	growing markets	shrinking markets
1	−0.53	+0.91
2	−0.19	+0.84
3	+0.98	+0.80
4	+0.10	−0.21
5	+0.51	+0.58
6	−0.39	+0.41
7	+0.55	+0.66
8		+0.82
9		+0.86
Average	+0.15	+0.63

markets and eight out of nine observations (one-sided p=0.0195) with shrinking markets point in the same direction.[7] Table 3.5 shows the outcome of this analysis. The null hypothesis of no trend can be rejected in favor of the alternative hypothesis of increasing prices for shrinking markets, but not for growing markets.

Visual examination of Figure 3.3 and the distribution of Pearson correlation coefficients suggest that the upward trend in prices is much more pronounced in shrinking markets. We test this conjecture by checking whether the Pearson correlation coefficients listed in Table 3.5 are significantly greater in the treatment with shrinking markets. If this is so, then we interpret this as evidence for a stronger tendency towards increasing prices in the shrinking market condition. Again using the coefficients as summary statistics, we apply Fisher's two-sample randomization test to check for significance. Indeed, the test rejects the null hypothesis of equal coefficients with a one-sided p-value of p=0.028.

This result is consistent with the explanation we propose for the treatment difference in prices. Initial behavior is relatively similar in both treatments. In fact, Fisher's two-sample randomization test applied to the market prices in the first round does not reject the null

---

[7] Since the probability of each event is 0.5, the binomial distribution is symmetric, and thus the two-sided p-values are exactly twice the one-sided ones.

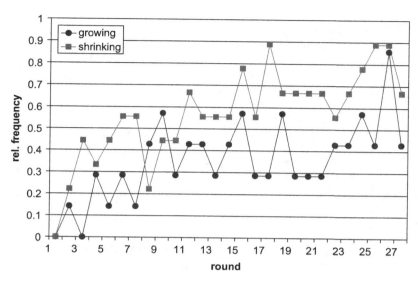

Figure 3.4 Coordination on a common price

hypothesis of equal prices (one-sided p=0.132). Thus, the difference between the two treatments is not due to initial conditions, but to faster coordination in shrinking markets. This supports our conjecture that the expectation of rapidly diminishing profit opportunities disciplines firms to establish collusion quickly.

3.3. Coordination on a common price

The analysis of coordination provides some additional support for the above reasoning. Figure 3.4 shows the number of markets in which both firms submit the same price, over the twenty-seven rounds of the experiment. Coordination on the same price, as typical in collusive agreements, is higher in shrinking markets than in growing ones. For most of the twenty-seven rounds of the experiment, the frequency of coordinated prices in shrinking markets is above the corresponding figure for growing markets. The difference is weakly significant at p=0.094 (one-sided), according to Fisher's two-sample randomization test.

Both growing and shrinking markets exhibit a tendency towards better coordination over time. In a manner analogous to our analysis

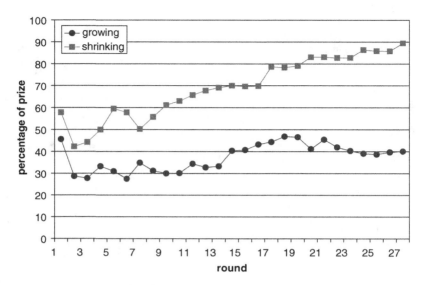

Figure 3.5 Average posted price

of market price dynamics, we compute Pearson correlation coefficients for the coordination in the independent markets. In both
treatments the majority of coefficients are positive. All six observations with growing markets to which this analysis can be applied[8] are
positive; in the shrinking markets condition this holds for seven out of
nine observations. The binomial test rejects the null hypothesis that
positive and negative coefficients are equally likely at a $p=0.016$ (one-
sided) for growing and a weakly significant $p=0.090$ (one-sided) for
shrinking markets.

The high degree of coordination implies that firms' individual asking
prices and the resulting market prices are very similar. Figure 3.5 shows
the evolution of the average asking prices, which include those
demands that have not been the lowest. Naturally the average asking
prices are higher than the average market prices. Besides that we can
observe a picture that is very similar to that of the average market
prices, as depicted in Figure 3.3.

---

[8] In one market no coordination was ever achieved, so a Pearson correlation
coefficient cannot be computed.

Table 3.6 *Number of rounds with a market price of 100*

No.	growing markets	shrinking markets
1	0	3
2	0	17
3	1	11
4	0	0
5	0	0
6	0	23
7	24	4
8		0
9		16
Average	1.92	8.22
% of rounds	13.22%	30.44%

3.4. Perfect collusion

The purest form of collusion is a price set to 100 by both firms, in which case the whole prize is shared equally without deduction. Both firms then make a profit of half of the prize. This is the only way to collude in which firms extract the entire surplus from the market.[9] We rarely observe this type of collusion in growing markets. In only one of the seven markets, firms established coordination on the maximum price. This is the most collusive of our experimental markets: Both firms set the maximum demand from round 4 onwards without deviation. However, this market is an exception in the treatment with growing markets, as Table 3.6 shows. The table lists in how many of the twenty-seven rounds the market price was 100, i.e. both firms had set this price.

Figure 3.6 shows the evolution of perfect collusion over the twenty-seven rounds of the experiment. In the shrinking markets condition, collusion steadily increases after an initial period. Thus, the increased coordination observed earlier coincides with coordination on the

---

[9] In a repeated setting, other forms of collusion are also possible. For instance, firms could agree to take turns in setting the lower price and extracting the surplus. However, the maximum feasible price is 100, thus the firm with the lower price needs to submit a price lower than 100 and thereby leave some money on the table. Apart from being inefficient, such forms of collusion are also less natural and focal than perfect collusion. So it may not be surprising that we do not observe them in the data.

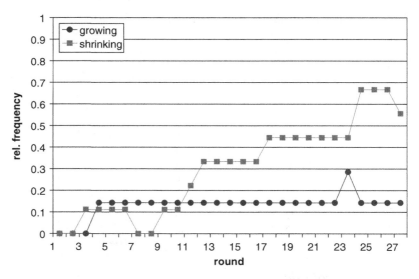

Figure 3.6 Markets with perfect collusion

maximum price. In the growing markets condition, perfect collusion is almost constant over time, with one market perfectly colluding most of the time and all others virtually never.

3.5. Average profits

Naturally in our game, profits are directly linked to the prices set, thus we would expect firms to make higher profits in the treatment with shrinking markets. Table 3.7 shows that, overall, this is the case. The table lists the average per-firm profit in the individual markets, totalled over the twenty-seven rounds of the experiment.

While we do observe higher profits in shrinking markets, the effect is not as pronounced as the difference in average prices would suggest. Indeed, Fisher's two-sample randomization test does not reject the null hypothesis of equal payoffs. The reason is that firms in shrinking markets do not benefit from the upward trend of market prices over time in the same way as firms in growing markets do. When they achieve the highest degree of cooperation, towards the end of the experiment, demand has already decreased so much that the gains from collusion do not add as much to the firms' profits as they would do in earlier rounds.

Table 3.7 *Total profit per firm*

No.	growing markets	shrinking markets
1	4717	27754
2	806	38267
3	68394	28253
4	11383	7790
5	31447	42128
6	1861	54542
7	73307	33904
8		44540
9		18629
Average	27416	32867

4. Summary and conclusions

We report a simple experiment on collusion in duopolies. We analyze whether collusion is more likely to occur in markets with growing or shrinking demand. Game-theoretic reasoning suggests that, if no entry or exit is possible, growing markets should be more prone to collusive behavior. The intuition behind this argument is that short-term gains from deviation from the collusive agreement are small in comparison with long-term losses from retaliation. In a shrinking market, on the other hand, future profits are relatively small, such that the short-term gains from deviating are much more attractive.

In our experiment we observe the exact opposite. Collusion is much more frequent in shrinking markets, leading to average prices that are more than twice as high as in growing markets. In shrinking markets coordination on the maximum price is almost three times as frequent as in growing markets. Further, we observe a strong and significant upward trend in shrinking markets that is much more pronounced than in growing ones.

We conjecture that this is due to a strong disciplining effect that is exerted by the prospect of shrinking profits. If cooperation is not achieved early, then profit opportunities melt away at a fast pace. In growing markets, however, early rounds are worth relatively little, which might tempt firms to "play around" and try out different strategies, rather than strive for the collusive outcome immediately. This behavior can then easily be interpreted as aggressive by the competitor. This perceived aggressive behavior may destroy trust between the firms in early rounds. Without trust cooperation is not possible. As a consequence, when the prize becomes precious in the later rounds of the experiment, collusion is difficult to establish.

The policy implications of our results are straightforward. Antitrust authorities should be advised to be particularly vigilant towards markets that are shrinking or stagnating. As our experimental results show, firms find it easier to establish collusive cooperation in those markets than in markets that are especially dynamic in their development. Our experiment exhibits a pure behavioral effect, but in real life other factors might even reinforce these tendencies. Shrinking markets are often long-established markets for product families that have passed the peak of the product cycle. Thus, firms know each other typically quite well and can anticipate each other's behavior better than competitors in growing markets that are newly emerging.

Of course, our experiment is not the last word in the matter. To focus on the behavioral effect we were examining, we used an extremely simplified market model, abstracting from much of the richness of real-life oligopolies. In our experiment firms sold a homogeneous good without product differentiation. Further, we abstracted from the effect that different costs structures might have on collusion. We also did not address the effect of possible entry and exit, taking the number of firms as exogenously given. In order to obtain a complete picture of collusion in dynamic markets, more research is needed that takes these issues into account. Nevertheless, we believe that our counterintuitive results are a good starting point for a comprehensive analysis.

Appendix A: Instructions

General information

We thank you for coming to the experiment. The purpose of this session is to study how people make decisions in a particular situation. During the session it is not permitted to talk or communicate with the other participants. If you have a question, please raise your hand and one of us will come to your desk to answer it. During the session you will earn money. At the end of the session a show-up fee of €3 plus the amount you will have earned during the experiment will be paid to you in cash. Payments are confidential; we will not inform any of the other participants of the amount you have earned. In the following, all amounts of money are denominated in talers, the experimental currency unit.

During the experiment you will be paired with another participant. You will be paired with the same participant throughout the experiment. You will not be informed of the identity of the person you are paired with.

The experiment consists of a number of separate rounds.

Prize per round

In each round there will be a "prize". This prize will increase (decrease) from round to round. The prize in round 1 will be 89 (29448) talers and increase (decrease) at a constant rate of 25% (20%). The prize in round 2 will be (111) 23558, in round 3 (139) 18846... At the beginning of each round you will be informed of what exactly the prize of the round is.

Decisions

In each round you and the other participant that you are matched to will each separately make a decision. This decision will consist of choosing a percentage between 0 and 100. When you have decided on the percentage please enter it into the computer.

Earnings

After each round, the earnings for each pair will be determined as follows. If the two percentages of the two participants in a pair are the same then each participant obtains half the prize of the round multiplied by the percentage. If the two percentages are not the same then the participant who chose the lowest percentage obtains the percentage multiplied by the prize of the round and the participant that chose the higher percentage obtains nothing in that round.

Information about earnings

After each round, your round earnings are credited to your talers account. At any moment during the experiment you will be able to check your talers account on the screen.

At the end of the experiment your total earnings in talers will be converted into euros at the exchange rate of €1 for every 1500 talers.

Appendix B: Prices in the individual markets

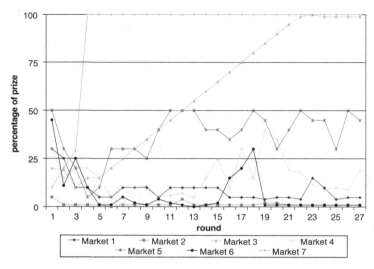

Figure 3A.1 Market prices (growing demand)

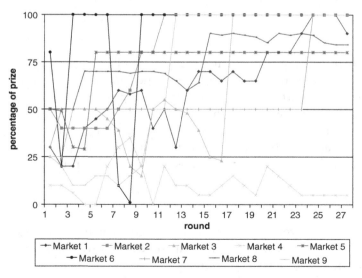

Figure 3A.2 Market prices (shrinking demand)

References

Abbink, K., and J. Brandts (2008), Pricing in Bertrand competition with increasing marginal costs. *Games and Economic Behavior*, 63, 1–31.

Abbink, K. and H. Hennig-Schmidt (2006), Neutral versus Loaded Framing in a Bribery Experiment. *Experimental Economics*, 9(3), 103–21.

Abbink, K., and A. Sadrieh (1995), RatImage – Research Assistance Toolbox for Computer-Aided Human Behaviour Experiments. SFB Discussion Paper B-354, University of Bonn, Bonn.

(1996), RatDemo – A Ready-to-Run Experiment in 99 Program Lines. SFB Discussion Paper B-325, University of Bonn, Bonn.

Alm, J., G. McClelland and W. Schulze (1992), Why do people pay taxes? *Journal of Public Economics*, 48, 21–38.

Apesteguía, J., M. Dufwenberg and R. Selten (2006), Blowing the Whistle. *Economic Theory*, 50, 143–166.

Baldry, J. (1986), Tax Evasion is Not a Gamble – A Report on Two Experiments. *Economic Letters*, 22, 333–335.

Bertrand, J. (1883), Théorie Mathématique de la Richesse Sociale. *Journal des Savants*, 67, 499–508.

Burnham, T., K. McCabe and V. Smith (2000), Friend-or-Foe, Intentionality Priming in an Extensive Form Trust Game. *Journal of Economic Behavior and Organization*, 43, 57–74.

Camerer, C. (2003), *Behavioral Game Theory, Experiments on Strategic Interaction*, Princeton University Press, Princeton, N.J.

Dastidar, K. G. (1995), On the Existence of Pure Strategy Bertrand Equilibrium. *Economic Theory*, 5, 19–32.

Davis, D., G. Harrison and A. Williams (1993), The Effects of Non-stationarities on the Convergence to Competitive Equilibria. *Journal of Economic Behavior and Organization*, 22, 305–326.

Dufwenberg, M., and U. Gneezy (2000), Price competition and market concentration, an experimental study. *International Journal of Industrial Organization*, 18, 7–22.

Dufwenberg, M., U. Gneezy, J. Goeree, and R. Nagel (2007), Price Floors and Competition. *Economic Theory*, 33(1), 207–224.

Holt, C. (1995), Industrial Organization, A Survey of Laboratory Research, in: J. Kagel and A. Roth (eds.), *The Handbook of Experimental Economics*, Princeton University Press, Princeton, N.J., 347–443.

Holt, Charles A., L. Langan, and A. P. Villamil (1986), Market Power in Oral Double Auctions. *Economic Inquiry*, 24, 107–123.

Huck, S., H. T. Normann, and J. Oechssler (1999), Learning in Cournot Oligopoly – An Experiment. *Economic Journal*, 109, C80–95.

Huck, S., H. T. Normann, and J. Oechssler (2004), Two are few and four are many, On number effects in experimental oligopolies. *Journal of Economic Behavior and Organization*, 53, 435–446.

Isaac, R. M. and S. Reynolds (1992a), Schumpeterian Competition in Experimental Markets. *Journal of Economic Behavior and Organization*, 17 (1992), 59–100.

(1992b), Stochastic Innovation and Product Market Organization. *Economic Theory*, 2 (1992), 525–545.

Ivaldi, M., B. Jullien, P. Seabright, and J. Tirole (2003), The Economics of Tacit Collusion – Report for DG Competition, European Commission. IDEI Working Paper, University of Toulouse.

Ledyard, J. H. (1995), Public Goods, A Survey of Experimental Research, in John Kagel and Alvin E. Roth (eds.), *Handbook of Experimental Economics*. Princeton University Press, Princeton, N.J., 111–194.

Moir, R. (1998), A Monte Carlo Analysis of the Fisher Randomization Technique, Reviving Randomization for Experimental Economists. *Experimental Economics*, 1, 87–100.

Motta, M. (2004), *Competition Policy*. Cambridge University Press, Cambridge.

Offerman, T., J. Potters and J. Sonnemans (2002), Imitation and Belief Learning in an Oligopoly Experiment. *Review of Economic Studies*, 69, 973–997.

Rotemberg, J. J., and G. Saloner (1986), A Supergame-Theoretic Model of Price Wars During Booms, *American Economic Review*, 76, 390–407.

Selten, R., and J. Apesteguía (2005), Experimentally Observed Imitation and Cooperation in Price Competition on the Circle. *Games and Economic Behavior*, 51, 171–192.

Smith, V. L. (1982), Markets as Economizers of Information, Experimental Examination of the Hayek Hypothesis. *Economic Inquiry*, 20, 165–179.

Vives, X. (1999), *Oligopoly Pricing*. MIT Press, Cambridge, Mass.

4 | Price ceilings as focal points? An experimental test

DIRK ENGELMANN AND
HANS-THEO NORMANN*

In this experiment, we analyze whether price ceilings can have a collusive effect in laboratory markets. Our main interest is the focal-point hypothesis which says that a price ceiling may facilitate tacit collusion and lead to higher prices because it resolves a coordination problem inherent to collusion. Our results reject the focal-point hypothesis. Markets with price ceilings have lower prices than markets with unconstrained pricing. The static Nash equilibrium predicts the data accurately.

1. Introduction

Price ceilings are a common instrument of competition policy. They have been used at least since ancient Greek times and are known from today's markets as diverse as food, steel, rents, fees for physicians, interest rates and electricity spot market prices.

The prevalence of price ceilings and the temptation for policy makers to impose them is easily explained. One can go as far back as Roman Emperor Diocletian (*The Edict on Prices*, AD 301) to find

In response to the needs of mankind itself, we have decided that maximum prices of articles for sale must be established. We have not set down fixed prices since many provinces occasionally enjoy the fortune of welcome low prices. [E]very person shall take note that the liberty to exceed them [maximum prices] has ended, but that the blessing of low prices has in no way been impaired.

In short, this policy prevents prices from getting higher than the ceiling but does not harm competition possibly pushing them below the ceiling. To be precise, only non-binding price ceilings (that is,

---

* We are grateful to Wieland Müller for substantial contributions at various stages of the chapter. Armin Schmutzler's comments much improved the chapter.

61

those above the competitive equilibrium price) have this property. Binding price ceilings actually lower welfare.[1]

Industrial economists have challenged the conclusion that price ceilings cannot weaken competition with the theory of focal points (Scherer and Ross, 1990). The Folk Theorem (see for example Tirole, 1988) predicts that infinitely many prices can occur as outcomes of collusive equilibria in infinitely repeated games if the discount factor is sufficiently high. This suggests a coordination problem when firms attempt to collude. Here, a price ceiling may serve as a focal point on which firms coordinate. If that is the case, price ceilings would facilitate tacit collusion and lead to higher prices — contradicting the logic captured in the above quote.

Given that the focal point counter argument itself has become rather widespread (for example, the European Commission recently made use of it in the EMI/Time Warner and Sony/BMD merger cases), it has received surprisingly little attention in the literature. First of all, there is no formal model strengthening it. Second, there is a remarkable absence of evidence from field markets. A recent exception is Knittel and Stango (2003).

Knittel and Stango investigate interest rates of US credit cards in the 1980s. In this market, various price ceilings were effective. Most states (81% in 1979) imposed a ceiling of an 18% interest rate, 11% had a ceiling below that level, 3% were above the 18% level, and 6% had no ceiling at all. It is this very heterogeneity of price ceilings that makes the analysis of this market promising. Indeed, Knittel and Stango find that interest rates in markets with an 18% ceiling were on average higher than interest rates in markets with a higher ceiling. The lowest interest rates were observed in markets with a ceiling lower than 18%. This suggests the following conclusions which the authors underpin with a number of sophisticated econometric regressions. Ceilings lower than 18% are binding whereas those of 18% and above are not. Since the relative incentive to deviate from a collusive interest rate increases with the interest rate, markets with a ceiling higher than 18% are less often

---

[1] Binding price ceilings have the negative effect of reducing supply since they are set below the market clearing price. Such negative effects were observed during the California electricity crisis where price ceilings on the spot market worsened the shortage of electricity. See Rassenti *et al.* (2001).

collusive than those with a ceiling of 18%. Since, in addition, markets with an 18% ceiling have higher interest rates than markets without ceilings, this is convincing evidence that the focal point story is empirically relevant.

In this chapter, we analyze whether price ceilings can have a similar collusive effect in laboratory markets. Our main interest is the focal point hypothesis. In the laboratory, we can control whether a price ceiling is non-binding (by setting it above the equilibrium prediction) and we can impose different ceilings in our design. Our chapter builds on three previous experimental papers. Isaac and Plott (1981) and Smith and Williams (1981) analyze double auction markets with price controls (both price ceilings and floors). They clearly reject the focal point hypothesis. By contrast, their data suggest that non-binding price ceilings actually lower prices, consistent with the traditionally expected effect. Prices often failed to converge to the competitive equilibrium, leaving a "buffer" between the price ceiling and actual prices which prevented full convergence. Coursey and Smith (1983) analyze price ceilings with posted-offer markets. They obtain qualitatively the same results as Issac and Plott (1981) and Smith and Williams (1981). Markets converge to the competitive equilibrium and price ceilings as focal point do not play a role. A maximum price may lower average prices as prices cannot converge from above anymore but markets still converge to a price below the ceiling.

Despite this experimental evidence against the focal-point hypothesis, we believe that further experimental research is warranted. First, the results by Isaac and Plott (1981) and Smith and Williams (1981) are hardly surprising because of the well-known strong tendency of double auction markets to converge to the competitive equilibrium. Here, non-binding price ceilings cannot be expected to have an effect. Coursey and Smith's (1983) posted-offer markets appear to present stronger evidence against the focal point hypothesis. Posted-offer markets often have prices above the competitive equilibrium, possibly due to collusion, so a price ceiling may reduce average prices but might also facilitate collusion. However, in their design the incentives to collude are extremely small. The highest price ceiling they study is only $0.05 above the competitive equilibrium ($5.25) and as a result each seller would increase his or her profit by only $0.05 or $0.10. The total collusive profit would be less than 10%

above the equilibrium profit.[2] In contrast, deviating from collusion by lowering the price by $0.01 yields additional profits of at least $0.13. Furthermore, due to the random sequencing of buyers, the competitive equilibrium is not a Nash-equilibrium.[3] In the Nash-equilibrium of their design, prices above the price ceiling are played with positive probability, such that it is possible that the price ceiling in Coursey and Smith is indeed binding with respect to the Nash-equilibrium prices. This could explain why a price ceiling that is non-binding (with respect to the competitive equilibrium) still leads to lower prices.[4]

Our design, in contrast, establishes the upper end of the competitive price range as the unique Nash-equilibrium and provides substantial incentives to collude at the price ceiling, as profits would increase by about 40%. We therefore believe it is better suited to test the hypothesis. In our design, there are many prices at which firms could collude. This coordination problem might be resolved with a price ceiling since it presents a focal point for coordination. Moreover, incentives to deviate from collusive arrangements are often substantial which makes attempts to collude risky. Our design ensures that collusion at the price ceiling reduces the incentive to undercut relative to

---

[2] Unfortunately, details of the design of Coursey and Smith (1983) are not reported, but it appears that at least one buyer would actually *lose* from colluding because of a forgone commission fee that is not compensated by the price increase.

[3] Given that the number of sellers is only four, Nash-equilibrium (understood as Nash-equilibria in a game between the sellers, assuming that buyers maximize their payoffs and randomize between sellers who post the same price) is arguably more appropriate than competitive equilibrium as solution concept in this framework. The lack of detail in Coursey and Smith (it is not evident what the individual sellers' cost schedules look like) makes it impossible to calculate Nash-equilibria. Standard distributions of cost schedules (such that no seller sells more than two units in the competitive equilibrium), however, imply that there is no pure strategy Nash-equilibrium. Mixed strategy Nash-equilibria involve positive probability on prices above the competitive equilibrium.

[4] Kujal (1999) also studies price ceilings in posted-offer markets. The highest price ceiling he studies, however, is at the upper end of the competitive price range. Moreover, he shows that the supports of the (mixed) Nash-equilibria are above the competitive price range and hence his "non-binding" price ceiling is binding with respect to the mixed Nash-equilibrium prices. Therefore, it cannot serve as a focal point for collusion at supra-competitive prices. His methodology is seriously flawed because he deceived his subjects by not informing them that buyers were simulated. Apart from general concerns about deception, this is problematic because it might have influenced the sellers' willingness to collude if they assumed that other subjects might be harmed by their actions.

the collusive profits, which should increase stability of a collusive agreement.

2. Experimental design

We implement posted-offer markets with four symmetric sellers and simulated buyers. Sellers post their prices simultaneously and only once in every period. Other details of our implementation deviate from the usual posted-offer markets. Sellers are automatically committed to sell (given sufficient demand) the maximal quantity such that marginal costs do not exceed the price. Automated buyers are rationed efficiently, that is they buy in order of decreasing willingness to pay and from sellers in order of increasing price.

If several sellers charge equal prices, buyers split their demand equally and units sold are not restricted to integers. This is an important design issue. Posted-offer markets are often plagued by a multiplicity of Nash-equilibria. Moreover, these are often derived assuming that buyers split their demand equally between sellers with identical prices (see, e.g. Davis and Holt, 1993), which even rational human buyers have no reason to do (and the experimental software would usually not even allow them to do so). Abolishing this assumption in general destroys all pure strategy Nash-equilibria. By employing computerized buyers who follow the above assumption, we eliminate this problem which simplifies the calculation of expected profits, and eliminates any randomness.

The marginal costs for the sellers are given in Table 4.1. There were twenty-four simulated buyers who could buy one unit each. Their willingness to pay is given in Table 4.2. The sellers were restricted to state prices that were multiples of 0.01 and costs were incurred only for units that were actually sold. Figure 4.1 displays the supply and demand schedules implied by these marginal cost and willingness to pay schedules.

We study the effect of price ceilings in three treatments. Each treatment runs over sixty periods and is split into two halves. In our two main treatments LowNo and NoLow, we implemented a low price ceiling $p^l = 2.20$ either in the first thirty periods (LowNo) or in the second thirty periods (NoLow). In the third treatment HighLow we started with a high price ceiling $p^h = 2.80$, which was lowered to $p^l = 2.20$ in the second half. See Table 4.3 for an overview.

Table 4.1 _Marginal production costs for the sellers_

Unit	1	2	3	4	5	6
Marginal Cost	0.50	0.90	1.30	1.70	2.10	2.50

Table 4.2 _Willingness to pay of the simulated buyers and the according number of buyers_

Willingness to pay	3.60	3.00	2.40	1.80	1.20	0.90
Number of buyers	4	4	4	4	4	4

Table 4.3 _Overview of the price ceilings in the three experimental treatments_

Treatment	Ceiling Periods 1–30	Ceiling Periods 31–60
LowNo	Low (2.20)	None
NoLow	None	Low (2.20)
HighLow	High (2.80)	Low (2.20)

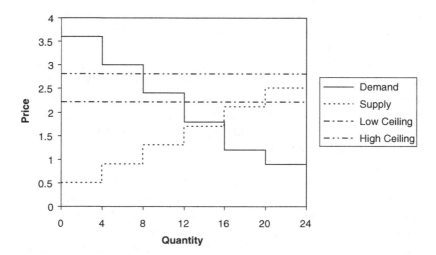

Figure 4.1 Supply and demand schedules in the experimental markets and price ceilings imposed in treatments High and Low

3. Predictions

We need several predictions for our experiments: the competitive equilibrium, the noncooperative static Nash equilibrium, and finally predictions for cooperative outcomes at various prices including the two ceilings. Consider these in turn.

The competitive price range where supply equals demand is easily seen to be $p^* \in [1.70, 1.80]$. The competitive equilibrium quantity is $q^* = 16$ with each seller selling 4 units. At these competitive prices, sellers make a profit $\Pi^* = 4p^* - (0.50 + 0.90 + 1.30 + 1.70) = 4p^* - 4.40$ such that $\Pi^* \in [2.40, 2.80]$.

The *unique* Nash-equilibrium of the price setting game between sellers is the price of 1.80, the upper end of the competitive price range. To see this, note first that all prices below 1.80 are strictly dominated by 1.80. Let seller 1 choose a price of 1.80. Market demand at this price is 16 units. Even if the other sellers all choose prices below 1.80, seller 1 can still sell 4 units since in that case the total supply by the other sellers is at most 12 units. Since he could not profitably sell more than four units at any lower price, deviating below 1.80 always leads to a lower profit. Now assume all sellers charge 1.80. If seller 1 deviates to any price $p > 1.80$, he sells nothing. The reason is that market demand at this price is $D(p) \leq 12$ and the other sellers supply 12 units.[5] Hence all sellers choosing $p = 1.80$ is a Nash-equilibrium. The noncooperative Nash equilibrium profit at this price is 2.80.

To establish uniqueness of this Nash-equilibrium, recall that no bidder would choose a strictly dominated price of $p < 1.80$ in a Nash-equilibrium. Then consider the case that $n \in \{1,2,3,4\}$ sellers choose $p^{\max} > 1.80$ and the remaining seller(s) choose prices $1.80 \leq p < p^{\max}$. Since total market demand $D(p^{\max}) \leq 12$ and each seller charging a price below $p^{\max}$ supplies at least 4 units and demand is split equally between sellers who choose the same price, the demand for the sellers at the maximal price is at most $(12 - 4(4 - n))/n = 4 (n - 1)/n \leq 3$.

[5] While this argument holds for our market with simulated buyers and efficient rationing, it would not hold for a posted-offer market with random sequencing of buyers since a seller might find a buyer with high willingness to pay even after the first 12 units have been sold. In particular, by deviating to $p = 2.40$, a seller would almost for sure be able to sell at least one unit.

If the highest-price sellers sell nothing (which is always, but not exclusively, the case if $n = 1$) any highest-price firm could profit by deviating to $p = 1.80$, which yields a guaranteed profit of $\Pi = 2.80$. Otherwise, let each of the highest-price firms sell d. In that case, by deviating to $p^{\max} - 0.01$ a highest-price seller would lose only $0.01d$, but, since it could now capture the whole demand previously shared by the highest-price sellers and since it always has excess supply of at least one unit (at cost of at most 1.70), it would increase its sales by at least min$\{d, 1\}$ and hence its profits by at least $(p^{\max} - 1.70)$ min $\{d, 1\} > 0.1$ min$\{d, 1\} > 0.01d$ since $d \leq 3$. (Note that if one or more other sellers charge $p^{\max} - 0.01$, the deviating seller has to share the d units he can capture from the seller(s) who charge(s) $p^{\max}$, but at the same time he gets a share of their sales as well and he always gains at least min$\{d, 1\}$.) Hence it always pays to deviate for the highest-price seller(s), so no other configuration of prices can be a pure strategy Nash-equilibrium. By the same line of argument there is also no mixed-strategy equilibrium. Let $p^{\max} > 1.80$ be the maximum among the upper ends of the supports of the sellers' mixed strategies (this permits assymmetric equilibria). Let d be the expected number of units sold when charging $p^{\max}$. As above, if $d = 0$, then it pays to deviate to 1.80. And if $d > 0$, then as above it pays to charge $p^{\max} - 0.01$ instead of $p^{\max}$ since in each possible constellation where a quantity q (which never exceeds 3) is sold at $p^{\max}$, the gains are $(p^{\max} - 1.70)$ min$\{q, 1\} > 0.1$ min$\{q, 1\}$ which again exceed the losses of $0.01q$. Therefore, the upper end of the support of at least one of the players is not a best reply, which cannot be true in a mixed equilibrium.

The joint-profit maximizing outcome is all sellers choosing a price of $p^c = 3.00$, each seller selling 2 units. (Intuitively, the joint-profit maximizing outcome price is where there is a step in the demand function. Since the profits on the third unit in case sellers charge 2.40 is $2.40 - 1.30 = 1.10 < 2 \cdot 0.60$, it pays to raise the price to 3.00 and sell only two units each.) The profits are $\Pi^c = 2 \cdot 3.00 - (0.50 + 0.90) = 4.60$. The gains from colluding are thus $\Pi^c - \Pi^* = 1.80$ or about 64% of Nash-equilibrium profits. By undercutting slightly to $p^u = 2.99$ a seller can sell six units and make a profit of $\Pi^u = 6 \cdot 2.99 - (0.50 + 0.90 + 1.30 + 1.70 + 2.10 + 2.50) = 8.94$, hence the incentive to undercut is $\Pi^u - \Pi^c = 5.34$ or about 116% of collusive profits. Hence, both the gains from collusion as well as the incentives to undercut are substantial. Note, furthermore, that if only one seller deviates to p^u the profit of the remaining sellers drops to $2(3.00 - 0.50)/3 = 1.67$ and if two undercut, it drops to 0.

Next, consider collusion at the next step in the demand function, $p = 2.40$. This is only slightly less profitable than collusion at $p = 3.00$, yielding a profit of $\Pi = 3 \cdot 2.40 - (0.50 + 0.90 + 1.30) = 4.50$, and hence gains from collusion of about 61%. Moreover, it is much less risky. The profit from undercutting to $p = 2.39$ is $\Pi = 5 \cdot 2.39 - (0.50 + 0.90 + 1.30 + 1.70 + 2.10) = 5.45$, implying incentives to undercut of about 21% of collusive profits. Profits in case one seller undercuts are $7 \cdot 2.40/3 - (0.50 + 0.90 + 1.30/3) = 3.77$ and in case two sellers undercut they are $2.40 - 0.50 = 1.90$. Hence three sellers alone can increase their profits from colluding at $p = 2.40$, no matter what the last seller does.

Collusion at price ceiling $p^l = 2.20$ would yield profits $\Pi^l = 3 \cdot 2.20 - (0.50 + 0.90 + 1.30) = 3.90$ and hence gains from collusion of $\Pi^l - \Pi^* = 1.10$ or about 39%. Undercutting to $p = 2.19$ yields a profit of $\Pi = 5 \cdot 2.19 - (0.50 + 0.90 + 1.30 + 1.70 + 2.10) = 4.45$, implying incentives to undercut of about 14% of collusive profits. Hence the incentives to deviate from the collusive agreement at p^l are slightly lower than for collusion at $p = 2.40$ and dramatically lower than for collusion at $p = 3.00$.

Collusion at price ceiling $p^h = 2.80$ would yield profits $\Pi^h = 2 \cdot 2.80 - (0.50 + 0.90) = 4.20$ and hence gains from collusion of $\Pi^h - \Pi^* = 1.40$ or 50%. Undercutting to $p = 2.79$ yields a profit of $\Pi = 6 \cdot 2.79 - (0.50 + 0.90 + 1.30 + 1.70 + 2.10 + 2.50) = 7.74$, implying incentives to undercut of about 84% of collusive profits. Thus the incentives to deviate from the collusive agreement at p^h are lower than for collusion at $p = 3.00$. The profits are, however, lower than for collusion at $p = 2.40$. Hence while the high price ceiling could also solve the coordination problem by providing a focal point, the coordination problem is not solved completely, because, opposed to collusion at the low ceiling, it is not maximizing joint profits among the admissable prices. Furthermore, it should be less robust since the incentives to deviate are substantially higher than at the low price ceiling.

4. Procedures

Written instructions were identical in all treatments and are reprinted in the Appendix. Subjects were informed at the beginning of the experiment that there would be a change in the market rules in the second half of the experiment without being informed about the nature of this change. Whenever a price ceiling was introduced, changed or abolished, subjects were informed about this by a message on the computer screen.

For our main treatments LowNo and NoLow we ran two sessions with twelve subjects each. Since fixed groups of four subjects interacted for the whole experiment, this implies six statistically independent observations per treatment. For the third treatment HighLow we conducted one session with twelve subjects or three independent observations.

The experimental software was developed and the experiments were run using z-Tree (Fischbacher, 2007). The experiments were run at the experimental laboratory at Royal Holloway, University of London in January and February 2005. The subjects were Royal Holloway students (90% undergraduates) of various disciplines (28% economics, 15% management, 57% others, including mathematics, media arts, history, etc.).

The experiments (including reading of the instructions and payment) took between 75 and 90 minutes. Subjects were paid in cash at the end of the experiment at a rate of 20 points = £1 plus a £4 flat fee. Average payoffs (including the flat fee) were £11.46 in LowNo and £11.87 both in NoLow and HighLow. For comparison, Nash-equilibrium profits are £12.40, whereas, if subjects colluded at $p=2.40$ if there is no (or a high) ceiling and at p^l if there is a low ceiling, profits would be £16.60. Hence subjects achieve profits substantially below collusive profits and even below Nash-equilibrium profits.

5. Results

Figure 4.2 and Table 4.4 show the results of our main treatments LowNo and NoLow. Prices are generally higher without price ceilings in both treatments. (We refer to posted prices throughout this section.) Prices without the ceiling appear to be higher particularly in LowNo when a ceiling in phase 1 was released in phase 2. This pattern confirms the findings by Coursey and Smith (1983).

The differences between treatment averages reported in Table 4.4 are statistically significant (where each of our six groups of four firms counts as one observation and data from all periods are used). In

Table 4.4 *Summary statistics of prices, standard deviations in parentheses; "second half" refers to periods 16–30 in phase 1 and periods 46–60 in phase 2*

		treatment LowNo			treatment NoLow	
		all periods	second half		All periods	second half
phase 1	Low Ceiling	1.789 (0.184)	1.782 (0.150)	No Ceiling	1.922 (0.313)	1.833 (0.101)
phase 2	No Ceiling	2.013 (0.599)	1.914 (0.636)	Low Ceiling	1.833 (0.093)	1.819 (0.071)

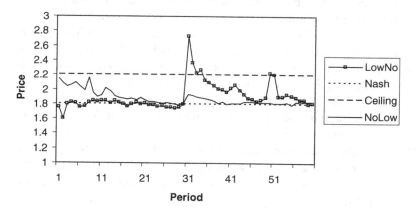

Figure 4.2 Development of average prices in treatments LowNo and NoLow across the 60 periods

LowNo, phase 2 prices are significantly higher (two-sided Wilcoxon signed-rank test, $p = 0.031$) whereas in NoLow phase 1 prices are higher (two-sided Wilcoxon signed-rank test, $p = 0.031$). This difference is not significant anymore if we only take data from periods 16–30 and 46–60 into account.

We can also compare prices across treatments. In phase 1, prices in NoLow are higher than those in LowNo (two-sided Mann-Whitney U, $p = 0.016$) and in phase 2 it is the other way around (two-sided Mann-Whitney U, $p = 0.024$). Again, this is not significant anymore if we only take data from periods 16–30 and 46–60 into account.

Finally, we do not observe an order effect. That is, phase 1 prices in NoLow are not significantly different from phase 2 prices in LowNo, and phase 2 prices in NoLow are not different from phase 1 prices in LowNo. This holds for all periods as well as the data from periods 16–30 and 46–60.

Result 1. Price ceilings cause lower prices. Average prices without a ceiling are significantly higher at the 5% level both within treatments and across treatments if data from all periods are taken into account.

The second feature of the data as shown in Figure 4.2 and Table 4.4 is that the competitive equilibrium, in particular the static Nash equilibrium prediction of 1.80, works remarkably well.[6] Prices converge towards 1.80 in both phases of both treatments. When a price ceiling is imposed, average prices are extremely well organized by the Nash prediction. After some five to ten periods, average prices are only marginally below or above 1.80. Without a ceiling, prices are "close" to 1.80 only in the final periods of the relevant phase. To statistically validate this claim, we compute 95% confidence intervals around the means reported in Table 4.4. The intervals are based on White (1980) robust standard errors which account for possible dependence of observations within groups. We find that the 95% confidence intervals include the Nash prediction of 1.80 in all cases listed in Table 4.4 except phase 2 of treatment LowNo when data from all periods are taken into account.[7]

The histogram in Figure 4.3 shows the frequency of choices with and without a price ceiling. It is based on data from periods 16–30 and 46–60 from both treatments. It reveals that the bracket including the Nash prediction (1.75 – 1.85) contains by far the most choices (70% and 58%, respectively). Moreover, when we ignore the somewhat arbitrary brackets and look at individual prices, it turns out that 1.80 is the most frequent choice both with a price ceiling (50%) and without (32%),

---

[6] Recall that the unique static Nash equilibrium is at the upper end of the competitive equilibrium range.

[7] There is only one group that manages to collude. Interestingly, this group was in treatment LowNo and colludes in the phase without a price ceiling at $p = 2.40$, after having converged quickly to the Nash-equilibrium in the first phase. Average prices were 1.90 and in decline towards the end though.

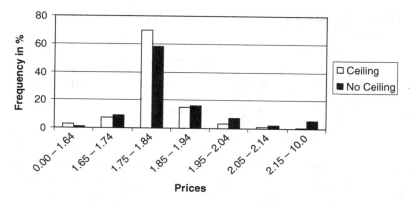

Figure 4.3 Histogram of prices in periods with and without a price ceiling ($p = 2.20$), based on data from second half of each phase (periods 16–30 and 46–60, respectively)

using periods 16–30 and 46–60 data. Moreover, the Nash price is also the median of the distribution with and without a price ceiling.

Result 2. The Nash equilibrium predicts average prices well. Average prices are not statistically different from the Nash prediction in both phases of all treatments (using periods 16–30 and 46–60 data). The Nash prediction is also the mode and median of the distribution of prices both with and without a price ceiling.

We now turn on the alleged focal-point effects of the price ceilings. From results 1 and 2 and Figure 4.2, it is clear that the price ceiling of 2.20 does not predict average prices well. The histogram in Figure 4.3 shows that the 2.20 bracket is of minor importance at best. We find that the price of 2.20 was set only 9 times (or 0.625%) when the ceiling was effective (where the total number of price observations is 1440).[8] Moreover, the price ceiling of 2.20 is never included in the confidence intervals mentioned above. We conclude

---

[8] For comparison, the number of choices for the candidate collusive price $p = 2.40$ when no price ceiling is in effect is much higher (32 or 2.2% of price choices). So there are more attempts at collusion without a price ceiling, contrary to the focal point hypothesis. Interestingly, even the ceiling price $p = 2.20$ is chosen more often (24 times) when no ceiling is in place than when it is.

Table 4.5 *Summary statistics of prices, standard deviations in parentheses*

		treatment HighLow	
		all periods	periods 16–30, 46–60
phase 1	High Ceiling	1.87 (0.21)	1.82 (0.06)
phase 2	Low Ceiling	1.81 (0.05)	1.80 (0.03)

Result 3. The price ceiling does not play a role in firms' price choices. There are virtually no attempts to establish 2.20 as a collusive price.

We finally report on our third treatment, HighLow. The rationale for this treatment was that collusion under the high ceiling may be too difficult to sustain because incentives to deviate are relatively higher. Collusion should be more likely in the second phase. However, see Table 4.5, we do not observe much collusion here. The Nash equilibrium prediction works well again and the ceilings have no apparent impact on behavior. The Nash equilibrium price 1.80 is again the mean and mode in both phases.

Result 4. The price ceiling does not have any influence on firms' price-setting behavior in treatment HighLow.

6. Discussion

Why does the focal point hypothesis fail in our data? It seems that subjects take the price ceiling as an upper bound from which to stay away rather than to coordinate on. They leave a "buffer" between the ceiling and their choices and never try to collude on this highest price possible. Note also the difference in behavior in the early periods of the second phase. Whereas in LowNo subjects jauntily set very high prices (higher than the price that would maximize joint profits, 3.00), in NoLow subjects are not even close to the maximum admissible price.

Perhaps the most surprising aspect of our data is the strong convergence to equilibrium. Generally, posted-offer markets sometimes converge to the competitive equilibrium, but often prices stay higher (Plott, 1989), possibly because Nash-equilibrium prices are higher. Here, however, we observe convergence to the competitive equilibrium in all treatments and all sessions. There was only one group that does not converge but manages to collude for a while. We see the following possible reasons for this surprisingly robust convergence:

- As opposed to the majority of posted-offer markets, our design implies a unique Nash-equilibrium which coincides with the upper end of the competitive price range.
- Sellers were restricted to setting prices but their quantity choice was automated. This may have prevented a collusive high-price low-quantity strategy, which might have made collusion comparatively difficult because it required exact coordination on a price.
- The fact that buyers were simulated eliminated non-maximizing behavior of the buyers. This in turn ensures that sellers obtain their equilibrium profits if they set equilibrium prices, which facilitates convergence. Put differently, in our experiment only the sellers needed to converge to equilibrium, while in posted-offer markets with human buyers, the behavior of both sellers and buyers has to converge.

7. Conclusion

In this chapter, we have reported on experiments designed to test the focal point hypothesis of price ceilings. This hypothesis argues that price ceilings may have the counter-intuitive effect of raising prices rather than lowering them. The logic is that price ceilings serve as a coordination device. Because the price ceiling is a focal point, firms will find it easier to collude than without the ceiling.

In our experimental data, we do not find such an effect at all. Prices are initially lower with a ceiling than without one, and later in the experiment they do not differ significantly. The maximum admissable price is virtually never chosen. Further, we find strong evidence that the Nash equilibrium price predicts the data very well.

Our results are consistent with previous findings by Isaac and Plott (1981) and Smith and Williams (1981) who analyze double auction markets with price controls and Coursey and Smith (1983) who do the same for posted-offer markets. Our results strengthen these earlier results, because we provide substantially higher potential gains from collusion and ensure that the price ceiling is not binding with respect to Nash-equilibrium prices. Our results are in contrast to the field-data study by Knittel and Stango (2003) who find a focal point effect of price ceilings.

Dufwenberg *et al.* (2007) analyze price floors in simple duopoly experiments with perfect Bertrand competition. They find that such a minimum bound may actually lower prices. Without the floor, subjects' choices are somehow bounded away from marginal cost pricing whereas, with the price floor, competition drives prices towards the price floor. As a result, average prices are higher without the floor. Their findings are not predicted by the Nash equilibrium or the quantal-response equilibrium generalization of Nash equilibrium. It seems surprising that a price floor can attract prices whereas sellers stay away from price ceilings.

Appendix: Instructions

This is an experiment on market decision-making. Take the time to read carefully the instructions. A good understanding of the instructions and well thought out decisions during the experiment can earn you a considerable amount of money.

In this experiment, you will be one of four sellers in a market. You will have to decide at which price you are going to sell a fictitious commodity. There will be 2 times 30 periods of trade. After the first 30 periods, we will change the market conditions. We will inform you in detail about theses changes after the first 30 periods are over.

During the 60 periods the other three sellers in the market are represented by the same subjects. That is, though there are 12 participants in the room, the same four sellers will serve the market for the entire course of the experiment. The other 8 participants will serve other markets.

The trade of the commodity determines your payoff in "Points". After the experiment, your payment in Pound Sterling will be computed and you will be paid immediately in cash. You will get £1 for every 20 Points you earned. In addition, you receive a payment of £4 independently of the points you earned.

In what follows, we will explain to you how sales in the market will be done and how your earnings are computed. After you have read the instructions, you will have the opportunity to ask questions. Before we start with the actual experiment, we will ask you a few questions in order to review these instructions and ensure everybody has fully understood them. Then we will begin the first trading period.

How sales are done

In every period, you and the other three sellers in the market choose a price at which you wish to sell units of the commodity. While you may sell more than one unit, you can post only one price. That is, you cannot sell different units at different prices. Prices may have two decimal points.

Each seller can produce and sell up to six units in every period. You have to pay production costs for each unit you sell. The production costs for each unit you may sell are as follows:

Unit	Costs in Points
1	0.50
2	0.90
3	1.30
4	1.70
5	2.10
6	2.50

What the table says is that, for the first unit you may sell, you have costs of 0.50 Points. If you sell a second unit, this second unit costs you 0.90 Points, and so on for units 3 to 6. For example, if you sell two units, your total costs are 0.50 + 0.90 = 1.40. You do not incur any costs for units which you do not sell. Note that all four sellers in the market have the same costs of production. (In fact, everybody in the room is reading the same instructions.)

The number of units of the commodity you offer will automatically be chosen by the computer in a way that ensures that you do not make losses. At most, you will sell the quantity that can be produced at costs below or equal to your chosen price. For example, if you post a price of 1.43, you will not sell more than 3 units. That is, the computer program ensures that you will never sell any units at a price below production costs. Note that this is the maximum quantity you may sell. The actual quantity you will sell will depend on the demand and on the prices that you and the other sellers choose.

How purchases are done

No buyers participate in this experiment. Instead, buyers are simulated by the computer. Each simulated buyer can buy exactly one unit. Each buyer has a certain (maximum) willingness to pay for the unit. This willingness to pay is simply the highest price at which the simulated buyer will purchase the commodity. These maximum prices buyers are willing to pay and the according number of buyers who have this willingness to pay are as follows:

willingness to pay	number of buyers with this willingness to pay
3.60	4
3.00	4
2.40	4
1.80	4
1.20	4
0.90	4

From the table you see that there are 24 buyers in total. 4 buyers are willing to pay up to 3.60 Points for their unit, 4 more buyers are willing to pay up to 3.00 Points for a unit, and similarly 4 buyers are willing to pay 2.40, 1.80, 1.20 and 0.90 respectively. Note that, given these values, no unit will be purchased from sellers who set a price higher than 3.60.

After you and the other sellers have chosen the prices, the simulated buyers make purchases according to the following rules:

1. Buyers purchase in decreasing order of their willingness to pay. That is, the first four buyers who purchase are those who pay up to 3.60 for their unit. Then come the buyers who pay up to 3.00, and so on.
2. Buyers start to purchase from the seller with the lowest price, then buyers purchase from the seller with the next lowest price, and so on.
3. Buyers purchase their unit only if the price of that unit does not exceed their willingness to pay. As long as a price posted by you or another seller does not exceed this maximum price, the buyer will buy.
4. If two or more sellers post the same price, the buyers who want to buy at this price will split their demand equally between these sellers.

    For example, assume that there are two sellers who charge a price of 2.89 (implying a total demand of 8 units at this price). Suppose further that the other two sellers charged lower prices such that these two sellers already sold 7 units. Then the two sellers charging a price of 2.89 face a demand of 1 unit jointly together, and our rule number four would imply that both sell half a unit. Each of them would incur costs for only half a unit, $(0.50/2 = 0.25)$. This is why we allow the commodity to be divisible.

Earnings and feedback

Your earnings are as follows. For every unit you sell, you earn the difference between your price and production costs for that unit. Total earnings in every period are the sum of earnings for all units sold. The computer will calculate the earnings for all units sold and also total earnings.

At the end of each period, you will see a screen informing you about the following:

- The prices charged by the other sellers in the market.
- The total quantity supplied by other sellers at prices lower than your price.
- The total demand at your price.
- The number of units you sold.
- Your total costs for the units you sold.
- Your resulting profit.

As an aside, the prices of the other sellers are given in decreasing order. Therefore you cannot identify other sellers by the position of their price in the feedback screen.

Summary of instructions

- Sellers:
  - Sellers can produce and sell up to 6 units. All sellers have the same costs of production.
  - Sellers earn the difference between the price and their unit costs.
  - By posting a price, sellers decide to sell any number of (up to six) units at this price as long as production costs do not exceed the price.
- Buyers:
  - Buyers are simulated by the computer.
  - Each buyer can buy one unit.

- Buyers buy as long as the price does not exceed their willingness to pay.
- Buyers shop in order of decreasing willingness to pay.
- Buyers start purchasing from the cheapest seller.
- The experiment is divided into a series of 2 × 30 trading periods. You and the same other three sellers will serve one market for the whole 60 periods.

References

Coursey, D. and Smith, V. L. (1983), Price Controls in a Posted Offer Market, *American Economic Review*, 73, 218–221.

Davis, D. and Holt, Ch. (1993), *Experimental Economics*, Princeton University Press, Princeton, N.J.

Dufwenberg, M., Goeree, J., Gneezy, U. and Nagel, R. (2007), Price Floors and Competition, *Economic Theory*, 33, 207–224.

Fischbacher, U. (2007), z-Tree – Zurich Toolbox for Readymade Economic Experiments, *Experimental Economics*, 10, 171–178.

Isaac, R. M. and Plott, C. R. (1981), Price Controls and the Behavior of Auction Markets, An Experimental Examination, *American Economic Review*, 71, 448–459.

Knittel, R. K. and Stango, V. (2003), Price Ceilings as Focal Points for Tacit Collusion, Evidence from Credit Cards, *American Economic Review*, 93, 1703–1729.

Kujal, P. (1999), Price Ceilings and Firm-Specific Quantity Restrictions in Posted-Offer Markets, *Information Economics and Policy*, 11, 389–406.

Plott, C. R. (1989), An Updated Review of Industrial Organization, Applications of Experimental Methods, in *Handbook of Industrial Organization*, eds. R. Schmalensee and R. Willig, Amsterdam, North-Holland, 1109–1176.

Rassenti, S. J., Smith, V. L., Wilson, B. J. (2001), Turning Off the Lights, *Regulation*, 24, 70–76.

Scherer, F. M., and Ross, D. (1990), *Industrial Market Structure and Economic Performance*, 3rd edn., Boston, Houghton Mifflin.

Smith, V., and Williams, A. (1981), On Non-Binding Price Controls in a Competitive Market, *American Economic Review*, 71, 467–471.

Tirole, J. (1988), *Theory of Industrial Organization*, Cambridge, MA, MIT Press.

White, H. (1980), A Heteroskedasticity-Consistent Covariance Matrix Estimator and a Direct Test for Heteroskedasticity, *Econometrica*, 48, 817–838.

5 | Transparency about past, present and future conduct: experimental evidence on the impact on competitiveness

JAN POTTERS*

Transparency relates to communication and information about the conduct of firms. Transparency can relate to the past, the present and the future and it can vary in format, content and reliability. In this chapter I review experimental evidence which relates to the impact of transparency on the competitiveness of markets.

1. Introduction

Competition, free and unfettered, is absolutely destructive to all stability of prices ... Knowledge regarding bids and prices actually made is all that is necessary to keep prices at reasonably stable and normal levels. (Arthur J. Eddy, as quoted in Scherer and Ross, 1990: 348)

In his book *The New Competition* Eddy suggested a policy of "open prices" in which competitors be actively stimulated to communicate and exchange price information or that industries set up trade associations to provide the service for them. Eddy's proposal fell on fertile ground. In the decades following his recommendation, open price associations formed in several industries. In the 1930s some 400 associations were approved by the National Recovery Administration in the United States. The practice of information exchange between competitors is still very much alive today. A significant recent example is the Airline Tariff Publishing Company set up by the major US airlines to exchange detailed information about fares, proposed fare changes, fare restrictions and other marketing data.

Ever since its initiation the open price policy has been under scrutiny of the antitrust authorities. Dissemination of information has met with varying degrees of hostility by the courts, in both the US and

* I would like to thank Bert Schoonbeek for helpful comments.

Europe. Two leading cases in the early 1920s testify of the troubled treatment of information exchange by the courts (see Scherer and Ross, 1990: 347–352, for a concise treatment of these and other landmark cases). In 1921 the Supreme Court found the reporting system enacted by the American Hardwood Manufacturers Association to be an illegal conspiracy in restraint of trade. In the Court's opinion "genuine competitors do not make daily, weekly and monthly reports about their business to their rivals, as the defendants did". Just two years later the Supreme Court took a more permissive stand toward information exchange. The Maple Flooring Manufacturers Association employed policies that were quite similar to those of the hardwood manufacturers. Now, however, the Court decided that "[p]ersons who unite in gathering and disseminating information … are not engaged in unlawful conspiracies in restraint of trade merely because the ultimate result of their efforts may be to stabilize prices and limit production through a better understanding of economic laws …" (quoted in Phillips, 1959: 23).

It must be admitted that economic science has been quite equivocal about information exchange as well (Kühn and Vives, 1995). In the model of perfect competition it is assumed that market participants have full information about prices and other relevant market variables. Therefore, some have argued, a system of communication and information exchange that brings a market closer to this ideal state will improve the efficiency of a market. Convergence to competitive prices will be quicker and the probability that extra-marginal units trade will decrease. Moreover, to the extent that buyers also enjoy the increased price transparency, there will be a positive effect on competitiveness.

More common among economists, however, is a concern about the potential anti-competitive effects of communication and information exchange among competitors. There are at least two reasons for this. First, communication may make it easier to coordinate and agree on a collusive price. Usually competing firms are not completely symmetric. Products are often differentiated to some degree and production costs may differ across firms. As a result, firms may disagree on what the preferred collusive prices are or on how they should react in case someone deviates from this price. Arriving at some coordinated course of action may be facilitated by direct communication. Second, information about the conduct of other firms is needed to monitor adherence to a collusive agreement (whether tacit or explicit). The central problem of any cartel is that participating firms have a constant temptation to cheat on the agreement. The longer it takes the other firms to find out that one firm has cheated, the larger the incentives will be to actually cheat. In the absence of reliable information about others' conduct there is also the danger that collusion breaks down because of a false positive. Therefore, the availability of quick and complete information on the conduct of other firms is important for the sustainability of collusion.

Many discussions about competition policy as well as actual anti-trust cases resolve around these issues of communication and information (Kühn, 2001). As we have just seen it is hard to settle the issue purely on the basis of theoretical arguments. Empirical studies on the impact of information exchange are scarce. Arguably the strongest evidence on price communication is by Albaek *et al.* (1997). The Danish anti-trust authority decided to gather and publish firm-specific transaction prices in the ready-mixed concrete industry. The aim was to promote competition by increasing transparency (in particular for buyers). The result of the policy, however, seemed exactly opposite to the authority's aim. Average prices increased by 15–20% within a year following the initial setup. This 'natural experiment' provides quite compelling support for the concern that *open* prices may well be *high* prices. This study is unique in its kind and unfortunately other evidence is much less convincing. This leads Kühn to the assertion that "unfortunately we know very little about how important communication is in practice to establish collusive outcomes".

In this chapter I review the experimental literature that deals with the effects of information and communication on market outcomes. This means that I take a rather broad perspective on transparency. Given the space limitations, taking such a broad perspective implies that I will have to take some short cuts on other accounts. First, I will focus attention on the impact of transparency on competitiveness and collusion, as measured by the level of prices. This means that I will mostly ignore the effects of transparency on other performance measures such as efficiency or convergence. Second, I restrict attention to experiments that have an explicit industrial organization orientation. I will not discuss the emerging experimental literature on transparency in financial markets which deals with somewhat

different issues (such as price efficiency and liquidity) than those of
competition policy (see, e.g., Bloomfield and O'Hara, 1999; Huisman
and Koedijk 1998). Also I will disregard the experimental literature
that deals with issues of communication and information in experimental settings other than markets, such as the provision of public
goods. Finally, I will pay relatively little attention to design issues and
obviously cannot do justice to the details and richness of the individual studies. I will focus on the results and how they relate to issues
of transparency. (See also the chapter by Haan, Schoonbeek and
Winkel in this volume on collusion issues in general.)

The information from the various papers will be organized by
formulating a series of *observations*. These observations should be
seen as my interpretations of a diverse set of results from a variety
of papers. They should not be taken as firmly established facts that
have passed the tests of replication and refinement. The aim is to
accessibly organize the experimental results on transparency contained in a wide set of papers with very different aims, designs and
interpretations.

The remainder of this chapter is organized as follows. The next three
sections will review the experimental evidence that deals with communication and information about future, present and past actions,
respectively. The final section contains a concluding discussion.

2. Transparency about future conduct of competitors

People of the same trade seldom meet together, even for merriment and
diversion, but the conversation ends in a conspiracy against the public.
(Adam Smith, *Wealth of Nations*, Book I, Chapter 10)

Explicit price-fixing agreements are illegal per se under the Sherman
Act and under Article 85 of the European Union. As a consequence,
price-fixing agreements or other restraints on competition are not
contractible, simply because such contracts are not enforceable by a
court of law. From this perspective conspiracies are merely talk, no
more and no less. Agreements and promises about future conduct can
be regarded as "soft" information. Hence, from an economist's point
of view the proposition that such information will affect market outcomes is far from trivial. However, if there are multiple equilibria —
which is not unlikely in repeated games — then even cheap talk may

help to coordinate on a certain equilibrium. Moreover, talk is perhaps less cheap than economists tend to think and reneging on a promise may involve a direct disutility. Therefore, promises and agreements may reduce strategic uncertainty and increase transparency about the likely course of future action.

Before we discuss the effects, let us first see whether and how subjects use communication possibilities in the first place.

Observation 2.1 When given the opportunity to communicate, competitors will use it to conspire and often they manage to come to some form of price fixing agreement.

Friedman (1967) was the first to examine experimental markets in which competitors were allowed to communicate. He set up duopoly markets with price competition and product differentiation. Demand was simulated, and the relation between prices and profits was presented to the subjects in bi-matrix form. Before prices were set, one seller could send a written message to the other seller who could then send one written response. The results indicated that in 75% of the cases a collusive agreement was formed.

Unstructured face-to-face communication was allowed in Isaac and Plott (1981), Isaac *et al.* (1984) and Davis and Holt (1998). Sellers and buyers were in different rooms and they were instructed that they could speak to each other except during brief periods of recess between trading rounds. They could discuss anything they wished except that they could not mention side payments, threats or reveal their private payoff information. Isaac and Plott report that sometimes it took a few periods but then often quite specific collusive strategies were discussed. The following quote illustrates this: "So, let's try starting the bidding like up at a dollar at the beginning and see if they go for it, and then, like, keep it between 90 cents and a dollar ..." (Isaac and Plott, 1981: 18). Often the discussions were intertwined with conversations about items of personal interest.

Also when communication is more structured, competitors often manage to come to an agreement. For example, in Andersson and Wengström (2007) communication between duopolists was restricted to one subject suggesting "I consider ... to be the appropriate price," and the other subject responding by "I agree" or "I disagree." They find that in about 50% of the cases the two competitors managed to come to an agreement.

Observation 2.2 Direct communication can have a substantial impact on prices.

Friedman (1967) is an early paper suggesting that communication between competitors can lead to highly collusive outcomes. As we saw 75% of the duopolies managed to agree on some collusive price, and this agreement was subsequently honored in 90% of the cases. Friedman did not run a control treatment without communication, so we cannot attribute the collusion he observed to such communication. Strictly speaking it could also be due to the market structure.

Isaac *et al.* (1984) is the first study that finds a substantial and significant price increasing effect of seller conspiracies. They implemented posted-offer markets with four sellers and four buyers, who each could trade up to three units. At the beginning of a trading period the sellers independently posted take-it-or-leave prices and the number of units they were prepared to sell at this price. Then buyers were selected in a random order and could decide if and from whom they wished to buy units. Market sessions consisted of somewhere between fifteen and twenty periods. Isaac *et al.* ran a control treatment in which sellers were not allowed to communicate directly and one conspiracy treatment in which in between periods, and without the buyers knowing this, sellers were given the opportunity to talk about the market. The results show that in the control treatment prices tended to converge toward the competitive equilibrium price while in the conspiracy treatments, average prices were significantly above the competitive price at a level about halfway toward the monopoly price.

Davis and Holt (1998) employ a very similar posted-offer design with three sellers and three buyers and treatments with and without conspiracies. Also their results are very similar. In the control treatment average transaction prices were very close to the competitive equilibrium price. In the markets with conspiracies, on the other hand, average prices were above the competitive price (39.4 above it to be precise) and approaching the joint profit maximizing price (which was 55 above the competitive price).

Observation 2.3 Conspiracies do not always have a (lasting) effect on prices.

Isaac and Plott (1981) study double-auction markets with four sellers and four buyers which were open for eight periods. They compare a control treatment without conspiracies with treatments in which either the buyers or the sellers are allowed to communicate face-to-face in between periods, as described above. Isaac and Plott find very little effect of the communication possibilities on the average price level. Compared to the control treatment, prices moved only about 6% in the direction of the conspiring side. As we have discussed under Observation 2.1, it is not that the traders did not attempt to conspire, it is just that their attempts were not successful.

Holt and Davis (1990) is a study that finds only a transitory effect of communication (see also Cason, 1995; Cason and Davis, 1995). They set up markets in which three sellers simultaneously posted prices and demand was simulated. First, there were fifteen periods without communication and then there were at least ten periods with price announcement and a random stopping rule after this tenth period. The communication proceeded over the computer and was very structured. At the beginning of a period one of the three sellers was selected at random to make an announcement of the form: '$ ... is the appropriate for this period.' The other two sellers could then respond with A (agree), H (price should be higher) or, L (price should be lower). The results indicate that the announcements had a clear initial effect on prices. The effect however was only temporary and by the tenth period prices were almost back at the level where they were before the announcements were introduced.

Observation 2.4 Factors found to affect the effectiveness of communication include: (a) the market institution (posted prices versus double auctions), (b) the market environment (demand and supply structure), (c) the communication format (face-to-face versus impersonal), and (d) the cost of communication.

Factor (a) is based on Isaac and Plott (1981) and Isaac *et al.* (1984). The former employ double-auction markets and find very little effect of conspiracies, while the latter find that prices are significantly affected by conspiracies in posted-offer markets. Moreover, Isaac *et al.* also conduct double-auction markets with conspiracies and find prices to be lower than in posted-offer markets with the same demand and supply configuration. Clauser and Plott (1993) examine the reason for this difference and find evidence for the following explanation. In posted-offer markets sellers can only submit price offers at the beginning of a period and cannot revise these offers once the market has opened for trading. In double-auction markets sellers have much more flexibility and can revise their prices continuously. This flexibility makes it the more difficult for conspiring sellers to resist the temptation to renege on an agreement.

Factor (b) follows from Holt and Davis (1990); see also Cason (1995). The former paper compares the effect of conspiracies in two different environments: a "power design" and a "no power" design. The former design was expected and found to make conspiracies more effective as it made the joint profit maximizing price more focal and reduced the temptation to cheat (in either case the effect seemed rather transitory as was just discussed).

There is no direct evidence for factor (c). Yet, comparing across different studies it is noticeable that posted-offer studies with face-to-face and free-form communication (Isaac *et al.* 1984), Davis and Holt, 1998) tend to find a more substantial impact than those with impersonal and structured communication (Holt and Davis, 1990, Cason, 1995, Harstad *et al.*, 1998, Andersson and Wengström, 2007).

Finally, factor (d) is based on Andersson and Wengström (2007). They study price-setting Bertrand duopolies with structured pre-play communication. Markets were repeated with a random continuation probability and an expected length of fourteen periods. As in Holt and Davis (1990), before each period one seller had the opportunity to send a message saying "I think ... is the appropriate price" and the other seller could respond with "I agree" or "I disagree." In the study the per-period cost of sending these messages was systematically varied. In one treatment the cost was zero, in a second treatment the costs were low (about a quarter of the stage game monopoly profits), and in a third treatment the costs were high (equal to the stage game monopoly profits). The results indicate that when the cost of communication increased its frequency decreased while its effectiveness increased. The net effect implied that the incidence of collusion went up dramatically as the cost of conspiring increased. This result suggests that players feel more committed to an agreement if substantial costs had to be borne to reach the agreement.[1] One cause for an increase in the costs of conspiring is a more strict enforcement of competition policy. Therefore, the authors argue that such an enforcement may

---

[1] This result is similar to the finding that the likelihood of collusion increases with an increase in entry costs (Offerman and Potters, 2006).

actually be counterproductive. This interpretation seems a bit bold though. For one thing, competition policy imposes an uncertain (i.e., expected) cost rather than a fixed cost like in the experiment.

3. Transparency about current prices

Prices change with varying frequency, and, unless a market is completely centralized, no one will know all the prices which the various sellers (or buyers) quote at any given time. (Stigler, 1961: 213)

In this section we will review the experimental evidence that relates to transparency about current prices. At least two potentially conflicting effects may be at work here. On the one hand, if sellers can immediately and reliably observe each other's prices, the incentive to undercut prices of competitors may be seriously weakened. Competitors will detect the price cut immediately and in order to prevent a price war, it is perhaps better to refrain from the price cut in the first place. On the other hand, if buyers are better informed about sellers' current prices they will be better able to make price comparisons, which may make stimulate competition among the sellers. Hence, it is important to distinguish which side of the market gets better information about sellers' current prices: only the sellers, only the buyers, or both.

Observation 3.1 If information about current prices is public, i.e., available to both sellers and buyers, then there is no unambiguous effect on competitiveness.

A paper which presents (weak) evidence for a negative effect on competition is Hong and Plott (1982). This is the first study to use experiments for a practical question of market regulation. This paper was motivated by a new price-setting policy proposed (by the railroads!) for the inland water transportation industry. Rather than using private bilateral negotiations, it was proposed that shippers post their prices with a central agency. The railroads argued that the public information feature of prices would make the market more competitive. The regulator was skeptical about the argument and commissioned an experimental study (Plott, 1987).

This experimental study is remarkable for a number of reasons. It consisted of four sessions of three hours each with the same thirty-three subjects, which included engineers, students, secretaries and housewives. Considerable effort was taken to bring the demand and supply parameters of the experimental market in line with those of the waterways barge industry. A price-posting institution was used for two experimental sessions. At the beginning of a period, sellers posted their prices. These prices were then listed on a piece of paper and photocopied for all traders in the market. When the market opened ("at the sound of a horn"), subjects were free to call another subject and make a purchase or sale at the price posted by the seller. A telephone market was used on the other two days. Buyers and sellers could call each other and negotiate contracts privately. No one but the two traders involved would know about the contract, although subjects were free to discuss (or lie) about deals made with other subjects.

The results suggest that the skepticism of the administrators was warranted. The posted-price policy resulted in higher prices and lower efficiency. In the posted-price sessions the prices were from 5 to 9% above those in the telephone markets (and also a little above the competitive price). The price effect seems rather modest in size. Whether it is statistically significant is hard to say.

Grether and Plott (1984) is another experimental study commissioned by a government agency. The Federal Trade Commission brought action against four chemical companies and asked them to stop using several marketing practices that the FTC believed to be anticompetitive. One of these practices was that firms publicly announced prices. Another is the use of a most-favored customer clause, which effectively rules out private price discounts from the announced prices. The results reveal that in combination these practices led to substantially higher prices. Each individual practice did not seem to have a strong anti-competitive effect, but the design does not really allow for a clean assessment of the effects of the different practices in isolation.

Both Joyce (1983) and Kirchsteiger *et al.* (2005) compare double-auction markets and decentralized-bargaining markets. In a double-auction market, a seller (buyer) can continuously submit price offers to the market which indicate he (she) is prepared to sell (buy) at that price. All offers are public information and at any time a buyer can accept an offer from a seller and vice versa. A decentralized-bargaining market is like a "telephone market" in Hong and Plott. Buyers and sellers can contact each other on a bilateral basis and can try to negotiate a mutually acceptable transaction price. No trader other than the two bargaining parties is informed about current price offers.

Hence, one can say that in moving from a decentralized-bargaining market to a double-auction market, transparency on price offers increases for both sides of the market. No effect on the average level of transaction prices was observed in these markets though. In both studies the average prices were very close to the competitive price. For example, in Joyce average transaction prices were 2.589 in the double-auction market and 2.597 in the decentralized-bargaining market (with the competitive price at 2.6). At the same time, efficiency usually increased significantly with the increase in transparency.

One might argue that in view of the symmetric role of sellers and buyers in both the double-auction and the decentralized-bargaining market no effect on average price should be expected. Posted-offer markets could be more relevant to examine a potentially negative effect of public information about sellers' prices. Davis and Holt (1994) is the only paper I know that speaks to this issue (at least indirectly). In a standard posted-offer market, sellers post prices and buyers then decide from whom to buy at these posted prices. No trades can occur at prices other than the ones publicly listed. In particular, sellers cannot grant private discounts to individual buyers. In line with Stigler (1964) one might conjecture that the absence of secret discounts, whether by contract or by industry custom, impedes competition and fosters collusion. To examine this Davis and Holt compare a standard posted-offer market with a posted-offer market with private discounts. At the beginning of the period sellers post prices publicly and simultaneously. Then buyers are selected in random sequence. In the standard market, the buyer simply decides from whom to buy at posted prices. In the market with discounts, each buyer can buy at the posted price or request for a private discount. Sellers are free to grant such a discount which will be observed by no one but the buyer involved. All the sessions involved two sellers and three (human) buyers, and markets lasted for at least fifteen periods. The results indicate that the presence of secret discounting increased the variance across different sessions, but no effect on average transaction prices was discernible. The fact that the transaction prices were public information (and not just the "list prices") did not reduce seller competition.

Observation 3.2 If price transparency improves only for sellers (and not buyers), or if sellers are involved in an active conspiracy then competitiveness will be restricted.

Davis and Holt (1998) examine markets which are characterized by explicit conspiracies among the three sellers (see also the previous section). In one treatment, after the seller discussions, the market proceeded along standard posted-offer trading rules, implying that all trades must be made at the posted prices. In the second treatment, the sellers were given an opportunity to give private secret discounts. Upon contacting a seller a buyer could request a discount. The seller could then respond by offering a price below the list price. As in Davis and Holt (1994) discounts were observed only by the buyer concerned and not by other buyers or sellers.

As we have already seen in the previous section, the posted-offer markets with conspiracies and without secret discounts were very collusive. The average price in the last five periods was 39.4 (with the competitive price at 0 and the joint profit maximizing price at 55). As soon as the possibility for secret discounts was introduced, however, the posted-offer markets with conspiracies generated significantly lower prices with an average of 14.9 in the last five periods. In fact, cartels failed in five of the six markets. This was in spite of the fact that sellers could discuss and conspire not just once but each time before the market opened. Hence, the possibility to offer prices privately and selectively was an important impediment to successful conspiracies.

Kirchsteiger *et al.* (2005) examine endogenous rather than exogenous information about current prices. They set up two-sided auction markets with six buyers and six sellers, who each could trade at most one unit. When submitting a price offer to the market, sellers decided whether or not to inform their competitors about this price offer. Kirchsteiger *et al.* found that high (supra-competitive) price offers were more likely to be communicated to competing sellers than low price offers. This suggests that price sharing was at least partly driven by collusive intentions. It is as if sellers wanted to send a message to keep prices at a high level by informing each other about their high price quotes. When posting a relatively low price sellers were less likely to inform their rivals. Price communication also had a discernible effect on transaction prices. Prices were higher in periods with relatively frequent information exchange about price offers than in periods with relatively infrequent information exchange. The effect is small in size but statistically significant. At the same time, there is no evidence that increased price communication among sellers reduced price dispersion, speeded up convergence or increased efficiency.

Another interesting result in Kirchsteiger *et al.* is that price communication tended to have a public good character. As we have just seen, sellers as a group benefited from price communication. Individually, however, sellers were better off to conceal their price offers from competitors as this reduced the probability that an offer would be undercut by a rival. Kirchsteiger *et al.* found that price communication was unlikely to arise endogenously when sellers could decide to conceal or reveal price offers individually and freely. Only when price communication was "sponsored" was it getting of the ground to some extent. This suggests that some (trade) association may be needed to stimulate or organize price communications.

Observation 3.3 If price transparency increases for buyers only, then there is a positive effect on competition.

In the competition policy debate, improved transparency is typically viewed as promoting competition if it affects only the buyer side of the market. If buyers get better information about sellers' current prices, while sellers' information is not affected, a downward pressure on prices will be effectuated. The experimental evidence supports this view.

Davis and Holt (1996), for example, study markets with three buyers and three sellers. At the beginning of a trading period sellers simultaneously post their prices. Then the buyers were randomly selected one at a time and given the opportunity to approach a seller and make a purchase. A buyer incurred a cost when approaching a seller (like a travel cost). There were two treatments. In the posted-offer treatment, a buyer could see all sellers' prices, while in the search treatment a buyer could only see a seller's price offer after this seller had been approached. Sellers could not see one another's posted prices in either treatment. Davis and Holt find that in the search treatment the transaction prices were significantly higher than in the posted-offer treatment. If it was more difficult for buyers to make price comparisons, the competitive pressure on sellers was clearly lower. Cason *et al.* (2003) compare haggling (decentralized-bargaining) markets and posted-offer markets, and find a result that is much in line with Davis and Holt (1996). Competitive pressure was lower in the haggling markets in which it was more difficult for buyers to make price comparisons.[2]

More evidence for the observation comes from studies that vary the exogenous search costs of buyers or the costs from switching to another seller (Cason and Friedman, 1999, 2002, 2003; Cason *et al.* 2003). For example, Cason and Friedman, (1999) study posted-offer markets in which buyers costlessly observe one or two of the posted prices but have to pay a cost if they wish to observe price offers from more sellers. Results indicate that competition softens and prices increase if buyer search costs increase (at least when inexperienced human buyers are used in the experiment).

Related results are reported in studies that vary the fraction of informed consumers (Morgan *et al.* 2006a) or studies that vary the costs of sellers to advertise their prices (Cason and Datta, 2006; Morgan *et al.* 2006b). A special feature of these studies, however, is that buyer behavior is simulated. For example Morgan *et al.*, 2006b, employ markets in which sellers simultaneously choose prices and decide whether or not to advertise their prices in each period. One half of the buyers are bargain hunters who buy from whichever seller advertises the lowest price; the other half of the buyers are price insensitive and always buy from the same seller. Morgan *et al.* find that higher advertising costs decrease demand for advertising and raise advertised prices. This comes at the expense of consumers.

Finally, note that the (search) models on which the experiments mentioned above are based are all static models. The impact of buyer transparency on tacit collusion has not been investigated much. A recent model by Schultz (2005) shows that there may be two opposing effects. An increase of transparency increases the benefit from undercutting a rival's price, but it also decreases the punishment profit. Schultz shows that in a market with product differentiation the first effect tends to dominate, making it harder to sustain collusion. This prediction still awaits experimentation however.

---

[2] As in Davis and Holt (1996), seller information about competitors' prices is held constant across the two treatments in Cason *et al.* (2003). This is why the results in these two studies are discussed here and not under Observation 3.1.

4. Transparency about past conduct of competitors

Several experimental studies are related to this issue of information on past conduct of competitors. Some studies directly address the antitrust concerns; others speak to the issue in a more indirect manner.

Observation 4.1 Reliable information feedback about competitors' prices fosters the stability of explicit conspiracies.

Experiments show that conspiracies are less successful and less stable when feedback information about competitors' conduct is lacking. The first piece of evidence is contained in Holcomb and Nelson (1991) who studied twenty repeated symmetric quantity-setting duopolies. In the first phase of the experiment firms were allowed to conspire and they also received perfect information feedback about their competitor's quantity choice. In the second phase of the experiment, information feedback became imperfect: in each period, there was a 50% probability the feedback received corresponded to the choice made by the competitor and a 50% probability the feedback provided was a random draw from the set of possible quantities. Profits were determined by the reported choice (whether real or random). The results show that in the first phase with perfect monitoring no less than seventeen out of the twenty pairs were perfectly collusive (joint profit maximizing) in at least the last ten periods of the game. As soon as monitoring became imperfect though, collusion became very unstable and sixteen of the seventeen previously collusive duopolies moved toward the Cournot equilibrium. This result clearly suggests that reliable information feedback about what competitors are doing is essential for the stability of cartels.[3] Another interesting result of this study is that the cartels did not fail so much because some firms started to defect from the collusive outcome. Rather, the cartels failed due to false positives, that is, firms increasing quantity in reaction to the incorrect information that a competitor had defected.

---

[3] It must be noted that there is a potential confusion here. In the first phase of the experiment the duopolies had perfect information feedback *and* were allowed to communicate to each other directly. From the paper it is not entirely clear whether this communication was still allowed in the second phase of the experiment.

Davis and Holt (1998) is another paper showing the importance of reliable information feedback about competitors' conduct. As was already discussed in support of the previous result, conspiracies tend to break down when secret discounts on the posted prices are possible. One further treatment in the exceptionally rich study by Davis and Holt implements a situation in which secret discounts are still possible but all sellers receive feedback information on each other's sales volume. This situation was intended to parallel the information that is often collected and disseminated by trade associations. Although competitors' sales volumes are not a perfect signal of any discounts offered, still they appear to be a useful indicator of the degree to which competitors abide by a cartel agreement. The results reveal that average prices increase from 14.9 to 24.8 when feedback information on competitors' sales are provided. This outcome shows that the availability of this feedback information restores to some degree the stability of collusion that was undermined by the possibility of secret discounts.

Observation 4.2 Firm-specific information feedback about competitors' conduct is in some cases found to foster tacit collusion, but these cases are relatively infrequent, particularly so if the information provided includes details about profits, and if the firms compete in quantities rather than in prices.

Here the evidence is quite mixed. Some papers suggest that more detailed or more explicit information feedback on competitors' conduct reduces competition, while several others show that it may actually increase competition.

A first piece of evidence comes from Benson and Feinberg (1988), who examine price-setting duopolies with product differentiation. There are two treatments: one in which subjects received information about the rival's price after each round, and one in which feedback information was restricted to market shares. The results indicate the tacitly collusive outcomes are more frequent with explicit feedback information about rivals' prices, but the evidence is not overwhelming.

Stronger evidence that reliable information feedback on competitors' past conduct can facilitate tacit collusion is provided by Feinberg and Snyder (2002). They study repeated duopolies in which price choices were restricted to three values: a collusive price (C), an undercutting price (U) and a punishment price (P). Both (U,U) and

(P,P) are Nash equilibria of the stage game, but the payoff-dominating outcome (C,C) is not. In the game, random demand shocks were introduced which gave the same payoff as when a competitor would undercut on a collusive price (C,U). In one treatment the players knew when a demand shock had occurred, while in a second treatment they did not and could not distinguish a demand shock from a cheating competitor. The results indicated that the latter feature made tacit collusion much more difficult. In the first treatment, 68% of the choices corresponded to the collusive price, while in the second treatment this was only 21%.

Further evidence is given by Dufwenberg and Gneezy (2002). They examine a series of Bertrand duopolies. Two firms simultaneously set a price and the one with the lowest price gets a positive profit which is decreasing in the level of the price, while the firm with the highest price gets no profit.[4] In each session of the experiment the game is played ten times by twelve participants and in each period the participants are randomly matched in pairs. The experiment uses three feedback-information treatments: one in which the participants only learn whether they had the lower price of the two, one in which the participants learn all the low prices of the six duopolies and one in which they learn all prices of all six pairs. The results show a large treatment effect. When participants learn the whole set of prices, the markets are quite collusive with average transaction prices about halfway between the competitive price and monopoly price. In the other two treatments prices converge toward the competitive price. Apparently the dissemination of information about the high prices of competitors stimulates participants to charge higher prices as well.

Offerman *et al.* (2002) examine symmetric quantity-setting triopoly markets in which the same three participants interact for 100 periods. In one treatment (Q) information feedback after each period is restricted to own profits and aggregate quantity. In a second treatment (Qq) information is also provided about the individual quantities set by the two competitors. In the third treatment (Qqπ) in addition the realized profits of competitors are given. The experimental results reveal that the average levels of outputs are almost identical in the

---

[4] The game can also be interpreted as a symmetric procurement auction with complete information. This interpretation also makes a random matching protocol more realistic.

three treatments and very close to the Cournot–Nash equilibrium. A closer look at the individual triopolies (eleven in each treatment) and at the dynamics over time revealed some remarkable differences, however. In treatment Q the only frequent and stable outcome was the Cournot equilibrium. In treatment Qq apart from the Cournot outcome also the collusive joint profit-maximizing outcome was reached quite frequently by some triopolies and turned out to be very stable. In treatment Qqπ the results were even more dispersed. The Cournot outcome lost all its drawing power and outcomes were either very competitive or very collusive. So with more detailed information feedback the *range* of outcomes increased dramatically, even though the *average* degree of competition did not.

The fact that the availability of firm-specific information on past conduct and performance can increase competition is most clearly illustrated by Huck *et al.* (1999, 2000). Comparable results have been obtained by Altavilla *et al.* (2006) and Davis (2002), and these studies have an excellent predecessor in Fouraker and Siegel (1963). Huck *et al.* (1999) set up markets in which four firms compete in quantities and implement two different information treatments: one (BASIC) in which information feedback is restricted to aggregate conduct of competitors and one (EXTRA) in which individualized information about past conduct and profits of competitors is available. Huck *et al.*, find that the availability of more detailed information feedback about competitors actually increases the competitiveness of the markets. In the last half of the forty periods, average quantity is 74.7 in the BASIC treatment, which is very close to the theoretical Cournot–Nash equilibrium quantity of 74.5. In the EXTRA treatment the market becomes even more competitive with an average quantity of 83.4. And even though the range of outcomes increases somewhat in the latter treatment, very few are anywhere near the joint profit maximizing quantity of 49.7. Huck *et al.* (2000) also conduct similar experiments for markets in which the four firms compete in prices (Bertrand) rather than in quantities (Cournot). Here they find that the degree of competitiveness is about the same for the BASIC and EXTRA treatments and again very close to the noncooperative equilibrium. So also for the case of price competition they find no evidence that individualized information about past conduct and performance reduces competition. The main theoretical explanation for the competition-enhancing effect of the EXTRA treatment is that it allows firms to compare profits. This may stimulate them to imitate the conduct of the more successful competitor in the market. Typically the more successful form is the one that produces the largest quantity or charges the lowest price. Copying the behavior of this firm then tends to increase the quantity and reduce the price.

In sum, there is quite conflicting evidence on the effects of firm-specific information feedback (see also Bosch-Domenech and Vriend, 2003). Two opposite forces seem to be at work. On the one hand, detailed information on competitors' past conduct allows for signaling of intentions and monitoring of conduct. Both of these may reduce competition. On the other hand, detailed information about competitors' profits allows for an assessment of relative performances. This may stimulate imitation and make markets more competitive. The net effect seems to depend on the content of the information (does it include profit information?), the number of competitors (little collusion is observed with more than three firms) and the type of interaction (price or quantity competition).[5]

5. Concluding discussion

One lesson that can be drawn from the experimental results is that establishing and sustaining collusion is not easy. Tacit collusion in particular is not very frequently observed in experiments, even with relatively few competitors and repeated interaction. And even when competitors have a possibility to conspire, collusion is often quite unstable. This holds in particular when talk is, literally and figuratively speaking, "cheap", that is, when communication bears no cost, occurs frequently and involves little commitment. If the opportunities to defect are frequent, lucrative and hard to detect, then even explicit conspiracies often tend to be quite unstable. Hence, it seems that some form of explicit communication about future conduct is required as well as reliable information on present or past conduct.

---

[5] Furthermore, the extent to which imitation of successful other firms tends to make markets more competitive also depends on the sample taken. If the sample firm is taken from another market or from a more distant past then the competition-inducing force of imitation is weakened (Apesteguia *et al.* 2007; Bru *et al.* 2002).

One of the important issues for competition policy is whether and when information exchange on past conduct should be allowed among competitors. The experimental evidence does not provide unambiguous results on this issue. Observation 4.2 suggests that often there is little harm and in some experimental settings it was even found to increase competition. On the basis of this one might argue (and some have done so) that there is little reason to be hostile towards information exchange on past conduct, even if this involves firm-specific information.

This conclusion may be too naïve though. Observation 4.1 indicates that information exchange is important for the support of explicit collusion, and Observation 4.2 indicates that in a certain fraction of the cases information exchange does in fact stimulate tacit collusion. In the field, information exchange is not some exogenous feature of a market (like it is in an experiment). In most cases, firms or associations *choose* to have such an exchange of information.[6] Hence, a natural question to ask is: when is information exchange more or less likely to be set up? In view of Observations 4.1 and 4.2 one might expect that information exchange is more likely to be set up in markets which are characterized by some degree of explicit conspiracy. Put bluntly, information exchange is perhaps even more likely to be a *consequence* of (explicit) collusion than to be a *cause* of (implicit) collusion.

Finally, looking at the experimental methodology a lesson we learn from the experiments is that there is often a substantial variance in outcomes — across studies with similar designs and even across repetitions with an identical design (see e.g. the discussion of Observations 3.1 and 4.2). This just reiterates the importance of strategic uncertainty. It is not just the controllable variables that exert an impact on outcomes, but also uncontrollable variables. Arguably, the most important among those are the ones that relate to differences between people. Some students are just more risk averse, more confident, more patient, more competitive, or more fair than others. This

---

[6] This relates to a more general methodological issue. In experiments we tend to assess the impact of an institutional variable by comparing different treatments in which this variable is manipulated, that is, the variable is *exogenously* changed. In the field, however, the (non)occurrence of a change is often endogenous rather than exogenous, so there is a possible selection effect which is absent in the lab.

may hint at a potential drawback of experiments. To the extent that the distribution of relevant qualities is very different across students than across the target population of interest (through self-selection or learning), experiments may give a biased picture. However, it is not obvious that matters are much different in the real world. Also consumers, shop-owners, managers and CEOs differ on dimensions that may have an impact on the way they go about their business. Surely unexplained variance is a fact of life in the social sciences.

References

Albaek, Svend, Peter Møllgaard and Per Overgaard (1997), Government-Assisted Oligopoly Coordination? A *Concrete* Case, *Journal of Industrial Organization* 65 (December), 429–443.

Altavilla, Carlo, Luini, Luigi, and Sbriglia, Partizia (2006), Social Learning in Market Games, *Journal of Economic Behavior and Organization* 61, 632–652.

Andersson, Ola, and Erik Wengström (2007), Do Antitrust Laws Facilitate Collusion? Experimental Evidence of Costly Communication in Duopolies, *Scandinavian Journal of Economics* 109, 321–339.

Apesteguia, J., Huck, S., and Oechssler, J. (2007), Imitation – Theory and Experimental Evidence, *Journal of Economic Theory* 136, 217–235.

Benson, B., and Feinberg, R. (1988), An Experimental Investigation of Equilibria Impacts of Information, *Southern Economic Journal* 54 (3), 546–561

Bloomfield, Robert, and O'Hara, Maureen (1999), Market Transparency: Who Wins and Who Loses?, *Review of Financial Studies* 12 (1), 5–35.

Bosch-Domenech, A., and Vriend, N. (2003), Imitation of Successful Behavior in Cournot Markets, *Economic Journal* 113, 495–524.

Bru, L., Gomez, R., and Ordonez, J. (2002), Information in Repeated Experimental Cournot Games, in: M. Isaac and C. Holt (eds.), *Research in Experimental Economics, Volume IX. Experiments Investigating Market Power*, JAI Press, Elsevier, Amsterdam.

Cason, Timothy (1995), Cheap Talk Price Signaling in Laboratory Markets, *Information Economics and Policy* 7, 183–204.

Cason, Timothy and Datta, Shakun (2006), An Experimental Study of Price Dispersion in an Optimal Search Model with Advertizing, *International Journal of Industrial Organization* 24, 639–665.

Cason, Timothy, and Davis, Doug, (1995), Price Communications in a Multi-Market Context. An Experimental Investigation, *Review of Industrial Organization* 10, 769–787.

Cason, T., and Friedman, J. (1999), Customer Search and Market Power. Some Laboratory Evidence, *Advances in Applied Microeconomics* 8, 71–99.

(2002), A Laboratory Study of Customer Markets, *Advances in Economic Analysis and Policy* 2 (1).

(2003), Buyer Search and Price Dispersion: A Laboratory Study, *Journal of Economic Theory* 112, 232–260.

Cason, T., Friedman, J., and Milam, G. (2003), Bargaining versus Posted Prices in Customer Markets, *International Journal of Industrial Organization* 21 (2), 223–251.

Clauser, Laura, and Plott, Charles (1993), On the Anatomy of the 'Non-facilitating' Features of the Double Auction Institution in Conspiratorial Markets, in: *The Double Auction Market: Institutions, Theories, and Laboratory Evidence*, eds. D. Friedman and J. Rust, Reading, Mass.: Addison-Wesley, 333–353.

Davis, Douglas D. (2002), Strategic Interaction, Market Information, and Predicting the Effects of Mergers in Differentiated Product Markets, *International Journal of Industrial Organization* 20, 1277–1312.

Davis, Douglas D., and Charles A. Holt (1994), The Effects of Discounting Opportunities in Laboratory Posted-Offer Markets, *Economics Letters* 44, 249–253.

(1996), Consumer Search Costs and Market Performance, *Economic inquiry* 34, 133–151.

(1998), Conspiracies and Secret Discounts in Laboratory Markets, *Economic Journal* 108 (May), 736–756.

Davis, Douglas D., Wilson, Bart J. (2002), Experimental Methods and Antitrust Policy, in: *Research in Experimental Economics: Experiments Investigating Market Power*, Vol. IX, C. Holt and R. M. Isaac (eds.), Greenwich: JAI Press.

Dufwenberg, M., and Gneezy, U. (2002), Information Disclosure in Auctions: An Experiment, *Journal of Economic Behavior and Organization* 48, 431–444.

Feinberg, R., and Snyder, C. (2002), Collusion with Secret Price Cuts: An Experimental Study, *Economics Bulletin* 3 (6), 1–11.

Fouraker, L. E., and S. Siegel (1963), *Bargaining Behavior*. New York: McGraw-Hill.

Friedman, James W. (1967), An Experimental Study of Cooperative Duopoly, *Econometrica* 35, 379–397.

Grether, David M., and Plott, Charles R. (1984), The Effects of Market Practices in Oligopolistic Markets: An Experimental Examination of the Ethyl Case, *Economic Inquiry* 22, 479–507.

Harstad, Ronald, Stephen Martin and Hans-Theo Normann (1998), Intertemporal pricing schemes. Experimental tests of consciously parallel behavior in oligopoly, in: Louis Phlips (ed.), *Applied Industrial Economics*, Cambridge: Cambridge University Press.

Holcomb, James, and Paul Nelson (1991), Cartel Failure: A Mistake or Do They Do It to Each Other on Purpose?, *Journal of Socio-Economics* 20(3), 235–249.

Holt, Charles A., and Davis Douglas (1990), The Effects of Non-binding Price Announcements on Posted-Offer Markets, *Economics Letters* 34, 307–310.

Hong James T., and Plott, Charles R. (1982), Rate Filing Policies for Inland Water Transportation: An Experimental Approach, *Bell Journal of Economics* 13, 1–19.

Huck, S., H.T. Normann, and J. Oechssler (1999): Learning in Cournot Oligopoly – An Experiment, *Economic Journal*, 109, C80-C95.

(2000): Does Information about Competitors' Actions Increase or Decrease Competition in Experimental Oligopoly Markets?, *International Journal of Industrial Organization* 18, 39–57.

Huisman, Ronald, and Koedijk, Kees (1998), Financial Market Competition: The Effects of Transparency, *De Economist* 146 (3), 463–473.

Isaac, R. Mark, and Charles R. Plott (1981), The Opportunity for Conspiracies in Restraint of Trade, *Journal of Economic Behavior and Organization* 2, 1–31.

Isaac, R. Mark, Valerie Ramey and Arlington Williams (1984), The Effects of Market Organization on Conspiracies in Restraint of Trade, *Journal of Economic Behavior and Organization* 5, 191–222.

Joyce, P. (1983), Information and Behavior in Experimental Markets, *Journal of Economic Behavior and Organization* 4, 411–424.

Kirchsteiger, G., Niederle, M., and Potters, J. (2005), Endogenizing Market Institutions. An Experimental Approach, *European Economic Review* 49(7), 1827–1853.

Kühn, Karl-Uwe., and Xavier Vives (1995), *Information Exchanges Among Firms and their Impact on Competition*, Luxembourg: European Commission.

Kühn, Karl-Uwe (2001), Fighting Collusion by Regulating Communication Between Firms. *Economic Policy* 16, 169–204.

Morgan, John, Orzen, Henrik, and Sefton, Martin (2006a), An Experimental Study of Price Dispersion, *Games and Economic Behavior* 54(1), 134–158.

(2006b), A Laboratory Study of Advertizing and Price Competition, *European Economic Review* 50(2), 323–347.

Muren, A., and Pyddoke, R. (2006), Collusion Without Communication *Information Economics and Policy* 18(1), 43–54.

Offerman, T., and Potters, J. (2006), Does Auctioning of Entry Licenses Induce Collusion. An Experimental Study, *Review of Economic Studies* 73(3), 769–791.

Offerman, T., Potters, J., Sonnemans, J. (2002), Imitation and Belief Learning in an Oligopoly Experiment, *Review of Economic Studies* 69(4), 973–997.

Phillips, A. (1959), A Critique of United States Experience with Price-Fixing Agreements and the *Per Se* Rule, *Journal of Industrial Economics* 8(1), 13–32.

Plott, Charles (1987), Dimension of Parallelism: Some Policy Applications of Experimental Methods, in Roth, A., (ed.) *Laboratory Experimentation in Economics. Six Points of View*, Cambridge: Cambridge University Press.

Scherer, F., and Ross, D. (1990), *Industrial market structure and economic performance*, Boston: Houghton Mifflin.

Schultz, C. (2005), Transparency on the Consumer Side and Tacit Collusion, *European Economic Review* 49, 279–297.

Stigler, G. (1961), The Economics of Information, *Journal of Political Economy* 69, 213–225.

(1964), A Theory of Oligopoly, *Journal of Political Economy* 72, 44–61.

PART II

6 | Abuse of a dominant position: cases and experiments

ERIC VAN DAMME, PIERRE LAROUCHE
AND WIELAND MÜLLER

This chapter reviews EU competition cases related to abuses of dominant positions. It then reviews the experimental literature that deals with market dominance. It is concluded that little experimental work has been done and that, hence, the link is weak between competition policy practice and experimental economics in the area of market dominance. The chapter concludes by answering the following three questions: (i) Is there scope for further experiments within the sphere of abuse of dominance? (ii) Is the gap between experimental research results supplied by the literature and the demand of case handlers due to the inherent boundaries of experimental research as such? (iii) What are the lessons for using experimental research in antitrust enforcement?

1. Introduction

Article 82 of the EC Treaty states that any abuse of a dominant position is prohibited, and mentions four examples of abuses: (i) directly or indirectly imposing unfair prices or other unfair trading conditions; (ii) limiting production or development to the prejudice of consumers; (iii) unequal treatment of trading parties, thereby placing some at a competitive disadvantage; and (iv) making use of tying contracts, hence, forcing unnecessary supplementary obligations on customers. Of course, other price or non-price strategies may be considered an abuse as well.

It is important to note that Article 82 EC does not forbid certain types of behavior as such; only dominant firms are forbidden from using such strategies. In two of the earliest cases arising out of Article 82, *United Brands*[1] and *Hoffmann-La Roche*,[2] the European Court of

---

[1] Case 27/76, *United Brands Co and United Brands Continental BV v. Commission* [1978] ECR 207, [1978] 1 CMLR 429, para. 65.
[2] Case 85/76, *Hoffmann-La Roche & Co AG v. Commission* [1979] ECR 461, [1979] 3 CMLR 211.

Justice (ECJ) gave a definition of dominance that still stands today: a dominant position is a position of economic strength that enables a firm to prevent effective competition on the relevant market; a firm with a dominant position has the power "to behave to an appreciable extent independently of its competitors, its customers and ultimately of it consumers." In economic terms, one would, hence, say that a dominant position is one in which the firm has a "reasonably large" degree of market power.

In assessing whether or not a firm is dominant, the European Commission (EC) and the Court place great emphasis on the market share of the firm. Already in *Hoffmann-La Roche*, the Court held that very large market shares are in themselves, save in exceptional circumstances, evidence of dominance. While it is not possible to give an exact boundary, it is frequently stated that if the market share is above 50%, dominance is essentially presumed, while to date, there have been no cases where a firm with a market share of significantly less than 40% was found to be dominant. Of course, market shares are a very imperfect proxy for market power and, indeed, both the EC and the ECJ have frequently been criticized for attaching too much weight to market shares when assessing dominance, and for paying relatively little attention to other market characteristics, such as entry barriers. We will not deal with such issues here: we will deal with firms with large market share, presume dominance and focus on the question of whether certain types of behavior constitute an abuse.

Indeed, the text of Article 82 leaves this question open. A cursory reading might give the impression that the article deals primarily with straightforward monopolistic exploitation, hence, that the focus is on constraining monopolies. Such a narrow interpretation is also suggested by the French and German language versions of Article 82 that speak of "abusive exploitation." Obviously, in this case, there would be a clear contrast with Section 2 of the Sherman Act in the US that only seems to aim at preventing "monopolization" of markets, hence, at anti-competitive (exclusionary) behavior directed at competitors. This is not to say that the US is not concerned about exploitative behavior, rather in the US that behavior is usually countered by sector-specific regulation. As a large portion of the literature in experimental economics originates in the US, such a sharp contrast would be relevant for this chapter. On the one hand, one should not expect the "monopolization" experiments to deal with exploitative behavior, but rather be more focused on exclusionary behavior; on the other hand, the experimental literature on regulation would be relevant for this chapter as well. Fortunately for us, in practice the difference is not that large. EC competition law focuses also mostly on exclusionary behavior, as was evidenced recently again by the choice of the Commission to launch the discussion on the reform of Article 82 EC by a Discussion Paper on exclusionary abuses, which it considers to be the priority area.[3]

Two aspects contribute to EU policy in this domain not being fundamentally different from policy in the US. First of all, in *Continental Can*,[4] the ECJ made it clear for the first time that Article 82 does indeed apply also to anti-competitive conduct that weakens competition that is already weak. Since then this has been confirmed on various occasions. For example, in *Hoffman-La Roche*, the ECJ wrote that abuse relates to taking "recourse of methods different from these of normal competition" with the effect of hindering the competition still existing in the market or the growth of that competition. Second, in practice, the European competition authorities have been reluctant to intervene in cases of alleged exploitation. Consequently, although historical factors may explain a difference between the two sides of the Atlantic,[5] in practice policy focuses on anti-competitive behavior and so we will in this chapter. We did not have to look, and did not look, into the literature on regulation.

To summarize, under Article 82 EC, firms are not forbidden from having market power. However, firms with significant market power are banned from using certain business strategies that other non-dominant firms are free to use. Presumably, the idea is that welfare and consumer surplus can be hurt if dominant firms would be allowed to engage in such (anti-competitive) practices. As will be clear, the challenge now is how to separate normal competitive behavior from behavior that should be classified as anti-competitive and, hence, be forbidden (see also Vickers, 2005).

---

[3] EC, DG Competition Discussion Paper on the application of Article 82 of the Treaty to exclusionary abuses (19 December 2005).
[4] Case 6/72 *Europemballage Corp and Continental Can Co Inc* v. *Commission*, [1973] ECR 215, [1973] CMLR 199.
[5] The main goal of policy in the US was to prevent dominant firms coming into existence, whereas European industrial policy accepted that large firms may be necessary to successfully compete on world markets, as long as they are constrained.

Experimental economics could contribute to answering this question and, hence, to competition policy in three ways. First, if dominant firms have the ability to set prices above the competitive level, to sell products of an inferior quality, or to reduce the rate of innovation below the level that would exist in a competitive market, experiments can be conducted to see whether dominant firms will indeed engage in such practices. Second, where theories are too weak to distinguish normal competitive behavior from anti-competitive conduct, experiments might help out to see which theory is applicable, or which is the most relevant one. Third, since, when making their decisions, antitrust officials rely on a variety of formal and informal arguments, experiments may be useful to see to what extent these arguments hold water: if a certain type of behavior is termed abusive, is it indeed observed in the experimental laboratory and, if so, does it reduce welfare or consumer surplus?

Conversely, antitrust cases may be a source of inspiration for experimental economics. Real-life cases may demonstrate a variety of behaviors, which may or may not be profit maximizing, and one may investigate whether these behaviors are observed in the laboratory, and whether they can survive there. As we will see in this chapter, there are plenty of allegedly abusive strategies that do not seem to have been formally investigated in the laboratory. The agenda of experimental economics seems to be influenced internally (by other experiments) and by developments of theory, but not so much by real-life cases and problems, let alone by abuse cases. As we discuss more extensively in the concluding section, this is not to say that experimental economics is irrelevant for practitioners of competition law: since experiments may help in delineating the boundaries where various competition theories are relevant, they can be extremely relevant.

The remainder of this chapter is organized as follows. In Section 2, we classify various types of abuses on the basis of the real-life cases that have been dealt with by the EC and the ECJ. This allows addressing the second issue mentioned above: can antitrust cases serve as a source of inspiration for experimental economics? In Section 3 we review the experimental literature on anti-competitive behavior, thereby addressing the first issue. We will see that few experiments are directly inspired by actual abuse cases; most of the experiments are motivated by theory or by other experiments, hence, the link with Section 2 is not very intense. Nevertheless, some experiments contain important messages for antitrust practitioners. In Section 4 we put together the various threads and draw our conclusions. Specifically, we answer the following questions: (i) Is there scope for further experiments within the sphere of abuse of dominance? (ii) Is the gap between experimental research results supplied by the literature and the demand of case handlers due to the inherent boundaries of experimental research as such? (iii) What are the lessons from this chapter for using experimental research in antitrust enforcement?

2. Abuses

As is well known, Article 82 EC has given rise to far fewer cases than the other major provisions of EC competition law, such as Article 81 EC or the Merger Control Regulation. The Appendix provides an overview (as of March 2005) of the relevant case law of the ECJ/CFI and the decision practice of the EC under Article 82 EC (please bear in mind the methodological notes that accompany the table).[6]

That table indicates that, since the inception of the EC in 1958, there have been 50 relevant Commission decisions under this article, 26 of which were brought before the ECJ or the Court of First Instance (CFI) by way of judicial review (resulting in 9 annulments). In addition, there were 17 relevant ECJ decisions in preliminary ruling procedures, answering questions put by national courts.

In passing, we may note that, in the Netherlands, in 2003 alone, the Dutch competition authority (NMa) decided not less than 159 cases relating to the Dutch equivalent of Article 82 EC. In only two of these cases (*CR Delta* (case 3353) and *LOI* (case 3125)), the NMa came to the conclusion that a dominant position might have been abused. The latter case concerns predatory pricing and, after a more thorough review, in 2005, the NMa concluded that its initial assessment had been mistaken: LOI did not have a dominant position. The former case is about non-linear pricing, and loyalty discounts in particular, and still has to be decided on appeal. Of the remaining 157 cases,

---

[6] Since then, three new cases have been dealt with: (i) *Astra Zeneca* (which concerns a new type of abuse in the management of IP rights), (ii) the *Coca-Cola case* (traditional type, with exclusivity, etc., not unlike *Van den Bergh Foods*) and (iii) the opening of proceedings in the recent *Telefónica case*, involving margin squeeze.

in 79 of them the complaint was dismissed immediately, without any investigation; in the 78 other ones, that conclusion was reached after a brief investigation. We may conclude that there are frequent complaints about abuse, but that most often these apparently are not justified.

In light of the table in the Appendix, there are five broad groups of practices that have been dealt with by the Commission and the ECJ/CFI over the years:

1. pricing practices, including excessive prices, predatory pricing and price squeeze;
2. rebates, actually a subset of pricing practices, but which have received so much attention that it is worth treating them separately. They include loyalty rebates, non-linear rebates and selective ('fighting') rebates;
3. discrimination, comprising discrimination between customers (exploitative practice) and discrimination towards competitors in a vertical integration setting (which also has an exclusionary impact);
4. various forms of refusal to deal, concerning either the supply of goods, of IP rights or information, of physical facilities (including the so-called "essential facilities" cases) or refusal to enter into standard cooperative (and pro-competitive) arrangements for the industry in question;
5. various types of non-price contractual practices, including tying and exclusivity deals.

This classification has been established on the basis of available classifications, but it is not entirely in line with the most recent classification made by the Commission in its Discussion Paper of December 19, 2005. The Commission Paper is concerned only with exclusionary abuses, which it further splits between predatory pricing, "single branding" (a term used to cover all matters of rebates and exclusivity links), tying and bundling as well as refusal to supply. In the preparation of this chapter, all types of abuse — exclusionary but also exploitative or discriminatory (as the Commission calls them) — were surveyed. On the basis of the table in the Appendix, the information can be recombined to match the classification of the Discussion Paper. In what follows these groups of practices are discussed in more detail.

2.1. Pricing practices (excluding rebates)

2.1.1. Excessive pricing

This is the complaint that pricing is too high. Such complaints have to be dealt with under European antitrust law, but, as described above, there is no equivalent in US law. In any event, European competition authorities have repeatedly stated that they did not want to become price regulators, and accordingly few cases of excessive pricing have been pursued. The leading case remains the ECJ judgment in *United Brands*.[7]

In addition to the natural reluctance of competition authorities to engage in pricing inquiries, figuring out when a price is excessive remains a fundamental problem. As the ECJ stated, a price is excessive if it bears no more "reasonable relation to the economic value of the product."[8] Whereas pricing practiced by the dominant firm is easy to observe, the economic value of the product is usually not so readily ascertainable. The key empirical difficulty in applying competition law to pricing issues lies in determining that value. Note that in an experimental setting, the economic value can be precisely controlled; hence, experiments might be directly relevant here.

The easiest way, in practice, of assessing the underlying economic value is to make a price–price comparison, that is, to look at prices practiced by non-dominant competitors on the same market or at prices of similar products in other — as much as possible competitive — markets (Martinez, 2007). These prices are usually as accessible as the prices of the dominant firm, and they can be thought to provide some indication of the economic value of the product in question. Such a comparative approach was endorsed by the ECJ in *Bodson*.[9]

This price–price comparison approach raises an interesting question for experimental economics. Roughly speaking, standard economics predicts that the price that a firm charges depends on the firm's cost structure, c, as well as on the market conditions, m, hence $p = p(c, m)$.

---

[7] ECJ, Case 27/76, *United Brands* v. *Commission* [1978] ECR 207.

[8] See ECJ, Judgment of 13 November 1975, Case 26/75, *General Motors Continental* v. *Commission* [1975] ECR 1367 at Rec. 12, *United Brands*, supra, note 64 at Rec. 250 and Judgment of 11 November 1986, Case 226/84, *British Leyland* v. *Commission* [1986] ECR 3263 at Rec. 27.

[9] ECJ, Judgment of 4 May 1988, Case 30/87, *Bodson* v. *Pompes funèbres des régions libérées* [1988] ECR 2479.

The practical test for abusive pricing builds on p depending on m. One would like to know how strong this effect is according to experimental economics: is monopoly pricing substantially different from pricing in duopoly or oligopoly situations? It may be noted here that there are three experimental studies that analyze the pricing behavior in oligopoly when the number of firms in the market varies: two early studies by Fouraker and Siegel (1963) as well as by Dolbear *et al.* (1968), and a more recent study by Dufwenberg and Gneezy (2000). Unfortunately, none of these studies includes a monopoly so that they leave open the question whether or not monopoly pricing is substantially different from pricing in an oligopoly. In Section 3.1, we will return to this issue and refer to other experiments that illustrate that the extent to which monopoly power can be exercised depends on the institutional structure of the market and that the resulting price may well be lower than the one predicted by theory.

This comparative approach will be unavailable in a number of cases for lack of comparative data, that is, where the dominant firm enjoys a monopoly or no comparable competitive markets exist. In such cases, *United Brands* makes an inquiry into production costs, hence, a price–cost comparison, almost unavoidable. In its decision, the Commission had found, among others, that United Brands violated Article 82 EC (ex 86) by charging excessive prices for its bananas on the following grounds: there was a wide difference (up to 100%) in the prices charged by United Brands for Chiquita bananas on the Irish market — which were thought to cover costs — and elsewhere in the EC, and it recommended that United Brands reduce its prices.[10] This represents an interesting approach, but its value is limited since it involves a comparison of prices charged by a dominant firm in different geographical markets.[11] The ECJ annulled that part of the Commission decision, on the ground that the approach was flawed; the Commission

---

[10] Decision 76/353 of 17 December 1975, *Chiquita* [1976] OJ L 95/1 at 15–6. The Commission recommended that United Brands reduce its prices in Belgium, Luxembourg, the Netherlands, Germany and Denmark to a level at least 15% below its then current prices for Germany and Denmark.

[11] In the Decision, ibid., the Commission also mentioned that United Brands' prices were superior to those of its non-dominant rivals, which were still profitable. In *United Brands*, supra, note 64 at Rec. 266, however, the ECJ held that the difference to which the Commission referred to was not remarkable enough (some 7%) to support a finding of abuse.

could not simply rely on price comparisons without at least trying to support its findings by reference to the costs of production.[12]

In economic terms, in a price–cost comparison, one investigates what the costs, c, are in producing the product and next looks at the price–cost margin, or Lerner index: $L = (p - c)/p$. Once having calculated this index of market power, a judgment call has to be made: how high is L allowed to be, and what to make of fixed costs? This is not so easy; one gets into all kinds of accounting issues. It does not seem so obvious what the contribution of experimental economics could be in this domain. Of course, in the laboratory, one can investigate directly to what extent subjects are engaging in monopolistic pricing, and what the constraints on such pricing might be.

A third test for abusive pricing has been used by the Dutch competition authority and is inspired by the way regulators proceed. It involves an investigation of the rate of return. Consequently, this test does not look at prices, but at profits, or, more specifically, to returns on investment. One compares the Return On Capital Employed (ROCE) to the Weighted Average Cost of Capital (WACC), the return that investors in the company would be satisfied with, as it provides an adequate return for the risk that is taken. The idea is that if the ROCE is much higher than the WACC, the price must be too high. As said, this method of rate of return regulation originates in regulated industries. We are not aware of a laboratory investigation of such a regulation.

2.1.2. Predatory pricing

Predatory pricing is the practice in which the dominant firm charges prices that are so low as to drive competitors from the market, thereby aiming to obtain supranormal profits afterwards. There are conflicting theories about whether, or in which circumstances, the practice can be a rational business strategy; see Bolton *et al.* (2000) for an overview. As a result, predatory pricing has also attracted attention from experimentalists, who have tested the predictions of the various theories and have pitted these against each other.

Despite the theoretical interest in the phenomenon, predatory pricing seems to be rare in practice. The case law with respect to

---

[12] *United Brands*, ibid. at Rec. 251–2, 254 and 256.

predatory pricing in Europe is limited (four cases), but it has attracted remarkable attention, the *Akzo* and *Tetra Pak II* cases having become leading precedents under Article 82 EC. The last two cases, *DP AG (Parcels)* and *Wanadoo Interactive*, date from 2001 and 2003, respectively, and are likely also to have an impact, since they pick up on suggestions made in the Notice on Access Agreements in 1998 and update the law in the context of multi-service industries (including network industries). Until then, the law was reasonably clear and had remained unchanged since *Akzo*. According to the case law, a price is predatory if it is below marginal cost (AVC), or if it is below average cost (ATC) and is part of an explicit plan to eliminate a competitor. Note that the latter respect implies that predation cannot be inferred from market and cost data alone: one needs to know the intentions of the firm. For experimental economics, this has the consequence that the strategy method should be employed to test the practice.

In *Wanadoo Interactive*, the Commission conducted a very detailed analysis of the costs of Wanadoo Interactive. It applied the abuse test set out above, yet even where the Commission found that Wanadoo did not recover AVC, it still inquired into intent. Indeed a key factor in the decision was the evidence that Wanadoo intended to drive its competitors out of the market. Such evidence was found in explicit statements contained in company documents and in an objective analysis of Wanadoo's strategy. Furthermore, none of the justifications put forward by Wanadoo for its strategy was accepted by the Commission. A number of pronouncements are interesting, where the Commission adopted a broader perspective on predation than what is sometimes found in economic theory. For instance, the Commission held that behavior less radical than the exclusion of competitors, i.e. mere inhibition, could also constitute predation under competition law.[13] Similarly, according to the Commission, it was not necessary to prove that Wanadoo would, or could, recoup its losses, although it did show that the relevant market was characterized by entry barriers, which do make recoupment possible. In the US, the possibility of recoupment is an integral part of the test for predation.

The economic literature has focused on the question of whether the cost test as described above is suited to separate prices that are

---

[13] Commission decision of 16 July 2003, *Wanadoo Interactive*, available on the website of DG COMP, Rec. 266.

"really" predatory (i.e. profitable only because of induced changes in the behavior of competitors or of the market structure) from prices that are normally competitive. The literature argues that the test is misspecified: under a variety of conditions, a firm will wish to charge prices that are below cost. Second, there is an extensive literature dealing with the question of under which circumstances predatory pricing can be a rational business strategy. For more details, we refer the reader to Bolton *et al.* (2000). The main lesson coming out of that literature is that market structure may be more important than cost data, hence, that the test for predation should focus on, or at least also include this aspect; in particular, recoupment of the initial losses will be possible only if there are entry or re-entry barriers. Consequently, only in these cases can predation be profit maximizing.

In contrast to the Chicago view that predation will always be irrational, hence, that the practice should not be of concern to anti-trust agencies, the more recent economics literature has identified a certain number of situations (models) in which predation could indeed be rational. The experimental economics literature could make contributions to answering two questions:

- Does predation happen in the cases in which theory predicts it could happen?
- Does predation happen in other situations?

We will return to these questions in Section 3.6. We will see that the answers are ambiguous: predatory pricing can be observed in the laboratory, but not always in those cases where it is predicted by theory. One should, however, be careful with interpreting the experimental results: economists do not always adopt the same definition of predation as the one that is used in EU case law.

2.1.3. Price squeeze
Price squeeze, also called margin squeeze, refers to the situation where an entrant has to buy an input from the dominant firm in order to compete with it on the output market. If the dominant firm sells to the competitor at a price that is higher than the price it charges consumers for the final product, clearly even an efficient competitor faces a very difficult situation. The Commission defines price squeeze as "an insufficient spread between a vertically integrated dominant operator's wholesale and retail charges... especially where other providers

are excluded from competition on the downstream market even if they are at least as efficient as the established operator."[14]

There are only two relevant cases of price squeeze, namely *Napier Brown* and *Deutsche Telekom*. The latter case illustrates very well the current state of the law. The Commission decided that DT's wholesale and retail charges for access to the local loop amounted to a margin squeeze. That is, the spread between DT's wholesale tariffs for unbundled access to its subscriber lines and the weighted average of its corresponding retail services tariffs (analogue, ISDN and ADSL connections) left DT's competitors an insufficient margin to compete for retail subscribers, as the spread was lower than DT's own downstream product-specific costs.

2.2. Rebate practices

The practice of the Commission and the case law of the ECJ/CFI contain a remarkably high number of cases concerning rebate practices. EC law remains relatively strict on this issue to this day, allowing dominant firms very little margin to offer rebates to their customers, except for linear rebates which are directly linked with cost savings on the volume of the order. Recent decisions of the CFI in *British Airways*[15] and *Michelin II*[16] have only confirmed the state of EC law on the matter, despite the criticism levelled at earlier cases.

2.2.1. Non-linear pricing (quantity discounts)

At stake in *Michelin II*, among others, is the question of whether quantity discounts can be anti-competitive. A similar issue arose in the Dutch case *CR Delta*, already referred to above, and as that case is simpler, we use it here as an illustration.

CR Delta is a farmer cooperative trading in bull semen. In *CR Delta*, the NMa objected to a very simple discount scheme: if a farmer's annual expenses exceed certain thresholds, he gets a certain discount (ranging from 1% to 5%) over the entire volume. In general such discount schemes are allowed if they can be justified on the basis of cost savings. The NMa, however, was not convinced of this and

---

[14] Ibid. at Rec. 108.
[15] CFI, Case T-219/99, *British Airways* v. *Commission*, not yet reported.
[16] CFI, Case T-203/01, *Michelin* v. *Commission* [2003] ECR II-4071.

argued that, in fact, the discount scheme functioned as a loyalty scheme. In particular, it considered the period (1 year) and the cumulative nature (the fact that discount is given over the entire volume) to be anti-competitive. In its decision, the NMa did not refer to an economic model to substantiate this claim, however, and interestingly for this chapter, it refers to a behavioral aspect: farmers that are close to a threshold would be induced to stay with the dominant company in order to reach the next level. It would seem interesting to test whether this effect is real, or more generally, to investigate under what circumstances quantity discounts induce loyalty.

2.2.2. Loyalty rebates

Loyalty rebates increase the costs of switching to a competitor and a dominant firm is in principle forbidden from using such rebates. *CR Delta* also involved a loyalty rebate: a farmer that bought at least 90% of its supplies from CR Delta received a discount of 1%; a farmer that bought only from CR Delta got a discount of 2%. Interestingly, the scheme was never implemented, but it was announced and NMa argued that the announcement as such was anti-competitive. In this respect there is a relation with announcement effects and vapourware; we are not aware of experiments related to this practice. More generally, loyalty schemes play, at least in part, on certain consumer characteristics, hence, they might be a fertile ground for experimental economics. Again, we are not familiar with experimental literature investigating these aspects.

Interestingly, CR Delta was also offering a third type of rebate scheme, which was claimed to induce foreclosure. The company was offering two types of products: tested semen of known quality and semen of bulls that had not yet been used for breeding, or very little, and that still needed to be proven. CR Delta needed the cooperation of farmers to test semen of the latter type and, if successful, to possibly transform it into a profitable product on the tested market. To induce farmers to engage in such testing, it gave a reduction of 10% on tested semen to those farmers that were willing to do a certain amount of testing. The price reduction was viewed as a reward for participation in the testing program, but the NMa argued that it induced "testers" to buy from CR Delta, hence, that it foreclosed the market for competitors. Obviously, if the reward for testing had been a lump sum, farmers would indeed be more inclined to buy from competitors.

Again we do not know of papers in the experimental economics literature dealing with this or similar pricing strategies.

2.2.3. Selective rebates (fighting practices)

There are two cases of "fighting" practices, where the dominant firm systematically set out to underbid its competitors, namely *Irish Sugar*[17] and the *Cewal*[18] case. In the former case, the dominant Irish sugar producer and packer granted selective rebates to customers who were importing sugar from other Member States and offered rebates to customers of competing packers on condition that they source all of their needs from it. In the latter case, the various liner conferences reacted to the entry of new competitors on the Europe–West Africa cargo lines by departing from their tariff to offer cargo services at the same rate as the competitors at about the same sailing date (so-called "fighting ships").

2.3. Discrimination

In this section we focus on first-degree price discrimination and third-degree price discrimination. EC competition law deals with three broad types of discrimination:

- First-degree price discrimination: Discrimination among the customers of a dominant firm (see the classical cases *United Brands* or *Michelin I*). These are cases where price discrimination is used to extract the most profit from individual customers who are in the eyes of the competition authority in a similar position and should thus pay similar prices.
- Third-degree price discrimination: A sub-set of the former type, which is more likely to fall foul of EC competition law, is discrimination among customers according to the Member State where they are located. This type of practice, even if it may be linked to differing preferences amongst national markets in various Member States, runs against the market integration objectives of the EC Treaty. A pre-eminent example of this is found in the *Tetra Pak II* case.
- Another subset of first-degree price discrimination has appeared in recent times: here a vertically integrated firm with a dominant

---

[17] Decision of 14 May 1997, *Irish Sugar* [1997] OJ L 258/1.
[18] Decision of 23 December 1992, *Cewal, Cowal, Ukwal* [1993] OJ L 34/20, upheld on this point by the CFI and the ECJ.

position on, say, the upstream market, would discriminate in favour of its own downstream subsidiary and against the competitors of that subsidiary. The objective there is no longer just exploitation, but also exclusion. See here *HOV SVZ/MCN* for an example, where the German railway operator Deutsche Bahn applied different prices for the transport of containers from seaports to German destinations, favoring German ports (Hamburg, Bremen), which it served on its own, over Benelux ports (Antwerp, Rotterdam), which were served via a joint venture with other railway operators.[19]

The economics of price discrimination is well understood: if it leads to expanding the size of the market, it is most likely to be welfare improving; otherwise most likely it is not. Article 82 EC forbids any price discrimination by dominant firms; hence, the law might be more strict than is desirable from the point of view of economic welfare. EC competition law is, however, not only guided by that objective, but also by the — sometimes prevailing—objective of market integration.

2.4. Refusal to deal

Cases where a dominant firm refuses to supply an existing customer, or a potential competitor, probably offer the largest contrast between EU and US policy. Ordering the dominant firm to supply is a strong interference with business freedom and in this domain European policy has typically been much more interventionist. The numbers in the Appendix indicate that refusal to deal is the largest group of practices dealt with under Article 82. Refusal to deal cases can be split into a few sub-categories:

- "classic" cases where a dominant firm ceases to supply its competitors (*Hugin*, *Hilti*) or its established distribution channels (*United Brands*, *Commercial Solvents*);
- refusal to grant access to production facilities, including the so-called "essential facilities" cases. These were popular in the 1990s and include precedents such as *Bronner*, *London European/Sabena* and *Sea Containers/Stena*;

---

[19] Decision of 29 March 1994, *HOV SVZ/MCN* [1994] OJ L 104/34, upheld by the CFI.

- refusal to grant access to IP rights and other valuable information. These include cases such as *Magill*, *IMS Health* and the recent Commission decision in *Microsoft*;
- refusal to cooperate in normal industry practices, such as interlining (*British Midland*).

It is in this domain that the special responsibility towards competition that a dominant firm in Europe is said to have is playing an important role. In *Commercial Solvents*, for example, a pharmaceutical firm cancelled orders for a certain raw material, presumably expecting to be able to buy that material cheaper elsewhere. When the alternative supplies did not prove satisfactory, the firm turned to the original supplier, a dominant firm, again, but that supplier had meanwhile decided to vertically expand into the downstream product market, hence, it no longer wanted to supply. The ECJ ruled that thereby the dominant producer abused its dominant position as its strategy could eliminate all competition from the market. *Hugin* is essentially similar: a manufacturer no longer wanted to supply spare parts to a retailer as it wanted to build up its own spare parts business. In *United Brands*, the United Brands Corporation (UBC) wanted to punish a distributor for the fact that it had participated in a promotional campaign of a competitor of UBC. According to the ECJ, the countermeasure of no longer supplying this distributor was not proportional and, hence, abusive. It is remarkable that, in all these older cases, there is little attention to efficiency arguments: the dominant firm is simply said to have a responsibility to keep competition alive.

Essential facility cases are special cases of refusal to deal: a competitor needs access to the upstream production facilities of the dominant firm in order to be able to profitably compete on the downstream market. The question now is of under what conditions, and against which terms, the dominant firm should be forced to share its facilities. The so-called "essential facilities doctrine" that aims to answer this question originates in the US, and has been extensively criticized there (see Areeda, 1990, and the recent ruling of the Supreme Court in *Trinko* v. *Verizon Communications*).[20] Three important recent EU cases are *Magill*, *Bronner* and *IMS Health*.

---

[20] Docket No. 00–682 (13 January 2004).

In *Magill*[21] broadcasters were not willing to hand over their programming data to a publisher who wanted to publish a complete programming guide (as opposed to the single-broadcaster guides which the broadcasters themselves issued). The ECJ argued that the refusal to supply prevented a new product, for which there was apparent demand, from coming on the market, hence, that the refusal to supply constituted an abuse according to Article 82(b). This decision has been criticized for being too interventionist and for eliminating firms' incentives to invest. In the later cases, *Bronner* and *IMS Health*, the ECJ took a more reserved stance and sided more with the holder of the facility to which access was claimed.

In *Bronner*[22] the ECJ shows its awareness of the investment issue and it refused to grant a competitor access to the facilities of a dominant firm. *Bronner* deals with a small newspaper company, with low circulation, that wants to get access to the nationwide distribution system of a larger competition. Bronner argues that its circulation is too small for it to have its own viable system, hence, that it should get access to the unique nationwide distribution system, that of its competitor. The ECJ in essence argues that, given the current market shares, the claim might be true, but that this fact does not justify getting access. If Bronner would have an equal market share as the leading firm, then a nationwide distribution system would be viable for Bronner itself; hence, the competitor should not be forced to share. It has been argued that this *Bronner* test constitutes a formidable hurdle for new entrants: it may simply not be feasible to reach a comparable market share within a reasonable time frame (Bergman, 2000).

The latest instalment in this line of case law was *IMS Health*, issued by the ECJ in 2004.[23] In that case, a firm called NDC was trying to invoke EC competition law to obtain an order forcing IMS Health to license its "brick structure", i.e. the geographical breakdown in the reporting format used in the IMS report on the sales of pharmaceutical products. This structure was protected by copyright, and IMS refused to license it, preventing NDC from entering the market to compete

---

[21] Case C-241, 241/91P *RTE & ITP v. Commission*, [1995] ECR I-743, [1995] 4 CMLR 718.

[22] Case C-7/97 *Oscar Bronner GmbH & Co KG v. Mediaprint* [1998] ECR I-7791 4 CMRL, 112

[23] ECJ, Case C-418/01, *IMS Health* [2004] ECR I-5039.

with the dominant provider IMS. The ECJ restated the *Bronner* test, namely that

in order for the refusal by an undertaking which owns a copyright to give access to a product or service indispensable for carrying on a particular business to be treated as abusive, it is sufficient that three cumulative conditions be satisfied, namely, that that refusal is preventing the emergence of a new product for which there is a potential consumer demand, that it is unjustified and such as to exclude any competition on a secondary market.[24]

The ECJ also elaborated on the "new product" condition, stating that the competitor seeking access to the intellectual property must not "intend to...essentially duplicat[e] the goods or services already offered...but intend...to produce new goods or services not offered by the owner of the right and for which there is a potential consumer demand." After *IMS*, it seems unlikely that competition law will be often used to force access to the facilities of dominant firms.

Note that *IMS* is simply an example illustrating the general conflict between Intellectual Property Law and Competition Law and the trade-off between investment and diffusion of new ideas and technologies. It seems that this conflict area might be a fruitful one to study for experimental economists. At this point we are not aware of experimental work studying refusal to deal.

2.5. Non-price contractual practices

A number of non-price contractual practices have been found abusive over the years. Here as well, the *Tetra Pak II* case provides an illustration of a large number of such practices. The main ones are:

- tying and bundling;
- exclusive deals, in particular agreements whereby the dominant firm becomes the exclusive supplier of the other contracting party;
- display exclusivity.

In the 1970s, there were a number of cases where it was alleged that the enforcement of IP rights (essentially to prevent parallel trade) constituted an abuse of dominant position (*Deutsche Gramophon*, *Parke*

---

[24] At para. 38.

Davis). However, the ECJ always stood by its position that the mere exercise of IP rights did not constitute an abuse in the absence of concrete evidence of anti-competitive effect.

As mentioned in the Introduction, Article 82 specifically lists tying as a possible abuse. There is a rather large recent economics literature dealing with the question of whether, and in which circumstances, tying might be bad for welfare. Three leading cases in this domain are *Hilti*, *Tetra Pak II* and *Microsoft*. Quite surprisingly, despite the considerable interest by economic theorists in issues related to tying and bundling, we are not aware of experimental work that deals with this topic.

3. Experiments on abusing market power

We are not the first attempting to review the experimental literature that contributes to industrial organization with emphasis on antitrust issues. There are at least two other articles that should be mentioned here. The most comprehensive overview to date is Wellford (2002). Many of the experimental studies she reviews, however, are not directly related to the narrower focus of our overview. Nevertheless, there are some general conclusions that are interesting to reiterate here. First, institutional form matters more than theory implies. For example, under certain institutional settings the competitive outcome is more robust than theory would predict it to be. Second, often market power is not exercised to the full extent. Even single seller markets do not necessarily lead to monopoly outcomes and, although sellers with market power may set prices at supracompetitive levels, they do not always restrict production to the level predicted by theory. Third, Wellford points out that most laboratory studies to date have omitted two features that are crucial to antitrust issues, namely possible entry and the existence of antitrust agencies. Thus, it is likely that results are biased towards more collusive outcomes, or outcomes that violate antitrust laws. In the light of these two omissions, it is especially worthwhile mentioning that many market environments that Wellford reviewed are quite competitive.

Another, more personal, review is Davis and Wilson (2002), who propagate the incorporation of experimental work into the development of antitrust policy. We agree with their assessment that appropriately designed experiments can uniquely provide important insights relevant for competition policy. They illustrate this point by reviewing some of their experimental work on detecting price fixing in sealed bid auctions, enforcement standards for merger-specific efficiencies and differentiated product competition and the antitrust litigation model. Our chapter focuses on the abuse of market power by dominant firms and is complementary to theirs.

3.1. Monopoly pricing

Monopoly pricing has been tested in the lab using a variety of trading institutions; most prominently posted-offer markets[25] and to a lesser degree double oral auctions[26] and posted-bid monopolies.[27] Let us very briefly explain these institutions (for more details see e.g. Davis and Holt 1993). Each of these markets is divided into a series of trading periods. Subjects are assigned the role of a seller or a buyer. At the beginning of a period buyers are assigned unit valuations and sellers unit costs. Buyers' profits are given by the difference between the unit value and the contract price whereas sellers' profits are given by the difference between the contract price and the unit cost. In a double oral auction buyers call out bids at which they are ready to buy a unit whereas sellers call out offers at which they are ready to sell a unit. A buyer can accept any standing offer and a seller can accept any standing bid at any time. A posted-offer market follows a two-step procedure. First, sellers privately select a price for the current trading period and indicate the maximum number of units they are willing to sell at this price. Then these prices (but not the maximum number of units) are made public to the buyers and the other sellers. Then buyers are randomly and sequentially given the opportunity to make as many purchases as they like at any seller who has not yet sold his maximum number of units. When one buyer stops shopping another buyer is called to do his purchases. This continues until each buyer gets the opportunity to make purchases or until all units on offer are purchased. A posted-bid market works like a posted-offer market with the roles reversed. That is, in a posted-bid market it is the buyers who post bids at which they are willing to buy units from sellers.

---

[25] See Smith (1981), Isaac *et al.* (1984), Coursey *et al.* (1984), Harrison and McKee (1985), and Harrison *et al.* (1989).
[26] See Smith (1981) and Smith and Williams (1989).
[27] See Smith (1981).

Smith (1981) tests these three institutions and finds that monopolists in double oral and posted-bid markets are not able to exercise market power to the extent predicted by theory. In contrast to this, in the one posted-offer market reported in Smith, the monopolist performs as predicted. To illustrate these results, Holt (1995) computes the "monopoly effectiveness index": $M = (\pi^a - \pi^c)/(\pi^m - \pi^c)$, where π^a is actual profit, π^c is profit at the competitive equilibrium and π^m is monopoly profit, for the final period in the markets reported in Smith (1981).[28] The results are as follows: double-auction monopoly: $M = 0.36$; posted-bid monopoly: $M = 0.15$; posted-offer monopoly: $M = 1.0$. Plott (1989) remarks that the likely reason for the failure of the monopolist in the double auction to exercise market power is the fact that buyers in this institution do not behave passively as price takers but engage in withholding purchases. This behavior causes the monopolist to price more cautiously.

Holt (1995) also computes the monopoly effectiveness index M for other posted-offer monopoly experiments. These experiments vary the cost structure (decreasing or increasing), the type of buyers (human or simulated) and the level of experience of subjects. Holt finds that the index varies considerably. It is highest in the study by Harrison *et al.* (1989) with experienced subjects, simulated buyers and a decreasing cost function where $M = 0.78$ and it is lowest in another treatment of the same study where all features of the design are the same except that subjects are inexperienced. For the latter treatment Holt computes $M = 0.44$.

In a more recent contribution Engle-Warnick and Ruffle (2004) analyze the effects of buyer concentration on the pricing of a monopolist. They construct experimental posted-offer markets in which a monopolist faces either two or four buyers. They find that markets with two buyers achieve significantly lower prices, sometimes even below competitive levels, than those with four buyers. In particular they report $M = -1.88$ for the two-buyer treatment and $M = 0.005$ for the four-buyer treatment. With the help of additional control treatments they are able to isolate the source of the difference. They find that the lower prices in the two-buyer treatment are due to the

---

[28] Clearly, M = 1 (M = 0) means that the monopolist achieves monopoly (competitive) profits.

monopolist pricing more cautiously when there are fewer buyers in order to avoid costly losses in sales. Buyer concentration may thus be an effective source of countervailing power.

Holt (1995: 381) summarizes the results of monopoly experiments as follows:

Pricing in posted-offer monopolies is higher than in double-auction monopolies. Posted-offer monopolists are generally able to hold prices well above competitive levels, but on average, profits are significantly below theoretical monopoly levels. Monopoly pricing in posted-offer markets is facilitated by experience and by constant or decreasing costs. The effect of using simulated buyers, as compared with a small number of human buyers, is probably to facilitate monopoly pricing a little.

In the light of the results by Engle-Warnick and Ruffle (2004), one would have to add that monopoly pricing is facilitated by markets with a higher number of human buyers.

Given the clear deviations from profit maximization reported above, it is interesting to refer to the work by Kahneman, Knetsch and Thaler (1986). In this study the authors collect data from telephone surveys to analyze "community standards of fairness for the setting of prices and wages." Summarizing the results of various administered questions these authors find "that many actions that are both profitable in the short run and not obviously dishonest are likely to be perceived as unfair exploitations of market power" (p.737) and that "even in the absence of government intervention, the actions of firms that wish to avoid a reputation for unfairness will depart in significant ways from the standard model of economic behavior" (p.738). The conclusion, hence, is that "considerations of fairness or concerns for long-run reputation, may act as a constraint on profit maximization."

Finally, we briefly mention that there is also a small experimental literature on durable-good monopolists that is fuelled by Coase's (1972) seminal contribution. Coase argued that product durability can constrain a monopolist's power as consumers might be willing to delay purchasing in the expectation that the monopolist will reduce its price in later periods. Later theoretical contributions have tried to isolate circumstances under which this is indeed the case. Experimental contributions to this discussion include Güth et al. (1995), Rapoport et al. (1995), Reynolds (2000), Cason and Sharma (2001), and Güth *et al.* (2004).[29] We only mention some results of this literature. Arguably, the most interesting result is that contrary to Coase's conjecture, sometimes durability fails to constrain monopoly power in that prices for a durable good are higher than for a non-durable good (Güth *et al.* 1995, Reynolds 2000). Second, often trading extends over more periods than predicted due to demand withholding (Cason and Sharma, 2001). Third, durable-goods experiments are rather complex such that without a sufficiently high number of repetitions, observed prices may fail to conform to comparative-statics predictions (Güth *et al.* 1995).

3.2. Price discrimination

The only paper analyzing price discrimination by a monopolist we are aware of is the paper by Hudson and Lusk (2004) who report on "a Web-based experimental learning tool to assist instructors in conveying the central principles of (third-degree) price discrimination under asymmetric information." Unfortunately, given its purpose, the sample size is quite small (thirteen subjects). Furthermore, there is no comparison with a treatment in which price discrimination is banned and monopolists are forced to set uniform prices. Nevertheless, let us very briefly report on the results of this paper.

In the experiment, subject monopolists are told that they are sellers of a higher quality and a lower quality good and that there is a population of ten simulated consumers, six of which prefer the lower and four of which prefer the higher quality product. So there is asymmetric information. Furthermore, subjects are told that production costs differ for the two products and that their objective is to price the two products in order to maximize profits. Surely, the optimal solution is to price the lower quality good at a price that extracts the maximum willingness to pay from the "lower" consumers and to price the higher quality product such that the "higher" consumer is left with some "information rent" such that all "lower" ("higher") consumers purchase the lower (higher) quality good.

---

[29] These studies analyze a wide range of features including one buyer vs. several buyers; one period vs. several periods; finite vs. infinite horizon; complete vs. incomplete information; same discount factor for the seller and buyer(s) vs. different discount factors for the seller and buyer(s).

Hudson and Lusk (2004) only present graphical results of their small sample of thirteen subjects. In any case, subjects appear to learn very quickly to set prices that are very close to the optimal levels. It turns out, however, that convergence to the optimal price of the lower quality good is somewhat quicker and more complete than convergence to the optimal price of the higher quality product where observed prices are at times too low.

3.3. Price discounts

There seems to be only a handful of experimental papers that deal with price discounts — and most of them do not concentrate on abusive practices. For example Davis and Holt (1994, 1998) deal with price discounts in posted-offer markets. The later paper is particularly interesting as it shows the effect and the interplay of conspiratorial discussions among sellers, secret price discounts and ex-post information about other sellers' individual sales quantities. But both papers implement sellers of equal size and the second concentrates on collusion. In Davis and Millner (2005) different rebate schemes that participants can choose from are exogenously implemented and the focus, again, is not an antitrust issue.

A relevant contribution to the topic of price discounts granted by a dominant firm is the study by Normann et al. (2007). This paper studies whether or not — and if so, under what circumstances — large buyers (those who potentially purchase more than other things) are granted price discounts. The authors draw on the theoretical literature that states that whether such discounts are observed depends, among others, on the curvature of the total surplus function over which the parties bargain. (Here, the total surplus function is equal to total benefits minus total costs as a function of the quantity sold to buyers who reach an agreement with the seller). Theory predicts that: price discounts are granted to large buyers in case the total surplus function is concave; no discounts are granted to large buyers in case the total surplus function is linear; and this yields a variety of outcomes (including one with no discounts) in case the total surplus function is convex.

Normann et al. test these predictions in markets in which large and small buyers bargain simultaneously with a single seller. Here, large buyers' demand is twice as high as the demand of small buyers and different shapes of the total surplus function are achieved by varying the seller's marginal cost function. The timing is such that first each buyer makes a bid that represents the price at which she is willing to buy units, with buyers not being allowed to bid different amounts for different units. The seller, who is not capacity-constrained, observes each bid and then decides whether or not to accept it. Note that in this set-up there are no efficiency reasons that would suggest granting discounts.

The experimental results strongly support the theory. As predicted, large-buyer discounts are observed only when the total surplus function is concave. The main deviation from theory is that the absolute level of the bids sometimes differs from the theoretical predictions. Normann *et al.* do not offer specific policy implications of their results. However, it seems safe to say that their results support the view that under certain circumstances the ability of firms (even monopolists) to charge high prices depends on buyers' bargaining power.

3.4. Third-degree price discrimination: zone pricing

Deck and Wilson (2007) report results of an experiment regarding zone pricing. They concentrate on the gasoline market and refer to zone pricing as the practice of refiners setting different wholesale prices for retail gasoline stations that operate in different geographic areas or zones. They point out that this is an important public policy issue: refiners claim that they use zone pricing in order to be competitive with local rivals, while antitrust practitioners argue that zone pricing benefits the oil industry and harms consumers. Relevant for the current overview are the experiments on the competitive effects of zone pricing on consumers, retail stations and refiners and the comparison with the proposed policy prescription of uniform wholesale pricing to retailers.[30]

---

[30] The authors also investigate the "rockets and feathers" phenomenon (the perception that retail gasoline prices rise faster than they fall in response to movements in the world price for oil) as well as the issue of structural separation, i.e. the legal restriction that refiners and retailers cannot be vertically integrated. Concerning the latter, the authors compare behavior in the baseline treatment with a treatment in which refiners and their retail gasoline stations are vertically integrated. They find that vertical integration eliminates the double mark-up of prices such that all buyers, in clustered or isolated areas, pay significantly lower prices and have substantially higher utility when stations are company-owned. Thus, the conclusion is warranted that, in the laboratory,

In their experiments there are four refiners that each produce a specific brand of gasoline and four retailers that each operate two gas stations. More precisely, each retailer operates one station in the "clustered" area at the center and another station in an "isolated" area. Hence, the center area is contested, while each refiner/retailer combination is dominant in one isolated area. Simulated final consumers are uniformly distributed on the grid with each consumer having inelastic unit demand. The experiments have a rich design and we will only describe the main features. In the baseline treatment, refiners have the ability to set geographically different wholesale prices, that is, each retailer observes two location-specific wholesale prices, but they cannot shift inventory between locations. In the uniform pricing treatment, the refiners must charge the same wholesale price to each station selling its brand, hence, each retailer observes only one wholesale price that applies to both of its locations. The experiment lasts for 600 periods (of 1.7 seconds each), with both refiners and retailers being allowed to adjust their prices at any time. Retailers and refiners observe all current retail prices, including those set by rival outlets, but only the refiner and the associated retailer know the current wholesale prices.

Deck and Wilson report the following findings. First, under both zone and uniform pricing, retail transaction prices are statistically higher in the isolated areas than in the clustered area. Second and more important for this paper, when compared to zone pricing, uniform wholesale pricing increases retail transaction prices significantly in the clustered area, while it has no significant effect on transaction prices in the isolated areas. Uniform pricing actually reduces the welfare of those buyers residing closest to the clustered center area and of those who are on the border of the center and the isolated areas. Interestingly, Deck and Wilson find that refiners' profits are unaffected by the uniform pricing: it is the retailers that extract surplus from the consumers. The following explanation is offered (p.148):

Under uniform pricing, the refiners offer a price that is above the center area zone wholesale price and below the isolated area zone wholesale price. These refiners are balancing extracting economic rents from the isolated

legislation that bars refiners and retailers from becoming vertically integrated harms consumers.

stations and remaining viable in the competitive, center area. Thus, a refiner's gains in the center area, due to higher wholesale prices, are offset by reduced earnings in the isolated markets where wholesale prices have decreased and profits are unchanged. With uniform pricing, the retailers do not gain a profit margin in the center area but do receive a larger margin in the isolated regions where retail prices are unchanged but wholesale prices have declined.

To summarize, contrary to claims put forward by proponents of uniform pricing legislation, under uniform pricing consumers lose when compared to a zone-pricing regime. In this respect, the experiment confirms the general view of economists that one should not forbid price discrimination too soon.

3.5. Entry deterrence

3.5.1. Limit pricing

A firm engages in limit pricing if it sets its price and output so that there is not enough demand for another firm to profitably enter the market. Note that consumers benefit from lower prices in the phase of limit pricing, but that this advantage might be offset by higher prices due to less competition if entry is successfully deterred. Also note that, in contrast to predatory pricing (that focuses on driving existing competitors out), limit pricing aims at preventing entry altogether. As far as we know, there are no actual cases involving complaints of limit pricing.

Cooper *et al.* (1997a and 1997b) test a game based on the Milgrom and Roberts (1982) model of limit pricing. In this two-period model, an incumbent is confronted with a potential entrant. The market is one with a homogeneous good and linear demand. The privately known cost of the incumbent is either high or low (with equal probability) and entry is only profitable if the incumbent's costs are high. In the first period, only the incumbent is in the market. After having observed the price chosen by the incumbent, the potential entrant decides whether to enter or not. If he stays out, the incumbent remains a monopolist; otherwise the market becomes a Cournot duopoly. Due to the uncertainty about the incumbent's cost (that can only be inferred indirectly by the entrant, if at all, through the incumbent's first-period price), there is room for signaling through limit pricing in the first period.

Cooper *et al.* (1997a) consider two main treatments: one in which the entrant has "high", and one in which it has "low" costs. The game with a low-cost entrant has a unique (pure strategy) separating equilibrium: the low-cost monopolist sets a first period price below its myopic monopoly price and so low that it cannot be matched by the high-cost monopolist, hence, there is limit pricing in order to deter entry. Consequently, in equilibrium, the entrant correctly infers the monopolist's cost and enters if and only if the monopolist is weak. Note that entry occurs if and only if it is efficient. In the game with a high-cost entrant, the parameters are such that, given the prior distribution on cost, the entrant finds it optimal to stay out. Now multiple equilibria exist. Along with pure-strategy separating equilibria, there are pooling equilibria in pure strategies in which the high-cost monopolist engages in limit pricing to deter entry. In these pooling equilibria, the high-cost monopolist charges the same price as the low-cost monopolist, nothing about cost can be learned from first-period prices, and the potential entrant decides to stay out. Note that in this case, production is not always efficient.

The main finding of the Cooper *et al.* study is that "limit pricing reliably emerges in both types of games as the theory predicts with play consistently converging on a particular equilibrium as a function of the underlying treatment conditions" (Cooper *et al.*, p.663). The patterns of convergence are particularly interesting. Cooper *et al.* report (p.663):

Convergence to equilibrium follows a characteristic history of play. Initially, independent of potential entrants' costs, monopolists largely ignore any threats of entry. Given that entrants can then easily infer the monopolist's type, entry rates on high-cost monopolists quickly rise, fostering attempts to pool with low-cost monopolists who are not being entered on. In games where pure-strategy pooling equilibria exist, play settles into an "efficient" pooling equilibrium in which low-cost monopolists produce at their full-information output level and high-cost monopolists imitate them, forestalling entry. In games where no pure-strategy pooling equilibria exist, these "pooling" efforts are shattered by increased entry that induces low-cost monopolists to separate to higher output levels.

In all, Cooper *et al.* show that the strategic use of limit pricing to deter entry does emerge in the laboratory.

Müller *et al.* (in press) examine the strategic behavior of incumbents and entrants in experiments that involve two incumbents and one potential entrant. The games are based on Bagwell and Ramey's (1991) model of oligopoly limit pricing. Incumbents first learn about an industry parameter that determines whether their costs are low or high and they next simultaneously choose prices. Upon observing these two prices, an entrant who does not know the industry cost, tries to infer it, and next decides whether or not to enter. Higher costs are associated with lower profits implying that incumbents, presumably, wish to signal high costs. Consequently, one is tempted to expect that prices will be distorted upward when industry costs are low. However, Bagwell and Ramey isolate circumstances under which "no-distortion" exists and incumbents play as if there was complete information or no entry threat at all. In this separating equilibrium, costs are revealed and entry takes places only if it is profitable (i.e. when costs are low). Thus, with at least two firms already in the market, in the no-distortion equilibrium, incumbents are unable to coordinate deception; hence, no limit pricing exists.

Müller *et al.* (in press) run both full-information and private-information treatments. When the entrant's outside option is low such that only separating equilibria exist, Müller *et al.* find evidence for the "no-distortion" equilibrium emphasized by Bagwell and Ramey (1991). In particular, they find that behavior in the full- and the private-information treatments is very similar and that incumbents' first-period prices quickly converge to the levels predicted under no threat of entry. As the first-period prices signal industry costs quite reliably, entry thus occurs only when costs are low. When the entrant's outside option is high such that both separating and pooling equilibria exist, Müller *et al.* find that prices charged by high-cost incumbents in the private-information treatment are similar to those in the full-information treatment. However, in this case, under incomplete information, low-cost incumbents set higher prices than they would under full information. Consequently, entry rates are lower in the former case than in the latter.

3.5.2. Investment into capacity

Mason and Nowell (1998) consider a simple, complete-information, two-stage quantity-setting duopoly game based on Dixit (1980). There is one incumbent and one potential entrant. Upon observing the incumbent's quantity, the entrant has to decide whether or not to enter the market. If it enters it pays a (commonly known) fixed cost,

which is large enough to ensure that the subgame perfect equilibrium
has the incumbent choosing the smallest output that makes it in the
best interest for the entrant not to enter.

Mason and Nowell (1998) run three treatments varying this entry
cost. The experiments consist of twenty periods with random
matching and role switching. They find that attempted entry deterrence by incumbents is relatively common and that it becomes more
common as time unfolds. Also, the frequency of deterrence attempts
clearly rises with the level of fixed entry costs. However, a substantial
fraction of the incumbents do not try to exploit their first-mover
advantage: they chose quantities that are below the entry-deterring
level. Regarding entrants' behavior, Mason and Nowell find that,
conditional on the incumbent player deterring entry, about 75% of
the entrants stay out whereas 25% enter nevertheless. It is noteworthy
that both of these aspects are persistent even towards the end of the
experiments. It seems that the softer behavior of some of the incumbents might be explained by the fear of punishment which, given
entrants' behavior, did indeed occur in the experiments.

Brandts *et al.* (2007) report on a test of the entry-deterrence model
by Bagwell and Ramey (1996). The starting point of the latter paper is
the fact that models predicting incumbents installing entry-deterring
excess capacity perform poorly in empirical studies. Bagwell and
Ramey consider a three-stage duopoly game: First, the incumbent can
(partially) pre-commit to a certain level of (costly) capacity. Upon
observing this choice, the entrant can make a similar choice. In the
third stage, the two firms simultaneously decide whether or not to
compete in the market by bearing (the rest of) the costs of capacity.
This game has two subgame perfect equilibria in pure strategies: one
of the firms produces and becomes a monopolist while the other firm
shuts down. However, a forward induction argument selects the
entrant's preferred equilibrium, implying that there is second-mover
advantage.

Contrary to this prediction, Brandts *et al.* (2007) find that the
incumbent becomes the monopolist three times as often as the
potential entrant (and that costly pre-installation is relatively rare for
both the incumbent and the entrant). Moreover, over time play does
not converge in the direction of the Bagwell–Ramey prediction. An
explanation offered by Brandts *et al.* (2007) is that players might enter
the game being equipped with a social norm that says that first movers

have a greater entitlement.[31] This preconception is apparently not eroded as time unfolds and players gain experience.

Let us conclude this subsection by noting that Brandts *et al.* also run a simple Dixit-style control treatment. As in Mason and Nowell (1998), they find that the predicted first-mover advantage is strong even when the incumbent does not engage in entry-deterring investment. However, when the incumbent does pre-install capacity the advantage is substantially more pronounced.

3.6. Predatory pricing

The first paper investigating the possible emergence of predatory pricing in the laboratory is Isaac and Smith (1985). They implement a posted-offer duopoly market that is served by a large seller and a small one. The large seller has a cost advantage over the other seller, a higher capacity and a larger cash endowment. Sellers don't know demand, or each other's cost functions. After prices (but not the quantities) were made public, demand was simulated. In the experimental market, there is a predatory price range where the large seller provides ten units at a price that is (a) lower than the small seller's minimum average price; (b) lower than the large seller's marginal cost of his tenth unit, and (c) demand is exhausted. In this case, the small seller cannot earn positive profits, while the large seller does not suffer losses, although his profits at the predatory price–quantity combination are lower than at the competitive equilibrium. In these markets no predatory pricing is observed.

This "negative" result induced Isaac and Smith to make several design changes. In a first design change, sellers are required to purchase entry permits. But again, no predatory pricing is observed. As a second design change, sellers are given full information about each other's costs. Yet, again, no predatory pricing is observed. Thus, this first "search of predatory pricing" was unsuccessful. Isaac and Smith conclude: "We are unable to produce predatory pricing in a structural environment that, a priori, we thought was favourable to its emergence" (p. 342).

Harrison (1988) continues the hunt for predatory pricing. He modifies the Isaac and Smith (1985) design by implementing five

---

[31] This explanation was put forward in Huck and Müller (2005) who report on the "money-burning" game.

simultaneous posted-offer markets and introducing eleven sellers. Four sellers are told that they would become large sellers (with costs as introduced in the Isaac and Smith experiments) if they would choose to enter "their" market, but that they would become small sellers in case they entered any other market. The seven remaining sellers are small sellers no matter which market they chose to enter. Efficiency demands that each of the four large sellers enters their preferred market, each of which would also see entry of a small seller, and for the remaining three small sellers to enter the fifth market in which no seller would have a cost advantage. Note that the fifth market serves as an "active escape opportunity" for the small sellers. Again, demand (as in the Isaac and Smith experiments) is simulated in each market. Finally, at the beginning of each market period, firms choose a market to enter, a price and a corresponding maximum quantity. With this setup, Harrison reports cases of predatory pricing in the sense defined above.

However, Goeree and Gomez (1998) replicate the Harrison (1988) study with the result that only 3 out of 144 price decisions of large buyers could possibly be classified as predatory. Note that in this design entry, price and quantity decisions are made simultaneously. This means that e.g. a large seller never knows whether he would be a monopolist in his market or whether he would share it with a small seller.

Consequently, Capra *et al.* (2000) vary Harrison's design in two respects. (a) Small sellers first choose their markets (which become commonly known) before all sellers choose prices and quantities (large sellers can now react to entry and possibly raise prices after exit). (b) Large incumbent sellers have complete information about demand and others' costs whereas small sellers only know own costs. Presumably, this makes it more likely that a large seller prices more aggressively. And in fact, Capra *et al.* report that predatory pricing consistently arose in most markets.

Jung, Kagel and Levin (1994) report on tests of Selten's (1978) chain-store game and Kreps and Wilson's (1982) reputation model.[32]

---

[32] Jung *et al.* (1994) is not the first and only paper reporting experimental results on reputation building. Camerer and Weigelt (1988), Neral and Ochs (1992) as well as Brandts and Figueras (2003) also report on reputation building in the lab. However, they cast the Kreps and Wilson model in a lender–borrower

In the model by Selten, there is an incumbent (a chain store) who is a monopolist in several (finitely many) markets where it is operating the same technology and producing the same products. In each market, it faces potential entry. More precisely, in the first market, first the entrant decides about entry. Then, if entry occurs, the incumbent decides whether to fight or to accommodate. The outcome of this interaction becomes publicly known before in the second market the same stage game is played between the incumbent and a new entrant, etc. In Selten's model the incumbent is weak and prefers to share each market in which entry occurs. Applying backward induction, Selten shows that each entrant enters and is always accommodated.

Kreps and Wilson's model is similar to Selten's, however, now entrants have incomplete information regarding the type of the incumbent: with some probability the incumbent is strong (low cost) and would always fight entry; with the complementary probability the incumbent is weak (high cost) and, as in Selten's model, prefers to share each market. Kreps and Wilson derive a sequential equilibrium in which the weak incumbent fights entry in the first markets to make the entrants believe it is strong. Only towards the end of the game does it start to accommodate entry. The fact that weak incumbents fight entry in early periods of the game can be interpreted as predatory pricing. (In fact, Kreps and Wilson define predation exactly in this way.)

Jung *et al.* (1994) implement markets in which a monopolist plays a sequence of eight periods against different entrants. They implement both a version of the Selten set-up, as well as a version of the Kreps and Wilson model. Using the Kreps and Wilson definition of predatory pricing, they report that, for experienced subjects, predatory pricing occurred in 100% of the cases in the Kreps and Wilson model and in 85% of the games in the Selten model. Furthermore, entry rates during early periods of the game are reported to be near 0% in the Kreps and Wilson model and as low as 30% in the Selten model. In the Selten model, the experimental results thus differ markedly from what theory predicts. However, regarding the Kreps and Wilson

frame. The latter has some strategic consideration in common, but also important differences. For instance, whereas the lender–borrower game can be given a "cooperative" interpretation, the Kreps and Wilson game has more of a "competitive" flavor. We therefore refrain from providing details of these experiments, as they seem not to be directly related to the kind of situations we consider in this paper.

model, also some deviations are reported. First, entry rates increase constantly towards the end of a game while the Kreps and Wilson model predicts fixed entry rates during these periods of mixed-strategy play. Furthermore, entrants do not enter more often after periods in which no entry occurred than after periods in which entry and fighting occurred.

3.7. Essential facilities and foreclosure

Rey and Tirole (2003) define foreclosure as "a dominant firm's denial of proper access to an essential good it produces, with the intent of extending monopoly power from that segment of the market (the bottleneck segment) to an adjacent segment (the potentially competitive segment)." These authors, however, also point out that a monopolist on an upstream market, faced with competition on the downstream market, may not be fully able to exploit its monopoly power as a result of the fact that it may not be able to make a credible commitment to downstream firms that it will restrict output. As a consequence, downstream firms will not accept contracts that allow the producer to extract full monopoly profits. Of course, vertical integration can resolve this commitment problem and enable the upstream monopolist to fully exploit its market power, but such integration may be blocked by the merger regulation. Martin *et al.* (2001) study this commitment problem of such an upstream monopolist in an experimental setting. The basic structure that they consider has a single upstream firm that produces an input at constant average and marginal costs and two downstream firms that convert each unit of input into a unit of a homogeneous final good. The upstream monopolist can simultaneously make take-it-or-leave-it contract offers to each of the downstream firms specifying a quantity and a fixed payment it demands for the bundle.

In a first treatment these contract offers become publicly known before downstream firms decide. Public contracts serve as a commitment device such that the upstream monopolist can earn the monopoly profit for itself by offering contracts that consist of offering half the monopoly output at half the monopoly profit to each downstream firm. If, however, the contracts are negotiated privately, such that a downstream firm will not observe the contract the upstream monopolist offers to the other downstream firm, the upstream monopolist may no longer be able to obtain the monopoly profit. Predictions in this treatment depend on out-of-equilibrium beliefs of a downstream firm concerning the contract that is being offered to its rival. More precisely, if a downstream firm entertains passive beliefs, it thinks that its rival receives the equilibrium offer. In this case it can be shown that output is higher, and the upstream monopolists' profits are lower than in the joint-profit-maximizing outcome.[33] A third treatment implements the case where the upstream monopolist integrates vertically with one of the downstream firms. Here, the integrated firm can commit to sell the monopoly quantity through its downstream subsidiary and not supply the other downstream firm at all; hence, there is foreclosure.

Martin *et al.* find partial support for the arguments from Rey and Tirole (2003) and the foreclosure theory. When contracts are secret (i.e. in the presence of a commitment problem), outputs are higher and the upstream monopolists' profits are lower than in the case of public contracts or in the case of an integrated firm. However, the differences are not as pronounced as theoretically predicted. Moreover, the experimental results differ from the theoretical predictions with regard to the division of profits between upstream and downstream firms. Theory predicts that the upstream firm should have all the bargaining power (by making take-it-or-leave-it offers) such that it should be able to extract all of the industry profits. This is observed most of the time in the treatment with an integrated firm. However, in the two non-integrated treatments, with public respectively secret contracts, the upstream monopolist only obtains a fraction of industry profits. It seems that the threat of the downstream firms to reject the upstream firm's offer limits the latter firm's bargaining power.[34] This unpredicted bargaining effect provides another rationale for vertical integration, different from the ones that are usually discussed in the literature. As Martin *et al.* (2001: 479) conclude: "other vertical restraints may not allow the upstream firm to extract as much industry rent as full vertical integration."

---

[33] There is, however, another equilibrium (with symmetric beliefs) in which the outcome is the same as with public contracts. However, Rey and Tirole (2003) argue that the assumption of passive beliefs is theoretically more sound.

[34] Martin *et al.* (2001) discuss (dis)similarities of their treatments with the ultimatum game for which experimental results reject the subgame perfect equilibrium prediction with its extremely asymmetric payoff consequences.

4. Conclusion

When Sections 2 and 3 above are put side by side, one cannot help noticing the discrepancy between the issues dealt with in each section. Whereas, for instance, it appears from the survey of the case law that the application of Article 82 EC to rebate schemes or to access to facilities has attracted a lot of attention, these themes do not seem to have been featured prominently in the experimental economic literature. Conversely, experimental economists have devoted considerable resources to investigating predation theories, whereas the case law does not appear to indicate that this has been a significant issue in the application of EC competition law.

One can speculate on a number of competing explanations for this discrepancy. We will look into two different hypotheses: the first one is that experimental economists would be out of phase with market developments, and the second one is the mirror hypothesis, namely that the sample of case law studied in Section 2 is either not representative or biased in favor of certain types of issues.

With respect to the first hypothesis, experimental economists appear to work mostly on testing theories or improving on other experiments. Most experimental studies are motivated either by a theoretical paper or by another experimental study. The research agenda in experimental economics does not seem to be driven by the occurrences in real-life situations; very few experimental studies are directly inspired by a real-world phenomenon or problem. Anecdotal evidence for this observation comes from a quick look at the program of the 2005 International Meeting of the Economic Science Association (ESA), which is the professional organization of experimental economists. Only about 5–10% of the papers presented at that meeting are directly inspired by real-life problems. Clearly, there are many real-world phenomena that, in principle, might be of interest to experimental economists, hence, given the already small overall percentage, one can only expect a very small number of papers to deal with antitrust issues, or with issues in industrial organization more generally. In the past, within industrial organization, experimental economists have been enthusiastic about doing experiments on auctions or other aspects of market design, in contrast to market regulation. The current preference might still be in that direction. For example, one of the few experimental papers on industrial organization issues presented at the ESA 2005 meeting, Porter *et al.* (2005), reports on a commission from the State of Virginia to have experimental economists explore alternatives for the design of an auction that allocated bankable NOx allowances.

With respect to the second hypothesis, the last decades of Article 82 EC enforcement do not appear to have been driven by any specific agenda on the part of the Commission. The only exception is the use of Article 82 EC as part of the liberalization policy pursued in network industries such as telecommunications, post, energy or transport, which accounts for a fair number of cases. Leaving this aside, there is no evidence that the Commission systematically set out to identify the most pressing problems in the area of Article 82 EC and then to direct its enforcement activities at these problems. This might be changing now in the wake of the modernization brought about by Regulations 1/2003 and 139/2004, which highlighted the state of neglect into which Article 82 EC had fallen. In any event, a large number of the cases surveyed arose out of preliminary references to the ECJ, and these definitely do not follow any agenda.

The case law and the decision practice of the Commission could thus very well be affected mostly by the relatively haphazard flow of complaints to the Commission and preliminary references to the ECJ, so that the data derived from the table in the Appendix would not have much aggregate significance as an indication of which problems are truly pressing and should be addressed by experimental economics. At the same time, it is conceivable that the complaints and preliminary references themselves are statistically indicative of which issues are most significant in the European economy, since they are made at the initiative of aggrieved parties. Yet not all complaints are taken up by the Commission and not all cases before national courts are sent to the ECJ by way of preliminary reference. Both the Commission (in deciding which complaint to pursue) and the national courts (in deciding whether to send a preliminary reference to the ECJ) have some measure of discretion. In the case of the Commission, it is a question of assessing whether dedicating resources to a complaint is in the Community interest.[35] In the case of the national court, it must be

---

[35] See the Notice on the handling of complaints by the Commission under Articles 81 and 82 of the EC Treaty [2004] OJ C 101/67.

seen whether a preliminary reference is useful to the solution of the case and whether the issue to be referred to the ECJ has not perhaps already been conclusively settled by the ECJ.

It might thus be that the Commission and the ECJ are busy with cases that do not reflect the truly important issues surrounding the presence and use of market power in the European economy. For the Commission in particular, there might be a historical bias in favor of dealing with issues concerning relationships between competitors, such as rebates, refusals to deal, etc., arising out of the heritage of unfair competition laws and of the intellectual tradition of ordoliberalism.[36] Furthermore, in deciding which complaints to take up, the Commission might also be influenced by the lobbying efforts of complainants. That certain issues appear to be more of a concern for the Commission would then reflect more effective or persuasive arguments presented by the complainants on these issues, as opposed to an inherent significance of the issue.

Let us now come back to some of the questions that we have posed at the beginning of this overview. First, is there scope for further experiments within the sphere of abuse of dominance? As stated above, one of the things we were surprised about is the relatively limited number of experiments that deal with abuse of a dominant position in the strict sense. Perhaps, in retrospect, this is nothing to be surprised about: experimental economists have not let themselves be guided very much by Article 82 cases; they have their own research agenda and there is nothing wrong with that. Despite this, Section 2 of this chapter has indicated some of the issues that antitrust practitioners worry about and we believe that some of these problems might interest experimental economists. In particular, experimental work on the following topics is limited, or completely missing, at the moment and additional work on these may attract the interest of practitioners: price discrimination (non-linear rebate schemes, loyality rebates, etc.), bundling and tying, refusal to deal in a vertical relationship, exclusion and exclusivity clauses, and predatory product differentiation.

Second, is the gap between experimental research results supplied by the literature and the demand of case handlers due to the inherent

---

[36] See Gerber (1998) for an account of the history of competition law in Europe and its intellectual lineage.

boundaries of experimental research as such? Our preliminary answer to this question is "No", with some qualifications. It seems fair to say that competition authorities are using more and more economic reasoning when analyzing cases and that, in particular, the application of theoretical models of strategic behavior will become more widespread.[37] It is, therefore, important to have a wealth of empirical evidence showing that the theoretical models the competition authorities rely on are indeed valid. Such evidence would help policy makers and courts to distinguish "normal" competitive behavior from illegal practices. Surely, there is no shortage of theoretical models of strategic behavior. What is missing, however, is empirical evidence. This is not surprising: in general it is hard to come by empirical evidence, especially since both theoretical models and business practices crucially depend on private information (for example about costs) that is inaccessible for outside observers.[38] A unique advantage of experimental methods is that all parameters of a market are under control and, more importantly, observable. This is not only true for firms' private information such as costs, but also for conspiratorial activities as in Davis and Holt (1998). Consequently, the value of experimental economics for antitrust practitioners may be indirect: by separating the theories that are empirically relevant from those that are not.

Let us illustrate with an example. Huck *et al.* (2007) report on an experiment with bilateral mergers imposed in three- and four-firm Cournot oligopolies with constant unit costs. Theory predicts that these mergers are not profitable for the merged firms (see Salant *et al.*,

---

[37] Note for example eminent economic theorists' involvement in antitrust cases. See also Brennan (2000, p.12) who reflects on the increasing importance of game theory in antitrust economics.

[38] The lack of empirical evidence and the problems of obtaining it are acknowledged by leading economists in the field. In fact, Scherer and Ross (1990) state that it is "difficult to observe systematically the actions taken by incumbents to deter entry" (p. 392). Or consider Wilson (1992: p. 324) who states that "The plethora of predictions obtainable from various formulations indicate that empirical and experimental studies are needed to select among hypotheses. Many models present econometric difficulties that impede empirical work, but this is realistic: the models reveal that strategic behavior can depend crucially on private information inaccessible to outside observers. Estimation of structural models is likely to be difficult, therefore, but it may be possible to predict correlations in the data. Experimental studies may be more effective."

1983). While theory predicts aggregate output well, it fails to predict individual quantities. Contrary to the prediction, post-merger markets are not symmetric, as merged firms produce a larger output compared to unmerged firms, and unmerged firms yield to the more aggressive behavior of merged firms. As a result, in the markets with initially four firms the merger is profitable in the short run, and merged firms break even in the long run. This asymmetry of individual outputs has an interesting implication for the econometric merger analysis. Much of the econometric work on mergers using field data has involved structural estimation based on Nash equilibrium behavior. In such studies, deviations from symmetric Cournot outcomes might be accounted for by differences in firms' marginal costs. In the absence of direct evidence on costs, field-data studies might well conclude that the merger resulted in efficiencies that reduced marginal cost and caused the merged firm to increase output. As the alleged efficiency increase is part of the welfare effect of the merger, conclusions about the desirability of the merger are misleading. In the laboratory, the experimenter can control for the underlying parameters, such as marginal cost, and a behavioral hypothesis such as Nash equilibrium behavior can be accepted or rejected based on evidence.

Experimental economics can contribute to observation-based underpinnings of strategic-behavior issues that can inform both theorists and antitrust practitioners. We think this is important as some economists argue that that there is some "judicial skepticism" against certain kinds of strategic behavior such as predatory pricing that has led to dismissal of charges of such behavior in court cases until recently (see e.g. Bolton *et al.* 2000). But experimental economists have helped to isolate circumstances under which e.g. predatory pricing is likely to arise. So, all evidence obtained from carefully and appropriately designed experiments should be welcome.

Some caveats need to be mentioned. Clearly, there are many situations where experimental economics will not be helpful assessing antitrust issues. For example, it is not possible to decide in the laboratory the cost function that a firm under scrutiny has. In general, all aspects that define a particular market (like the number of firms, costs, demand or the strategic variables, e.g. price, quantity or advertising outlets) cannot be determined in the lab. One can only (and freely) specify these variables and experimentally investigate which effect particular realizations of these variables have on the (mis) behavior of firms.

Another qualification is in order with regard to the specific subject pool used in most experiments: college students. However, it is likely that recent attempts to extend the methods that experimenters usually use will prove successful in increasing the general relevance of experimental procedures obtained using convenient student samples. (See Harrison and List [2004] on the relationship of laboratory and field experiments.)

Third, what are the lessons from this paper for using experimental research in antitrust enforcement? In the wake of *Tetra Laval*,[39] experimental economics appears more relevant than ever for the enforcement of competition law. In that case, the ECJ made it clear (for example in paragraphs 39 and 42) that the Commission must be careful in its analysis, and in particular that the economic analysis used by the Commission must be solid. While *Tetra Laval* dealt with merger control, there is no reason to believe that the ECJ would expect less from the Commission in Article 82 EC cases. Against that background, experimental economics can prove very useful in supporting (or weakening) theoretical claims. In the face of competing economic models, it can be conceived that experimental economics could be used to try to assess, in an objective and verifiable fashion, which of the competing theoretical claims made by various parties in a case is most solid.

The ability of experimental economics to test theoretical models against real-world assumptions as to rationality and information, in particular, could greatly help to test theoretical claims. In the end, only the largest firms can be assumed to come close to the standard theoretical assumptions about rationality. Accordingly, in cases involving consumers (exploitative abuses) or smaller competitors (exclusionary abuses), experimental economics could make a worthy contribution.

On a general level, there is an indirect link between experimental research and the work of competition practitioners. As also stated above, there is a strong link between theory and experimentation in

---

[39] ECJ, Case C-12/03, *Tetra Laval* (2005) ECR I-987.

the lab, hence, experimental research can help to assess the usefulness of a theory's (behavioral) assumptions or proposed mechanisms. And to the extent that competition authorities rely on theoretical models of firm behavior, experimental economics can help to assess a model's validity. But we feel that much more work needs to be done here.

In recent years we see that the work of experimental economists and psychologists in conjunction with theorists and competition lawyers helps to shape the behavioral approaches to industrial organization as well as to law and economics. (For the former see for instance the conference on "Behavioural Industrial Organization" organized by the Wissenschaftszentrum Berlin (WZB) or the talk "Behavioural Industrial Organization" delivered by Timothy Cason at the Annual Meeting of the Economic Science Organization in Montreal 2005. For the latter see for instance Jolls, Sunstein and Thaler, 1998.) These efforts are based on the insight that human economic actors are far less perfect than the ideal neoclassical agent and try to explore the consequences of various limitations for the functioning of markets. These efforts will hopefully lead to a more realistic modeling of competition in markets.

On a more specific level, the review of experimental studies for example in the section "Predatory pricing" nicely illustrates how continuous efforts of experimental economists help to isolate conditions under which such practices are (un)likely to occur.

Vickers (2005) notes that the EU law on abuse of dominance is far from settled and that it could develop in either of two broad directions, with emphasis either on legal form or on economic effect. He sees advantages from an evolution in the latter direction but notes that these advantages will be realized only "if European competition law on abuse of dominance becomes more firmly anchored to economic principles, and where those principles are practically applicable by competition authorities, lawyers and the courts." He furthermore notes that "to be effective, economics must contribute in a way that competition agencies, and ultimately the courts, find practicable in deciding cases." In our view, experimental economics can definitely serve as a tool to make economics effective. In this respect, we note that Davis and Wilson (2002) also offer some thoughts as to how competition practitioners might benefit from applications of the experimental method.

References

Aghion, P. and P. Bolton (1987), Contracts as a Barrier to Entry, *American Economic Review* 77, 388–401.

Areeda, P (1990), Essential Facilities: An Epithet in Need of Limiting Principles, *Antitrust Law Journal* 58, 841–853.

Bagwell, K. and G. Ramey (1991), Oligopoly Limit Pricing, *RAND Journal of Economics* 22, 155–172.

Bagwell, K., and G. Ramey (1996), Capacity, Entry and Forward Induction, *RAND Journal of Economics* 27, 660–680.

Bergman, M. (2000), The Bronner Case – A Turning Point for the Essential Facilities Doctrine?, *ECLR* 59.

Bolton, P., J.F. Brodley, and M.H. Riordan (2000), Predatory Pricing: Strategic Theory and Legal Policy, *Georgetown Law Review* 88, 2239–2330.

Bonnano, G. (1987), Location Choice, Product Proliferation and Entry Deterrence, *Review of Economic Studies*, LIV, 37–45.

Boyer, M., P. Mahenc, and M. Moreaux (2003), Entry Preventing Locations under Incomplete Information, *International Journal of Industrial Organization* 21, 809–829.

Brandts, J., A. Cabrales, and G. Charness (2007), Entry Deterrence and Forward Induction: an experiment, *Economic Theory* 33, 83–209.

Brandts, J. and N. Figueras (2003), An Exploration of Reputation Formation in Experimental Games, *Journal of Economic Behaviour & Organization* 50, 89–115.

Brennan, T.J. (2000), The Economics of Competition Policy: Recent Developments and Cautionary Notes in Antitrust and Regulation, RFF Discussion Paper, Washington, DC.

Camerer, C. and K. Weigelt (1988), Experimental Tests of a Sequential Equilibrium Reputation Model, *Econometrica* 56, 1–36.

Capra, C.M., J.K. Goeree, R. Gomez, and C.A. Holt (2000), Predation, Asymmetric Information, and Strategic Behaviour in the Classroom: An Experimental Approach to the Teaching of Industrial Organization, *International Journal of Industrial Organization* 18, 205–225.

Cason, T. and T. Sharma (2001), Durable Goods, Coasian Dynamics and Uncertainty: Theory and Experiments, *Journal of Political Economy* 109, 1311–1354.

Coase, R.H. (1972), Durability and Monopoly, *Journal of Law & Economics*, 15(1), pages 143–49.

Cooper, D. J., S. Garvin, and J. Kagel (1997a), Signalling and Adaptive Learning in an Entry Limit Pricing Game, *RAND Journal of Economics* 28, 662–683.

Cooper, D. J., S. Garvin, and J. Kagel (1997b), Adaptive Learning vs. Equilibrium Refinements in an Entry Limit Pricing Game, *Economic Journal* 107, 553–575.

Coursey, D., R.M. Isaac, and V.L. Smith (1984), Natural Monopoly and the Contested Markets: Some Experimental Results, *Journal of Law and Economics* 27, 91–113.

Davis, D. D. and C. A. Holt (1993), *Experimental Economics*, Princeton University Press, Princeton.

Davis, D. D. and C.A. Holt (1994), The Effects of Discounting Opportunities in Laboratory Posted-Offer Markets, *Economics Letters* 44, 249–253.

Davis, D. D. and C. A. Holt (1996), Markets with Posted Prices: Recent Results from the Laboratory, *Investigaciones Económicas* 20, 291–320.

Davis, D. D. and C. A. Holt (1998), Conspiracies and Secret Price Discounts, *Economic Journal* 108, 736–756.

Davis, D. D. and Millner, E. L. (2005), Rebates, Matches and Consumer Behavior, *Southern Economic Journal* 72, 410–422 (2005).

Davis, D. D. and B.J. Wilson (2002), Experimental Methods and Antitrust Policy, in: *Research in Experimental Economics, Special Issue Experiments Investigating Market Power*, Volume IX, eds. C. A. Holt and R. Mark Isaac, JAI Press, Elsevier Science, Greenwich, 61–94.

Deck, C.A. and B.J. Wilson (2008), Experimental Gasoline Markets, *Journal of Economic Behaviour and Organization* 67, 134–149.

Dixit, A. (1980), The Role of Investment in Entry Deterrence, *Economic Journal* 90, 95–106.

Dolbear, F.T., L.B. Lave, G. Bowman, A. Lieberman, E. Prescott, F. Rueter, R. Sherman (1968), Collusion in Oligopoly: An Experiment on the Effect of Numbers and Information, *Quarterly Journal of Economics* 82, 240–259.

Dufwenberg, M. and U. Gneezy (2000), Price Competition and Market Concentration: an Experimental Study, *International Journal of Industrial Organization* 18, 7–22.

Engle-Warnick, J. and B.J. Ruffle (2004), Buyer Concentration as a Source of Countervailing Power: Evidence from Experimental Posted-Offer Markets, Working Paper, Ben Gurion University, Beersheba.

Fouraker, L. and S. Siegel (1963), *Bargaining Behaviour*, McGraw-Hill, New York.

Gerber, D. J. (1998), *Law and Competition in twentieth century Europe*, Oxford University Press, Oxford.

Goeree, J. K. and R. Gomez (1998), Predatory Pricing in the Laboratory, unpublished draft, University of Virginia, Charlottesville.

Goeree, J. K., R. Gomez and C. Holt (2004), Predatory Pricing: Rare Like a Unicorn?, in press in C. Plott and V. L. Smith (eds.), *Handbook of Experimental Economic Results*, Elsevier Press, New York.

Güth, W., P. Ockenfels, and K. Ritzberger (1995), On Durable Goods Monopolies: An Experimental Study of Intrapersonal Price Competition and Price Discrimination over Time, *Journal of Economic Psychology* 16, 247–74.

Güth, W., S. Kröger, and H.-T. Normann (2004), Durable Goods Monopoly with Privately Known Impatience, *Economic Inquiry* 42, 413–424.

Harrison, G. W. (1988), Predatory Pricing in a Multiple Market Experiment. A Note, *Journal of Economic Behaviour and Organization* 9, 405–417.

Harrison, G. and J.A. List (2004), Field Experiments, *Journal of Economic Literature* 42, 1009–1055.

Harrison, G. W. and M. McKee (1985), Monopoly Behaviour, Decentralized Regulation, and Contestable Markets: An Experimental Evaluation, *RAND Journal of Economics* 16, 51–69.

Harrison, G. W., M. McKee, and E.E. Rutstrom (1989), Experimental Evaluation of Institutions of Monopoly Restraint, Chapter 3 in L. Green and J. Kagel (eds.), *Advances in Behavioural Economics*, Volume II, Ablex Press, Norwood, 54–94.

Holt, C. A. (1995), Industrial Organization: A Survey of Laboratory Research, in J. Kagel and A. Roth (eds.), *Handbook of Experimental Economics*, Princeton University Press, Princeton, 349–443.

Huck, S. and W. Müller (2005), Burning Money and (Pseudo) First-Mover Advantages: An Experimental Study on Forward Induction, *Games and Economic Behaviour*, 51, 109–127.

Huck, S., K.A. Konrad, W. Müller, and H.-T. Normann (2007), The Merger Paradox and Why Aspiration Levels Let it Fail in the Laboratory, *Economic Journal* 117, 1073–1095.

Hudson, D. and J.L. Lusk (2004), What You Don't Know Can Cost You: A Web Based Experiment in Price Discrimination, *Review of Agricultural Economics* 26, 392–403.

Isaac, R. M., V. Ramey, and A.W. Williams (1984), The Effects of Market Organization on Conspiracies in Restraint of Trade, *Journal of Economic Behaviour and Organization* 5, 191–222.

Isaac, M. R. and V. L. Smith (1985), In Search of Predatory Pricing, *Journal of Political Economy* 93 (2), 320–45.

Jolls, C., C.R. Sunstein, and R. Thaler (1998), A Behavioural Approach to Law and Economics, *Stanford Law Review* 50, 1471–1550.

Jung, Y. J., J. H. Kagel, and D. Levin (1994), On the Existence of Predatory Pricing: An Experimental Study of Reputation and Entry Deterrence in the Chain-Store Game, *RAND Journal of Economics* 25, 72–93.

Kahneman, D., J. L. Knetsch and R. Thaler (1986), Fairness as a Constraint on Profit Seeking: Entitlements in the Market, *American Economic Review*, 76(4), 728–41.

Kreps, D. M. and R. Wilson (1982), Sequential Equilibria, *Econometrica*, 50(4), 863–894.

Martin, S., H.-T. Normann and C. M. Snyder (2001), Vertical Foreclosure in Experimental Markets, *RAND Journal of Economics* 32, Autumn, 466–496.

Martinez, M. (2007), Some Views on Pricing and EC Competition Policy, available at http://ec-europa.eu/comm/competition/index_en.html.

Mason, C. F. and C. Nowell (1998), An Experimental Analysis of Subgame Perfect Play: The Entry Deterrence Game, *Journal of Economic Behaviour & Organization* 37, 443–462.

Milgrom, P. and J. Roberts (1982), Limit Pricing and Entry under Incomplete Information, *Econometrica* 50, 443–460.

Motta, M. (2004), *Competition Policy: Theory and Practice*, Cambridge University Press, Cambridge.

Müller, W., Y. Spiegel, and Y. Yehezkel (2004), Oligopoly Limit Pricing: Experimental Evidence, Games and Economic Behaviour.

Neral, J. and J. Ochs, (1992), The Sequential Equilibrium Theory of Reputation Building: A Further Test, *Econometrica* 60, 1151–69.

Normann, H.-T., B. Ruffle and C. M. Snyder (2007), Do Buyer-Size Discounts Depend on the Curvature of the Surplus Function? Experimental Tests of Bargaining Models, *RAND Journal of Economics* 38(3), 747–767.

Plott, C. R. (1989), An Updated Review of Industrial Organization Applications of Experimental Methods, in *Handbook of Industrial Organization*, Volume II, R. Schmalensee and R. Willig (eds.), Elsevier Science Publishers B.V., Amsterdam, 1111–1176.

Porter, D., S. Rassenti, V. Smith, and A. Winn (2005), The Design, Testing and Implementation of Virginia's NOx Allowance Auction, mimeo.

Ramseyer, J. M., E. Rasmusen, and J. Wiley (1991), Naked Exclusion, *American Economic Review* 81, 1137–1145.

Rapoport, A., I. Erev, and R. Zwick (1995), An Experimental Study of Buyer-Seller Negotiation with One-Sided Incomplete Information and Time Discounting, *Management Science* 41, 377–94.

Rey, P. and J. Tirole (2003), A Primer on Foreclosure, in *Handbook of Industrial Organization*, Volume III, M. Armstrong and R. Porter (eds.), North-Holland, New York.

Reynolds, S. S. (2000), Durable-Goods Monopoly: Laboratory Market and Bargaining Experiments, *RAND Journal of Economics* 31, 375–94.

Salant, S. W., S. Switzer, and R. J. Reynolds (1983): Losses from Horizontal Merger: The Effects of an Exogenous Change in Industry Structure on Cournot–Nash Equilibrium, *Quarterly Journal of Economics*, 98(2), 185–199.

Scherer, F. and D. Ross (1990), *Industrial Market Structure and Economic Performance*, 3rd edn., Rand McNally & Co, Chicago.

Segal, I. and M.D. Whinston (2000), Naked Exclusion: Comment, *American Economic Review* 90, 296–309.

Selten, R., (1978), The Chain-Store Paradox, *Theory and Decision* 9, 127–159.

Smith, V. L. (1981), An Empirical Study of Decentralized Institutions of Monopoly Restraint, in J. Quirk and G. Horwich (eds.) *Essays in Contemporary Fields of Economics in Honor of E.T. Weiler (1914–1979)*, Purdue University Press, West Lafayette, 83–106.

Smith, V. L. and A.W. Williams (1989), The Boundaries of Competitive PriceTheory: Convergence, Expectations, and Transactions Costs, in *Advances in Behavioral Economics*, Vol. II, (eds) L. Green and J. Kagel, Ablex Publishing, Norwood, NJ.

Vickers, J., (2005), Abuse of Market Power, *The Economic Journal* 115, F244–F261.

Wellford C.P. (2002), Antitrust: Results from the Laboratory, in *Research in Experimental Economics, Special Issue Experiments Investigating Market Power*, Volume IX, (eds.) C. A. Holt and R. Mark Isaac, JAI Press, Elsevier Science, Greenwich, 1–60.

Wilson, R. (1992), Strategic Models of Entry Deterrence, in R. Aumann and S. Hart (eds.), *Handbook of Game Theory*, Volume I, Chapter 10, 305–329. Elsevier Science Publishers, Amsterdam.

Table 6A.1 *Case-law and Commission decision practice under Art. 82 EC*

Name	Date (1)	Procedure (2)					Impugned practice									
							Pricing					Rebates				
		ECJ-Prelim. ref.	Commission Decisions	→ to ECJ (-1988)	→ to CFI (1989-)	→ →Appeal to ECJ	Excessive	Predatory	Fixing	Squeeze	Cross-ubsidization	Loyalty	Non-linear	Quality	"Fighting"	Whole req.
IMS/NDC	29-04-2004	*														
Microsoft	24-03-2004		*		P											
GCG/FS	27-08-2003		*													
Wanadoo	16-07-2003		*		P			*								
DT AG	21-05-2003		*		P					*						
Michelin II	31-05-2002		*		+									*	*	
De Post	05-12-2001		*													
DP AG (X-border mail)	25-07-2001		*				*									
DP AG (parcel service)	20-03-2001		*					*			*					
NDC/IMS	03-07-2001		*		−	−										
DSD	20-04-2001		*													
BA/Virgin	13-12-1999		*		+							*				
Ilmailulaitos	10-02-1999		*													
BNP	21-01-1999	*														
Decca	21-12-1998		*													
Flat glass	07-12-1998		*		−					*						
BPB	05-12-1998		*		−							*				
London Europ./Sabena	04-12-1998		*													
Bronner	26-11-1998	*														
TACA	16-09-1998		*													
AAMS	17-06-1998		*													
Alpha Flight	11-06-1998		*		+	+										
Van den Bergh	11-03-1998		*		+											
FAG	14-01-1998		*													
GT Link	17-07-1997	*														
Tiercé Ladbroke (3)	12-06-1997		*		−											

Betw. Cust.	Towards comp. (Vert.)	Between MSt	Supply IP/info	Cooperate (interlining, etc.)	Access/EFD	Supply goods	Tying	Exploitative clauses	Exclusive binding	Exclusive purchase	Display exclusivity	Compulsory licensing	Excl. lic. of compet. prod	Restr. on downstr. sales	Unilat. Contract changes	Use of IP rights	Restriction of supply	Affecting market structure	Quotas	Disciplines/Penalties	Segmentation between MSt	Exclusionary tech specs	Collective dominance	Authority	Aftermarket	Remarks
			*																							
			*				*																			
					*																					
							*																			
*						*											*									
			*																							
												*														
*																										
*																								*		
														—												
										*											*					
																		*				*				
*																										
					*																					
					*																					
						*												*				*				
	*																		*							
	*																									
											*															
	*																									
*																									*	
			*																							

Table 6A.1 *(cont.)*

Name	Date (1)	ECJ-Prelim. ref.	Commission Decisions	→ to ECJ (-	→ to CFI (1989-	→ →Appeal to ECJ	Excessive	Predatory	Fixing	Squeeze	Cross-ubsidization	Loyalty	Nonlinear	Quality	"Fighting"	Whole req.
							Pricing					Rebates				
Irish Sugar	14-05-1997		*									*	*		*	
La Crespelle	05-10-1994	*					*									
Almelo	27-05-1994	*														
Corsica Ferries	17-05-1994	*														
HOV SVZ/MCN	29-03-1994		*		+											
Sea Cont. / Stena	21-12-1993		*													
Cewal	23-12-1992		*		+	-						*			*	
Warner Lambert/ Gilette	10-11-1992		*													
FWA Ship Comm.	01-04-1992		*													
British Midland	26-02-1992		*													
Tetra Pak II	24-07-1991		*		+	+		*			*					
Soda ash − Solvay + ICI(4)	19-12-1990		*										*			*
Tournier / Lucazeau	13-07-1989	*														
Ahmed Saeed Flugreisen	11-04-1989	*					*	*	*							
Magill	21-12-1988		*		+	+										
Volvo/Veng / Renault	05-10-1988	*														
Tetra Pak I	26-07-1988		*		+											
Napier Brown	18-07-1988		*							*			*			
Bodson	04-05-1988	*					*									
Hilti	22-12-1987		*		+	+						*				
BBI	29-07-1987		*													
AKZO	14-12-1985		*	+												
Brit Leyland	02-07-1984		*	+												
BT	10-12-1982		*	+			*									
GVL	29-12-1981		*	+												
Michelin I	07-10-1981		*	+									*			

Discr.			Refusal to				Contractual practices										Other									Remarks
Betw. Cust.	Towards comp. (Vert.)	Between MSt	Supply IP/info	Cooperate (interlining, etc.)	Access/EFD	Supply goods	Tying	Exploitative clauses	Exclusive binding	Exclusive purchase	Display exclusivity	Compulsory licensing	Excl. lic. of compet. prod	Restr. on downstr. sales	Unilat. Contract changes	Use of IP rights	Restriction of supply	Affecting market structure	Quotas	Disciplines/Penalties	Segmentation between MSt	Exclusionary tech specs	Collective dominance	Authority	Aftermarket	
	*																									
																								*		
										*													*			
*																								*		
	*																									
				*																						
																							*			
																		*								
																			*				*			
					*																					
		*					*	*	*	*							*				*					
										*																
*																				*						
			*																							
	*		*																						*	
													*													
	*				*	*																				
			*	*	*	*																			*	
						*																				
			*																							
	*				*																					
*																										
*																										

Table 6A.1 *(cont.)*

Name	Date (1)	ECJ-Prelim. ref.	Commission Decisions	↑ to ECJ (-	↑ to CFI (1989-	↑ →Appeal to ECJ	Excessive	Predatory	Fixing	Squeeze	Cross-subsidization	Loyalty	Nonlinear	Quality	"Fighting"	Whole req.
							Pricing					Rebates				
Hoffmann-LaRoche	23-05-1978	*														
Hugin	08-12-1977		*	−												
ABG	19-04-1977		*	−									*			
EMI	15-06-1976	*														
Vitamins	09-06-1976		*	+								*				*
United Brands	17-12-1975		*	+ (−)			*									
Gen Motors	19-12-1974		*	-			*									
BRT/SABAM	27-03-1974	*														
Sugar	02-01-1973		*													
Commercial Solvents	14-12-1972		*	+												
Continental Can	09-12-1971		*	−												
Deutsche Gramophon	08-06-1971	*														
GEMA	02-06-1971		*													
Sirena	18-02-1971	*					*									
Parke Davis	29-02-1968	*														
TOTAL		17	50	12	14	6	8	4	2	2	1	7	6	1	2	2
Aggregates							Pricing:			17	Rebates:					18
+				8	10	4										
−				4	4	2										

Notes: (1) Date of ECJ judgment (for preliminary references) or Commission decision (for others).
(2) The last three columns indicate which Commissions were brought before the ECJ (until 1988) or the CFI (as of 1989, with the possibility of further appeal to the ECJ) P: case still pending; +: CFI/ECJ confirms Commission decision; -: CFI/ECJ annuls Commission decision

	Discr.			Refusal to				Contractual practices											Other								Remarks
	Betw. Cust.	Towards comp. (Vert.)	Between MSt	Supply IP/info	Cooperate (interlining, etc.)	Access/EFD	Supply goods	Tying	Exploitative clauses	Exclusive binding	Exclusive purchase	Display exclusivity	Compulsory licensing	Excl. lic. of compet. prod	Restr. on downstr. sales	Unilat. Contract changes	Use of IP rights	Restriction of supply	Affecting market structure	Quotas	Disciplines/Penalties	Segmentation between MSt	Exclusionary tech specs	Collective dominance	Authority	Aftermarket	
																	*										
							*																				*
																	*										
	*						*							*													
										*	*																
							*															*					
																			*								
																*											
																						*					
																	*										
	10	8	1	7	3	5	8	5	2	3	3	1	1	1	1	1	4	2	3	2	1	4	1	5	4	3	
	Discr.:	19	Refusals:			23	Contractual practices:										22											

(3) Decision of the CFI on an action for annulment against a Commission decision rejecting a complaint.
(4) Annulled by CFI (confirmed by ECJ) on procedural rounds, re-issued in 2000.

7 | Buyer countervailing power: a survey of the theory and experimental evidence

BRADLEY J. RUFFLE[*]

The rise of mega-retailers and industry concentration levels has recently generated an interest among economists and antitrust policymakers in the effects of buyer countervailing power. There exists a considerable theoretical literature offering a range of sources of powerful buyers' ability to extract price discounts. The explanations that have been tested experimentally have all found laboratory support. This chapter surveys the theoretical literature on countervailing power, emphasizing experimental tests where available. The increasing policy relevance of this topic and the blossoming of theoretical models contrasted with the dearth of experimental tests point to fruitful directions for research.

1. Introduction

The industrial organization literature has traditionally focused exclusively on seller strategies. Buyers are typically assumed to act as passive price-takers, accepting all sellers' prices below their demand curves. While this assumption may accurately describe the individual consumer's purchasing decision, non-retail sales account for one-third of the gross domestic product. In industrial-product, wholesale and intermediate-product markets, a small number of sellers typically compete with one another for the business of a small number of large buyers. In such settings, there is no theoretical or even intuitive reason to believe that buyers should be any less influential in establishing the price than sellers.

Galbraith (1952) first introduced the notion of buyer countervailing power. Galbraith contended that powerful buyers constitute an active

* I thank Hans-Theo Normann for useful comments and Shai Bernstein for valuable research assistance. The author bears full responsibility for any remaining errors or omissions.

restraint to monopoly power. Galbraith claimed not only that such strong buyers were ubiquitous, existing in virtually every non-retail industry, but that free enterprise ensured their existence: wherever an industry had become too concentrated, economic incentives gave rise to powerful buyers to offset the trend toward seller concentration.

Galbraith's idea was initially criticized on numerous grounds. Stigler (1954: 9) expected

bilateral oligopoly to be relatively monopolistic in operation . . . it simply is romantic to believe that a competitive solution will emerge, not merely in a few peculiar cases, but in the general run of industries where two small groups of firms deal with one another suddenly all the long-run advantages of monopolistic behavior have been lost sight of in a welter of irrational competitive moves.

Prior to the advent of mega-retailers, Hunter (1958) found no evidence in Britain for the rise of large-scale retailers in response to an observed increase in the concentration of production of numerous consumer goods.

Competition authorities' recognition of the importance of powerful buyers long precedes Galbraith's. Section 2 of the 1914 Clayton Act prohibits price discrimination between different purchasers on all goods and services, but explicitly exempts quantity discounts. As a result of this loophole, the Federal Trade Commission succeeded in obtaining cease-and-desist orders in only eight of forty-three cases of price discrimination initiated between 1914 and 1936.[1] The rise of mass retailers in the 1930s like A&P, Sears, Roebuck & Co. and Woolworth's led their smaller competitors and their suppliers to pressure legislators to prohibit preferential pricing for selected buyers. These lobbying efforts produced the Robinson-Patman Act in 1936, an amendment to Section 2 of the Clayton Act. Thanks to this new legislation, the Federal Trade Commission succeeded in prosecuting and obtaining cease-and-desist orders in more than one thousand cases of third-degree price discrimination from 1936 to 1972.

In contrast to the aggressive legislative approach in the United States, European countries have historically chosen to treat buyer power on a case-by-case basis. Despite observed increases in buyer

---

[1] Scherer and Ross (1990: 508–516) and the references therein provide a fuller discussion of the history of antitrust policies toward price discrimination.

concentration in Europe, particularly in the retail sector,[2] Dobson and Waterson (1997) argue that "UK competition authorities have remained largely impassive" (p. 418), choosing instead to take a "benign view of consolidation in retailing ... in contrast to the position adopted in the United States ... [Consequently,] US concentration levels in retailing have generally risen at a much slower pace than in the United Kingdom" (p. 419). Dobson and Waterson further note that the UK Competition Commission has taken action to block only one proposed merger in recent years (p. 428). Similarly, the Netherlands Competition Authority (NMa) concluded abuse of a dominant position in only two cases in 2003, despite receiving 159 complaints of abuse, 79 of which were immediately dismissed. One of the cases of declared abuse concluded with the NMa fining CR Delta, the Netherlands' largest supplier of bull semen to cattle farmers, for employing three distinct discount schemes that could not be justified on the basis of cost savings and served to bind cattle farmers to its product and limit access to competing suppliers.[3] One is left to speculate whether similar supplier discount schemes would have been successfully prosecuted had the buyers been large.

US competition authorities also appear to have adopted a less antagonistic view of buyer power in recent years. In 1982 the US Horizontal Merger Guidelines were revised to cite the "ability of sophisticated buyers to devise long-term contracts to break collusive agreements" as a measure to evaluate the competitiveness of an industry. The 1997 revision to the Horizontal Merger Guidelines and the UK 1998 Competition Act both recognize efficiency gains and the possibility that they will be partially passed on to consumers as a defense for mergers among buyers. In practice, however, antitrust authorities lack clear guidelines regarding, for instance, buyer size or concentration levels sufficient to counteract powerful sellers.

The absence of clear empirically established criteria for evaluating countervailing power may explain what may be interpreted as the US

---

[2] See, for example, the European Commission's (1999) case studies of buyer power and its impact on national competition in food retailing.

[3] The chapter of van Damme, Larouche and Müller elsewhere in this volume discusses the specifics of CR Delta's quantity discount and customer loyalty schemes. Additional details concerning the legal aspects of the case can be found in the NMa's January 7, 2004 press release, available on its website at: www.nmanet.nl/en/.

courts' reluctance to approve mergers despite a seemingly concentrated buyer side of the market. For instance, in *United States* v. *Country Lake Foods, Inc.* (1990), the merger between two fluid milk processors was blocked, despite the court's recognition that three large customers who accounted for over 90% of all purchases had the ability to monitor milk prices, switch suppliers and to enter the milk processing market themselves. More recently, America's first and second largest pharmaceutical companies concurrently proposed to merge with the fourth and third largest firms, respectively. The justification put forth for these multi-billion dollar mergers was the claim that 80% of the estimated $306.9 million in fixed cost savings due to the elimination of redundancies would be passed onto large pharmaceutical buyers, mainly hospitals, purchasing blocs that represent groups of hospitals and retail chains like WalMart, in the form of lower prices. Again, the absence of guidelines for assessing large buyers' countervailing role and the Supreme Court's ruling on Section 7 of the Clayton Act that "possible economies cannot be used as a defense to illegality" in merger cases led the courts to block both mergers (United States District Court for the District of Columbia, 1998, p. 41).

This chapter surveys the experimental work on the role of buyers in markets. While experimental methods are not well suited to examine the dynamic evolution of industry structure inherent in Galbraith's countervailing power thesis, they are ideal for testing the static factors of buyer structure (e.g. buyer concentration and size) hypothesized to counteract seller market power.

The remainder of this chapter organizes the countervailing role of buyers according to source. Section 2 explores the ability of retail consumers motivated by fairness considerations to constrain seller market power. Section 3 examines a number of sources of buyer market power relevant for non-retail markets that fall within the categories of buyer concentration and buyer size. Section 4 concludes.

2. Non-passive buyers and fairness in retail markets

The starting point for this literature is the observation that individuals are not motivated solely by monetary considerations, but also by equity and fairness concerns. Kahneman *et al.* (1986) survey the perceived fairness associated with unconstrained profit-maximization by firms. Price increases that follow from excess demand (e.g., on snow shovels in a snowstorm) rather than cost increases are deemed unfair by the vast majority of respondents. The authors conclude from these perceptions that markets will fail to clear in the short run as consumers respond to what they see as unjustified price increases by foregoing purchases. A more skeptical interpretation is that sellers will always attempt to justify price increases by claiming cost increases.

Kachelmeier *et al.* (1991a) test whether these survey responses are robust to real economic incentives in market experiments. The five sellers and five buyers in their double-auction markets first participate in ten rounds in which a known 50% income tax is paid by the sellers only. Beginning in round 11, the income tax is replaced with a 20% sales tax that, relative to the first ten rounds, has the effect of increasing the equilibrium price and the fraction of the profits earned by the sellers. The authors compare the convergence properties in three information-disclosure treatments. Their results reveal modest support for the hypothesis that prices converge quickest to the new, higher-priced equilibrium when supported by known cost increases (the marginal costs of sellers are revealed), whereas the revelation of sellers' profits only impedes convergence relative to the no-disclosure treatment. Kachelmeier *et al.* (1991b) follow the first seven rounds of play in a double-auction market with a 50% profit tax on the sellers in rounds 8–20. Because sellers' marginal units trade at a profit of zero in their design, the profit tax does not affect the competitive-equilibrium price, but merely decreases the sellers' relative share of the available surplus. Nonetheless, their results show that when buyers are informed of the profit tax, prices are higher than when buyers are uninformed of the tax. Moreover, prices in these tax treatments exceed the pre-tax periods; although these differences shrink over time, indicating fairness considerations give way to competitive forces.

Franciosi *et al.* (1995) extend Kachelmeier *et al.*'s (1991a) design to a posted-offer market, claiming that this is the market institution Kahneman *et al.* (1986) have in mind in their consumer market examples. Consistent with Kachelmeier *et al.* (1991a), prices in the profit-disclosure (fairness) treatment are initially below those in the cost- and no-disclosure treatments. However, over time prices in all treatments converge to the competitive equilibrium, again implying that competitive forces trump fairness.

Ruffle (2000) creates more extreme earnings inequalities at the competitive equilibrium in an attempt to determine whether posted-offer market buyers are able to resist convergence to the Nash equilibrium or even the competitive price. Indeed, when the surplus inequality at the competitive equilibrium yields each of the duopoly sellers six times as much as each of the two buyers, buyers withhold demand intensely and succeed in maintaining prices significantly below competitive levels. Interestingly, profit disclosure, rather than provoking increased demand withholding, actually facilitates collusion by allowing sellers to post similar prices and extract more gains from trade.

Tyran and Engelmann (2005) design posted-offer markets with a known cost increase announced in round 16 of 30. The supply and demand parameters are such that in equilibrium the entire cost increase is passed on to consumers. In their baseline treatment, each of the five buyers individually decides how many of its five units of demand to purchase and withhold, while in their boycott treatment, at the beginning of each period buyers vote whether to boycott the market. A majority vote in favor of a boycott shuts down the market for that period and each market participant earns zero.[4] Otherwise, the period proceeds as in the baseline treatment, with each buyer choosing to purchase or withhold demand. Despite boycotts in 2.7 out of 15 post-cost-increase periods on average, Tyran and Engelmann (2005) find that neither boycotts nor individual attempts at withholding are able to prevent convergence to the competitive price.

Perhaps the general ineffectiveness of consumer boycotts at lowering prices explains why they are so infrequently used. Friedman's (1985) study of ninety consumer boycotts in the US between 1970 and 1980 reveals that perceived violations of worker rights and insensitivity to the concerns of various minority groups, rather than exploitative pricing practices, sparked the vast majority of these boycotts.

3. Buyer countervailing power in non-retail markets

Galbraith's countervailing buyer thesis was intended for wholesale and intermediate product markets. The theoretical industrial organization literature cites a number of reasons for buyer power relevant

---

[4] Kritikos and Bolle's (2004) theoretical model allows the number of consumers and the utility from rejecting the monopolist's offer to vary to derive the likelihood of a consumer boycott.

for such markets. The emerging experimental literature on this topic has tested and found support for some of these reasons; the remainder await testing. Before discussing the theoretical models and the empirical and experimental evidence of buyer countervailing power, I briefly retrace some of the earlier market experiments that, instead of conducting all experimental sessions with simulated, passive price-taking buyers, also included one or more sessions with human buyers for the sake of comparison.

The workhorse in all of the earlier experiments discussed below is the posted-offer market institution, according to which each seller simultaneously posts a sales price. After all prices are displayed to all buyers and sellers, the buyers proceed in a randomly determined order to purchase the quantity that each desires. Because buyers are unable to make counteroffers or negotiate a better price, their only recourse involves rejecting a profitable purchase, also referred to as demand withholding. In a repeated posted-offer game, a buyer may withhold demand out of fairness concerns (e.g., the seller's proposed split is "unfair") or strategic reasons (e.g., to induce the seller to lower its price next period). In all of these earlier experiments, the induced cost and valuation parameters are strictly private information, thereby eliminating fairness as an explanation of buyer withholding.

3.1. Early market experiments

Until recently, market experiments focused almost exclusively on the behavior of sellers. Like the theory the experiments are designed to test, buyers are assumed to act as passive price takers. Thus, human buyers are replaced by a computer algorithm that continues to purchase from the lowest-priced seller as long as the price is less than (or equal to) the buyer's valuation. In fact, this censorship of human buyers dates back to the earliest oligopoly experiments (Fouraker and Siegel, 1963; Friedman, 1967). Simulated buyers offer the advantage of reduced subject payments. More importantly, (the threat of) strategic buyer behavior can only confound the interpretation of the data when the research question of interest focuses on the sellers.

Studies with one or more sessions with human buyers include Smith (1981) who conducts a single session with a posted-offer, increasing-cost monopolist facing five human buyers, each with only one unit of demand. In his eleven-round experiment, not a single instance of withholding is observed and prices converge in period 5 to the monopoly price.

Coursey *et al.* (1984) and Brown-Kruse (1991) test the contestable markets hypothesis with a decreasing-cost monopolist facing either computer-simulated or five human buyers. The decreasing-cost schedule implies that demand withholding hits the monopolist's most profitable units first. Both studies find that prices approach or even converge to competitive levels. Moreover, while prices are lower in sessions with instances of demand withholding, the mere presence of human buyers is sufficient to bring about lower prices compared to sessions with simulated ones.

Cason and Williams (1990) test whether extreme earnings inequalities inhibit equilibrium convergence: in their two box-design treatments, one side or the other of the market earns the entire surplus at the competitive price. They conduct one posted-offer session with four human buyers. With only three instances of demand withholding over ten rounds and excess demand at the competitive equilibrium (implying subsequent buyers who do not withhold negate earlier attempts), prices are found to be similar to the other four posted-offer markets with simulated buyers.

Davis and Williams (1990) examine the conjecture that in posted-offer markets the power of the non-posting side is eliminated. To do so, they conduct four posted-offer experiments in which two of the five buyers are endowed with market power in the sense that by withholding two marginally profitable units, the market-clearing price on the remaining units decreases by $0.25. Notwithstanding, two or more profitable units are left unpurchased in only 3 of 65 periods, and even the purchase of marginally profitable units is foregone in a mere 10 of 521 instances. Furthermore, the mean contract price never deviates from the competitive equilibrium by more than $0.10 and prices converge to the competitive equilibrium within 15 periods.

Davis and Williams (1991) test whether seller market power might inhibit convergence to the competitive equilibrium in posted-offer experiments. They compare the results of four simulated-buyer with four human-buyer experiments. Prices exceed the competitive equilibrium by at least $0.30 after three periods in each of the simulated-buyer experiments, while only one human-buyer experiment yields sustained price deviations from the competitive price. They conclude that "...computer-simulated buyers may generate qualitatively different results than similar posted-offer markets using human buyers, even if human buyers fully reveal demand. Posted-offer sellers appear initially to employ more tentative strategies when facing human buyers than when facing simulated buyers. This conjecture bears further analysis" (p. 273).

In a recent paper, Davis and Wilson (2004) depart from earlier private-information posted-offer experiments by making the supply and demand curves common knowledge. They compare the impact of simulated buyers with that of two human buyers on the pricing of pre- and post-merger sellers that vary according the presence and kind of post-merger synergy. After 25 rounds of play, four sellers are merged into two where the merged sellers benefit from either reduced combined fixed or variable costs or no cost synergies at all. The authors find that human buyers obtain lower prices than simulated ones, both pre- and post-merger. What is more, human buyers are able to extract a portion of both fixed- and variable-cost synergies from the sellers.

In sum, despite a focus on seller pricing behavior, some of the experiments that permit human buyers illustrate a potential moderating effect on sellers' prices. In such cases, the mere presence of human buyers is often sufficient to discipline sellers.

3.2. Buyer concentration

Numerous cross-sectional empirical studies evaluate the relation between industry buyer concentration ratios and seller profitability.[5] Lustgarten (1975), LaFrance (1979), Martin (1983) and Schumacher (1991) all demonstrate lower price–cost seller margins, the more concentrated the industries to which they sold. Kling's (1988) time-series study of the trucking industry finds a progressive rise in concentration following deregulation in 1980. He argues that increased concentration in trucking has provided a measure of countervailing power against large shippers, not previously needed when rates were state regulated.

Ruffle (2000) is the first experimental study to focus exclusively on strategic buyer behavior not motivated solely by fairness considerations. This study explores three variables hypothesized to affect posted prices through buyer demand withholding: buyer concentration

---

[5] Scherer and Ross (1990: 533–535) provide a brief overview of the evidence.

(two or four buyers), the surplus division between buyers and sellers (each duopolist seller earns six times or three times as much as each buyer) and the degree of information disclosure (full information or full information plus profits). The combination of a highly concentrated buyer side of the market (two) and a six-to-one earnings inequality ratio favoring the sellers yields particularly intense demand withholding, resulting in persistently declining posted prices. The terminal-period posted prices range from 10 to 42 units below the competitive price of 1.90, and 26.5 to 58.5 units below the expected price of the unique mixed-strategy Nash equilibrium. Prices well below the competitive equilibrium constitute a rare departure from the robust posted-offer-market finding that prices "tend to converge to the competitive price prediction from above (if at all) (Davis and Holt, 1993: 217). This departure attests to the effective withholding of two buyers in these full-information markets.

One possible explanation for two buyers' efficacy is that if one of the two buyers withholds all of his units of demand, then the two sellers must compete in price for the business of the remaining buyer. This may have led to the observed downward spiral in prices. The four-buyer treatments, by contrast, require three of the four buyers to withhold their entire demand schedules for this fierce price competition between sellers to ensue.

Engle-Warnick and Ruffle (2005a) control for price competition between sellers by conducting experiments in which a monopolist faces either two or four buyers. A further design feature that allows them to focus on buyer concentration (also employed in Ruffle (2000)) is the endowment of each buyer in both the two-buyer and four-buyer treatments with the identical individual demand, thereby equating each buyer's opportunity cost of withholding. Engle-Warnick and Ruffle observe significantly lower posted prices in the two-buyer treatment. Interestingly, demand withholding per buyer, per period does not differ significantly between the two treatments. One interpretation of this finding is that the monopolist selects different price levels in the two treatments to calibrate demand withholding.

To determine the source of lower prices in the two-buyer experiments, the authors design a second pair of two-buyer and four-buyer treatments in which the monopolist only is uninformed about the number of buyers in the market. The disappearance of the price differential and the similar levels of withholding in these uninformed treatments support the cautious monopolist hypothesis; namely, the price differential observed in the original, informed treatments can be explained by the monopolist's cautious reaction to fewer buyers, rather than a reaction to more aggressive withholding at a given price by two buyers than four buyers. Whatever its source, buyer concentration indeed appears to be an effective counterweight to seller market power.

Engle-Warnick and Ruffle (2005b) develop a Bayesian strategy-inference technique and apply it to the dataset in Engle-Warnick and Ruffle (2005a) to estimate each buyer's unobserved withholding strategy that underlies his observed withholding decisions. For about one-quarter of the buyers, the subgame-perfect-equilibrium strategy of passive price taking best describes their behavior. For the remaining three-quarters of the buyers, the authors find active withholding strategies that condition on time, the posted price and a combination of the two variables that best characterize each buyer's behavior. Unconditional, intense withholding early in the game is found to be more effective at lowering the monopolist's price (and no more costly for the buyers) than strategies that trigger withholding above price thresholds or that intensify withholding over time. One plausible explanation for the success of early withholding is that it signals the buyers' unwillingness to accept existing prices. The monopolist thus responds by lowering her price to increase sales and profits. If buyers do not withhold early on, the monopolist, feeling encouraged, may raise her price and continue to do so until she is met with resistance.

3.3. Large-buyer discounts

There are a number of plausible reasons, many modeled theoretically, according to which large buyers obtain a unit-price discount compared to their smaller counterparts. I review this literature below,[6] and include experimental evidence where available.

Adelman (1959) appears to be the first to articulate the threat of vertical integration as an important source of large-buyer discounts. Adelman's study of the Great Atlantic & Pacific Tea Company (A&P) reveals that A&P's credible threat of profitable in-house production of

---

[6] See also Snyder (2008) for a survey of the theoretical work on large-buyer discounts.

corn flakes allowed it to leverage a near 10% reduction with its supplier. Porter (1980: 25) includes the credible threat of backward integration among the sources of bargaining power for buyers, noting the success with which General Motors and Ford have employed this strategy. Scherer and Ross (1990: 530–531) discuss several industry studies in which buyers exercised their threat to produce their own inputs. Reeves (2005) notes that several electric-power companies purchased their own freight cars to assure availability. Katz (1987) formally models large buyers' ability to obtain price concessions through their increased threat of vertical integration and self-supply with a production technology exhibiting increasing returns to scale. With applications to agricultural markets in mind, Sexton and Sexton (1987) contrast the deterrence strategies of a monopolist facing entry from either another for-profit firm or a cooperative consisting of downstream buyers. While the for-profit firm's entry decision hinges on the market's post-entry profitability, the pre-entry market price determines the cooperative's entry decision. As a result, limit-pricing strategies (i.e., price discounts to buyers) are usually effective deterrence strategies against a cooperative. In Scheffman and Spiller (1992), despite the presence of customer-specific sunk investments that deter entry, supplier limit pricing results from buyers' credible threat of vertical integration.

In Snyder (1996, 1998), large buyers' threat to a seller comes not from the possibility of self-supply, but from a competing seller. Snyder adapts the framework of Rotemberg and Saloner (1986) who demonstrate that periods of high demand (booms) are most conducive to price wars since current demand is high relative to future demand. Thus, the current benefit from undercutting can exceed the expected loss from future punishment or lost profits. Snyder (1996) allows buyers to accumulate a backlog of unfilled demand, which they may satisfy all at once, thereby endogenizing buyer size. In Snyder (1998), competing sellers face a different-sized buyer each period. Large buyers cause sellers to underbid one another aggressively in an attempt to supply the large quantities demanded. To prevent undercutting, sellers collude on lower prices when confronted with a large buyer. Both of Snyder's models are amenable to laboratory tests.

Furthermore, competition between suppliers is often cited as the principal source of superstores' lower costs compared to rival local retail shops. For instance, WalMart's 21,000 suppliers must concede to its mega-buyer's price demands and contract terms or else face replacement by a more conciliatory competing supplier (Fishman 2003). In an empirical study of wholesale prices charged by pharmaceutical manufacturers to buyers who vary in size and substitution opportunities, Ellison and Snyder (2002) show that price discounts depend more on the ability to substitute among alternative suppliers than on sheer buyer size. Ellison and Snyder also conjecture that the failure of numerous collective purchasing internet sites, like Accompany, Ipool, LetsBuyIt, Mercata and MobShop, resulted from these collectives first contracting with a specific manufacturer for a declining price schedule as a function of the number of consumers and only then seeking customers for the item. Their results suggest that a better business model would have been first to obtain the consumers for the item and then force manufacturers to compete in offering the best deal.

Inderst and Shaffer (2007) model two retailers with opposite preferences over the differentiated goods offered by the two suppliers. If the retailers merge, the suppliers are made homogeneous with respect to the merged buyer's preferences. Consequently, the merged buyer need carry only one of the two suppliers' products, causing the suppliers to compete aggressively in price for the merged buyer's patronage.

In addition to the threat of switching suppliers, the goal of maintaining profit margins may also force suppliers of large buyers to become more efficient. Government auctions for construction and defense contracts encourage competing sellers to become leaner. Likewise, Fishman credits WalMart with improving the customer focus, inventory management and speed to market of its supplier Levi Strauss. Moreover, these efficiency gains have benefited other retailers that buy Levi's clothing. The positive externality of buyer power on smaller buyers is the mechanism through which the competitive fringe, and ultimately final consumers, obtain lower prices in Chen (2003). Chen models a monopolist supplier who negotiates with a large downstream buyer and a competitive fringe. An exogenous increase in the large buyer's market power reduces the supplier's share of joint profits. In an attempt to compensate for the reduced profits, the supplier lowers its wholesale price to the fringe, shifting the latter's supply curve to the right. This translates into lower retail prices.

With the objective of lowering retail prices, the monopolist supplier in Tyagi's (2001) model charges a lower input price to the larger of the two downstream manufacturers. Increased differences in the buying firms' equilibrium sizes reduce their attainable level of tacit collusion in the output market. Thus, the supplier chooses to favor the larger buyer to widen the size differential, weaken collusion and maximize its input sales. An interesting implication of this model is that a ban on price discrimination facilitates tacit collusion in the output market and reduces consumer welfare.

Risk aversion is another source of large-buyer discounts. DeGraba (2005) models risk-averse sellers who observe the customer's quantity demanded, but not her valuation. A customer who demands a large quantity represents a riskier profit source than multiple customers with independent valuations whose quantities demanded sum to that of the large buyer. The result is that the risk-averse seller offers a quantity discount to the large buyer. Chae and Heidhues' (2004) setup involves two markets with a seller and a buyer bargaining over the price of a good in each market. If the buyers are risk averse, the authors show that by forming an alliance or merging, the integrated buyer obtains a lower equilibrium price than the separate buyers. The underlying logic is that buyers in the alliance prefer to risk half the negotiated amount in each of two negotiations with the sellers, rather than risk the full amount once as separate buyers in a single negotiation with a seller. Both of these models lend themselves to straightforward, comparative-static tests of the large-buyer-discount prediction.

There are a number of bargaining models that condition quantity discounts not on risk aversion but on the shape of the supplier's gross surplus function. In Chipty and Snyder (1999), a monopoly supplier engages in Nash bargaining with n independent buyers. The authors consider the incentives of two buyers to merge with one another. Absent efficiency effects, a merger confers a bargaining advantage to the merged buyer compared to separate buyers if and only if the supplier's gross surplus function is globally concave. If revenues external to the buyer–supplier contract do not vary with the supplier's total quantity sold, then concavity is equivalent to an increasing marginal cost function.[7] A convex surplus function, by contrast, places the merged buyer at a bargaining disadvantage compared to two separate

---

[7] In Chipty and Snyder's (1999) study of the cable television industry, program-service suppliers earn revenues from advertising that are external to the negotiations between program supplier and cable operators.

buyers. The intuition behind these results is that each buyer assumes that all others have reached an equilibrium agreement and views itself as negotiating over the incremental surplus. If the surplus function is concave (increasing marginal costs), then the separate buyer negotiates over a relatively small surplus and, as a result, earns little surplus per unit. The merged buyer, however, negotiates over a larger per-unit surplus and, as a result, earns a larger per-unit surplus in equilibrium by paying a lower per-unit price.

Inderst and Wey (2007) reach a similar conclusion in a bilateral oligopoly framework: buyers choose to merge if supplier production technologies exhibit strictly increasing marginal costs and prefer to stay non-integrated if the opposite holds. The authors also show that a buyer merger induces the supplier to adopt a more efficient production technology. Recall the disciplining effect that WalMart exerts on its suppliers, among them Levi Strauss. On a related note, Farber (1981) concludes from his empirical study of fifty US four-digit industries that for concentrated seller industries, sellers' R&D activities increase with buyer concentration. Peters (2000) obtains an analogous result using survey data on the innovation process of German auto parts suppliers.

In Inderst and Wey (2007), the supplier's concave surplus function stems from buyers facing downward-sloping demand in the final-product market. Thus, a merged buyer shrinks the available surplus in the case of negotiation failure, since the supplier must march down smaller buyers' declining marginal surplus functions.

Like Chipty and Snyder, Raskovich (2003) models a monopolist supplier that engages in simultaneous, bilateral Nash bargaining with each of n buyers in stage one of the game. If the negotiated contracts cover the supplier's non-sunk fixed costs, the supplier sinks these costs and executes the contracts in the second stage; otherwise, it declares bankruptcy and all payoffs are zero. Raskovich demonstrates that if neither of the two buyers is pivotal to the supplier's production decision pre-merger, but become pivotal post-merger, then the merged buyer pays more than the joint payments of the pre-merger buyers. The reason is that the merged buyer's pivotal position requires it to cover the supplier's shortfall to induce it to produce.

Normann *et al.* (2007) test experimentally these theories that demonstrate a dependence between buyer-size discounts and the curvature of the seller's cost function. They design three separate markets that differ only in the shape of the seller's marginal cost curve (increasing, constant or decreasing marginal costs). Total costs and buyers' valuations are held constant across markets. Three buyers face a single seller in each market. Two buyers are small, with unit demand for the good; the third buyer is large with demand for two units. Costs, valuations and the market structure are all made common knowledge by reading aloud the instructions. In these posted-bid markets, each buyer simultaneously enters a bid to fulfill its given quantity demanded. The seller in each market chooses which bids to reject and accept, with accepted bids yielding the buyer his consumer surplus and the seller his producer surplus; rejected bids yield both parties zero surplus. Each market was conducted for sixty rounds, with each subject's role as a buyer or a seller fixed. However, the cohort of three buyers and one seller and the designation of the large buyer in each market was randomly determined each round to minimize repeated-game effects and to provide within-subject observations across cost structures and buyer sizes.

The posted-bid institution suggests that the appropriate theoretical solution concept for these experiments is subgame perfection, rather than Nash bargaining as in Chipty and Snyder, and Raskovich, or cooperative game theory as in Inderst and Wey. In the case of increasing marginal costs, there exists a unique pure-strategy, sub-game-perfect equilibrium according to which the large buyer pays a lower per-unit price than the small buyers. The constant-marginal-cost case predicts no quantity discount, while the decreasing-marginal-cost case yields a continuum of equilibria, including no discounts.

The experimental results are consistent with the theory. In markets with increasing marginal costs, large buyers bid 12% less per unit than their small-buyer cohorts. Moreover, sellers are much more likely to reject a low small-buyer's bid than an equivalent large-buyer's bid, resulting in a 14% large-buyer discount when accepted bids are compared. In the constant-marginal-cost and decreasing-marginal-cost markets, large- and small-buyers' bids are not significantly different, and neither are sellers' acceptance probabilities.

The laboratory support for these theoretical models is surprising for a number of reasons. First, the demonstrated importance of fairness considerations in surplus-sharing experiments with small numbers of subjects and the considerable strategic uncertainty given the buyers' simultaneous bidding both provide scope for behavioral departures from the predicted buyer-size discounts. More importantly, the experimental confirmation that buyer-size discounts are restricted to markets with decreasing returns to scale contradicts the popular wisdom that large-buyer discounts are ubiquitous.[8] Moreover, when asked, economists typically express the belief that large-buyer discounts are most likely to arise in the presence of economies of scale. Porter's (1980: 24) statement that "large-volume discounts are particularly potent forces if heavy fixed costs characterize the industry – as they do in corn refining and bulk chemicals, for example – and raise the stakes to keep capacity filled" succinctly captures this intuition. Indeed, if the supplier's production function exhibits increasing returns to scale and the supplier serves one buyer each production period, per-unit production costs decline with buyer size.

Economies of distribution represent another cost-based explanation for large-buyer discounts. They exist when the seller's average cost of serving a large buyer is lower than serving a small buyer. For example, the average fixed costs of putting together an order, billing and shipping to a large retail outlet or its warehouse are lower than those associated with a smaller retailer. Additionally, the industrial price of electricity is substantially lower than the residential price because, compared to residential consumers, industrial consumers: i) connect higher up in the transmission and distribution networks; ii) involve the same fixed cost for reading and billing electricity meters but amortize this cost over a much larger volume; iii) consume a smaller fraction of their electricity during peak-load times.[9] The separation of the economies-of-distribution explanation from other previously discussed sources of bargaining power related to buyer size is a topic suitable for experimental investigation.

One question left unanswered by most of this literature is whether the lower prices obtained by a large buyer or a highly concentrated buying side of the market are passed on to final consumers. Von Ungern-Sternberg (1996) models a two-stage game in which a

---

[8] Indeed, collective purchasing websites spanning a range of consumer goods were established on the premise that the larger the buyer, the better the volume discount attainable from the manufacturer, irrespective of its cost structure. The uniform failure of these sites suggests that size is not sufficient to yield substantial discounts. See also Ellison and Snyder (2002) for a discussion of this point.

[9] I owe these insights on electricity distribution to personal communications with Faye Steiner and Frank Wolak.

producer Nash bargains with n identical retailers who then act either as Cournot competitors or price takers on the final-product market. As the number of retailers decreases, equilibrium consumer prices are unambiguously shown to increase in the Cournot model and to decrease in the perfect-competition model. Dobson and Waterson (1997) obtain an analogous result: in their two-stage game, a monopolist supplier negotiates with differentiated retailers in the first stage who then compete in price for customers in the second stage. They show that a decline in the number of retailers leads to lower final prices only when retailers' services are sufficiently substitutable. Finally, as previously discussed, Chen (2003) shows that in response to an increase in the large buyer's market power, the monopolist supplier lowers its price to the competitive fringe. Lower retail prices result. These theoretical models beg experimental tests that include not only the usual negotiation between wholesalers and retailers, but an additional stage of competition between retailers for consumer demand.

4. Concluding discussion

The recent rise in North America and Europe of the general merchandise mega-retailer (e.g. WalMart, Costco and Target) as well as specialized mega-retailers in areas like food, pharmaceuticals, electronics, toys, home renovation, car, gardening and office supplies appears to have spawned a spate of research on the countervailing role of buyers. Although intended as a survey of experimental evidence, this chapter also unavoidably devotes considerable space to outlining the burgeoning theoretical literature as well as some of the empirical evidence on buyer countervailing power. In doing so, the contrast between the wealth of recent explanations for buyer power and the dearth of experimental tests is striking. This gap between theory and experiments is unfortunate given the inherent facility with which many of these theories may be evaluated experimentally.

Buyer power is most relevant in non-retail markets, precisely those markets in which price contracts, and cost and demand data are most difficult to obtain. Accordingly, experiments allow the researcher to assign sellers' costs and buyers' valuations, and to select the market structure of interest; prices are then the behavioral outcomes of these chosen variables. By highlighting sources and specific theories of buyer countervailing power, it is my hope that researchers will take advantage of the control offered by experimental methods to test these theories for which, currently, no more than anecdotal evidence exists.

The main implications of buyer countervailing are a subject of much contention and recent debate. On the one hand, where effective, buyer power constitutes a valuable check against seller power and, in this regard, may be seen as a substitute for antitrust legislation. On the other hand, if powerful buyers are also powerful sellers in the final product market, then price discounts may not be passed on to final consumers. Whether final consumers ultimately benefit from countervailing power is a topic particularly ripe for experimental research. In addition to price discounts, countervailing power may manifest itself in less benign forms: antitrust authorities need to be concerned with vertical contractual arrangements like exclusive dealing, fees extracted for store shelf space and most-favored-customer clauses.[10]

Regardless of the overall welfare and efficiency effects of countervailing power, the increasing policy relevance of this topic is indisputable for two reasons. First, Steuer (2004) makes the point that the phenomenon of outsourcing creates countervailing power. Growing corporations strive to maintain their profit margins often by cutting costs and specializing production through outsourcing some aspect of their business (e.g., product distribution, supply of inputs). These corporations assume the role of powerful buyers toward their new suppliers, bringing to bear their buying power, knowledge of the cost structure and ability to self-supply or switch suppliers. Second, the worldwide trends away from industrial regulation (i.e., toward deregulation) and toward increased industrial concentration, resulting primarily from an ongoing horizontal merger wave (see, e.g., Pryor 2001), challenges buyers to respond strategically and exert a countervailing force. The aforementioned growth of mega-retailers is an indication that they have risen to the challenge.

References

Adelman, M. A. (1959), *A&P: A Study in Price–Cost Behavior and Public Policy*, Cambridge, MA: Cambridge University Press.

[10] These practices are discussed at length in the European Commission's (1999) report on buyer power and the food retailing industry in Europe.

Brown-Kruse, J. (1991), Contestability in the Presence of an Alternate Market: An Experimental Investigation, *RAND Journal of Economics* 22, 136–147.

Cason, T. N. and A. W. Williams (1990), Competitive Equilibrium Convergence in a Posted-Offer Market with Extreme Earnings Inequalities, *Journal of Economic Behavior and Organization* 14, 331–352.

Chae, S. and P. Heidhues (2004), Buyers' Alliances for Bargaining Power, *Journal of Economics and Management Strategy* 13, 731–754.

Chen, Z. (2003), Dominant Retailers and the Countervailing Power Hypothesis, *RAND Journal of Economics* 34, 612–625.

Chipty, T. and C. M. Snyder (1999), The Role of Firm Size in Bilateral Bargaining: A Study of the Cable Television Industry, *Review of Economics and Statistics* 81, 326–340.

Coursey, D., R. M. Isaac and V. Smith (1984), Natural Monopoly and Contested Markets: Some Experimental Results, *The Journal of Law and Economics* 27, 91–113.

Davis, D. D., and C. A. Holt (1993), *Experimental Economics*, Princeton, NJ: Princeton University Press.

Davis, D. and A. Williams (1990), Market Power and the Institutional Asymmetry of the Posted-Offer Trading Institution, *Economics Letters* 34, 211–214.

(1991), The Hayek Hypothesis in Experimental Auctions: Institutional Effects and Market Power, *Economic Inquiry* 29, 261–274.

Davis, D. D. and B. J. Wilson (2004), Strategic Buyers, Horizontal Mergers and Fixed Cost Synergies: An Experimental Investigation, mimeo.

DeGraba, P. (2005), Quantity Discounts from Risk Averse Sellers, Federal Trade Commission, mimeo.

Dobson, P. W. and M. Waterson (1997), Countervailing Power and Consumer Prices, *Economic Journal*, 107, 418–430.

Ellison, S. and C. M. Snyder (2002), Countervailing Power in Wholesale Pharmaceuticals, M.I.T. mimeo.

Engle-Warnick, J. and B. J. Ruffle (2005a), Buyer Concentration as a Source of Countervailing Power: Evidence from Experimental Posted-Offer Markets, Ben-Gurion University, mimeo.

(2005b), The Strategies Behind their Actions: A Method to Infer Repeated-Game Strategies and an Application to Buyer Behavior, Ben-Gurion University, mimeo.

European Commission (1999), *Buyer Power and Its Impact on Competition in the Food Retail Distribution Sector of the European Union*, Luxembourg: Office for Official Publications of the European Communities.

Farber, S. (1981), Buyer Market Structure and R&D Effort: A Simultaneous Equations Model, *Review of Economics and Statistics* 62, 336–345.

Fishman, C. (2003), The WalMart You Don't Know, *Fast Company*, December: 77, 68.

Fouraker, Lawrence E. and Sidney Siegel (1963), *Bargaining Behavior*, New York: McGraw–Hill.

Franciosi, R., P. Kujal, R. Michelitsch, V. Smith and G. Deng (1995), Fairness: effect on temporary and equilibrium prices in posted-offer markets, *Economic Journal* 105, 938–950.

Friedman, J. (1967), An Experimental Study of Cooperative Duopoly, *Econometrica* 35, 379–397.

Friedman, M. (1985), Consumer Boycotts in the United States, 1970–1980: Contemporary Events in Historical Perspective, *Journal of Consumer Affairs*, Summer, 96–117.

Galbraith, J. K. (1952), *American Capitalism: The Concept of Countervailing Power*, Boston, MA: Houghton Mifflin, chapter 9.

Güth, W., R. Schmittberger, and B. Schwarze (1982), An Experimental Analysis of Ultimatum Bargaining, *Journal of Economic Behavior and Organization* 3, 367–388.

Hunter, A. (1958), Notes on Countervailing Power, *Economic Journal* 68, 89–103.

Inderst, R. and C. Wey (2003), Bargaining, Mergers, and Technology Choice in Bilaterally Oligopolistic Industries, *RAND Journal of Economics* 34, 1–19.

(2007), Buyer Power and Supplier Incentives, London School of Economics, *European Economic Review* 51(3), 647–667.

Inderst, R. and G. Shaffer (2007), Retail Mergers, Buyer Power and Product Variety, *The Economic Journal* 117(1), 45–67.

Kachelmeier, S. J., S. T. Limberg and M. S. Schadewald (1991a), A Laboratory Market Examination of the Consumer Price Response to Information About Producers' Cost and Profits, *Accounting Review*, 66, 694–717.

(1991b), Fairness in Markets: A laboratory investigation, *Journal of Economic Psychology* 12, 447–464.

Kahneman, D., J. Knetsch and R. Thaler (1986), Fairness as a Constraint on Profit Seeking, *American Economic Review* 76, 728–741.

Katz, M. L. (1987), The Welfare Effects of Third Degree Price Discrimination in Intermediate Goods Markets, *American Economic Review* 77, 154–167.

Kling, R. W. (1988), Trucking Deregulation: Evolution of a New Power Structure, *Journal of Economic Issues* 22, 1201–1211.

Kritikos, A. and F. Bolle (2004), Punishment as a Public Good: When Should Monopolists Care about a Consumer Boycott? *Journal of Economic Psychology* 25, 355–372.

LaFrance, V. A. (1979), The Impact of Buyer Concentration – An Extension, *Review of Economics and Statistics*, 61(3), 475–476.

Lustgarten, S. H. (1975), The Impact of Buyer Concentration in Manufacturing Industries, *Review of Economics and Statistics* 57, 125–132.

Martin, S. (1983), Vertical Relationships and Industrial Performance, *Quarterly Review of Economics and Business* 23, 6–18.

McGuckin, R. and H. Chen (1976), Interactions between buyer and seller concentration and industry price–cost margins, *Industrial Organization Review* 4, 123–132.

Normann, H. T., B. J. Ruffle and C. M. Snyder (2007), Do Buyer-Size Discounts Depend on the Curvature of the Surplus Function? Experimental Tests of Bargaining Models, *RAND Journal of Economics* 38(3), 747–767.

Peters, J. (2000), Buyer Market Power and Innovative Activities: Evidence for the German Automobile Industry, *Review of Industrial Organization* 16, 13–38.

Porter, M. E. (1980), *Competitive Strategy: Techniques for Analyzing Industries and Competitors*, New York, NY: Free Press, chapter 1.

Pryor, F. L. (2001), New Trends in US Industrial Concentration, *Review of Industrial Organization* 18, 301–326.

Raskovich, A. (2003), Pivotal Buyers and Bargaining Position, *Journal of Industrial Economics* 51, 405–426.

Reeves, S. (2005), On Track for a Good Deal, *Forbes.com*, April 1.

Rotemberg, J. and G. Saloner (1986), A Supergame-Theoretic Model of Business Cycles and Price Wars During Booms, *American Economic Review* 76, 390–407.

Ruffle, B. J. (2000), Some Factors Affecting Demand Withholding in Posted-Offer Markets, *Economic Theory* 16, 529–544.

Scheffman, D. T. and P. T. Spiller (1992), Buyers' Strategies, Entry Barriers, and Competition, *Economic Inquiry* 30, 418–436.

Scherer, F. M. and D. Ross (1990), *Industrial Market Structure and Economic Performance,* 3rd edn., Boston, MA: Houghton Mifflin.

Schumacher, U. (1991), Buyer Structure and Seller Performance in US Manufacturing Industries, *Review of Economics and Statistics* 73, 277–284.

Selten, R. and R. Stoecker (1986), End Behavior in Sequences of Finite Prisoner's Dilemma Supergames: A Learning Theory Approach, *Journal of Economic Behavior and Organization*, 7, 47–70.

Sexton, R. J. and T. A. Sexton (1987), Cooperatives as Entrants, *RAND Journal of Economics* 18, 581–595.

Smith, V. L. (1981), An Empirical Study of Decentralized Institutions of Monopoly Restraint, in *Essays in contemporary fields of economics in honor of E.T. Weiler (1914–1979)*, J. Quirk and G. Horwich (eds.), West Lafayette, Ind.: Purdue University Press, 83–106.

Snyder, C. M. (1996), A Dynamic Theory of Countervailing Power, *RAND Journal of Economics* 27, 747–769.

(1998), Why Do Large Buyers Pay Lower Prices? Intense Supplier Competition, *Economics Letters* 58, 205–209.

(2008), Countervailing Power, in S. Durlauf and L. Blume (eds.), *The New Palgrave Dictionary of Economics*, 2nd edn., London: Palgrave Macmillan.

Steuer, R. M. (2004), Blindside Deconcentration: Outsourcing, Power Retailers, and Antitrust, *theantitrustsource*, 1–8 March, available at www.antitrustsource.com.

Stigler, G. J. (1954), The Economist Plays with Blocs, *American Economic Review*, 44, 7–14

Tyagi, R. K. (2001), Why Do Suppliers Charge Larger Buyers Lower Prices?, *Journal of Industrial Economics* 49, 45–61.

Tyran, J. R. and D. Engelmann (2005), To Buy or Not to Buy? An Experimental Study of Consumer Boycotts in Retail Markets, *Economica* 72, 1–16.

United States District Court for the District of Columbia (1998), *FTC v. Cardinal Health, Inc. and Bergen-Brunswig Corp.* and *FTC v. McKesson Corp. and AmeriSource Health Corp.*, available at http://www.ftc.gov/os/caselist/ca98595ddc.htm.

von Ungern-Sternberg, T. (1996), Countervailing Power Revisited, *International Journal of Industrial Organization* 14, 507–520.

PART III

8 | Merger policy: what can we learn from experiments?

LORENZ GÖTTE AND ARMIN SCHMUTZLER*

This chapter surveys experimental literature relating to mergers. We put particular emphasis on discussing whether this literature addresses the issues that are relevant for competition policy. We also include some suggestions as to how the fit between the experiments and the requirements of competition policy research might be improved.

1. Introduction

So far, the explicit laboratory analysis of merger policy has been limited to very few examples, even though during the last few decades experimental economists provided many contributions directed at understanding imperfectly competitive markets. One might expect such industrial organization experiments to provide some insight into merger policy, even when they were not designed immediately for this purpose. Therefore, this survey attempts to clarify the role that experiments can play in answering the following questions:

- What effects do mergers have on the profits of the inside firms, on their competitors, and on consumer welfare? On a related note, under which circumstances should a merger be allowed?
- Under which circumstances are mergers likely to occur? How close is the relation between conditions that are likely to generate mergers and conditions under which mergers are desirable? In other words, under which conditions do the decisions of firms lead to the "right kind of mergers"?
- When policy decisions about mergers have to be taken without precise information about whether the theoretical conditions for allowing them are fulfilled, what kind of simple proxies should be used to determine that the circumstances are right?

* We are grateful to Stefan Bühler, Jan Potters and Dario Sacco for helpful comments.

- What kind of remedies might be useful to alleviate the negative competition effects of certain mergers while preserving whatever synergies there may be?

To analyze these questions, two aspects of mergers must be taken into account. First, a merger creates a new entity that differs in some important way from each of its components. The new firm typically controls more assets than each of its predecessors: it may have more capacity or a greater product spectrum. Also, it may have access to more technological and organizational knowledge, which should increase its efficiency. Negative effects are also conceivable: the larger firm may be harder to manage; the organizational cultures might not fit, etc. Second, just like the exit of a firm, a merger between two firms means that the total number of firms is reduced, at least if the merger does not spark off new entry.

A useful starting point for the analysis of mergers, whether in theory or in the lab, is to focus on the second effect and abstract from the important fact that a merger creates an entity that differs from its predecessors in some sense. Specifically, one of the most influential theory papers in the area (Salant, Switzer and Reynolds 1983, henceforth SSR) treats a merger between symmetric firms in much the same way as the exit of one of its constituent parts: Only one of the two original firms remains in the market, which is completely indistinguishable from its predecessors. In this case, we use the terminology pseudo-merger as opposed to a real merger where the new firm differs in some way from at least one of its components. While a full-fledged analysis of mergers must ultimately take into account that the new firm differs from each of its predecessors, decomposing the effects of a merger into the exit of one firm and a change in the assets of the other one helps to understand what is going on.

Similarly, the timing aspects of mergers can be simplified. In the real world, mergers involve the transformation of an old market structure into a new one: each firm has a pre-merger history, on the basis of which expectations about the post-merger situation are formed. A large chunk of theoretical and experimental work in the field simplifies the analysis by ignoring the time dimension. In this literature, market structures are investigated in a comparative-statics fashion rather than in an explicitly dynamic way. The papers consider several versions of static oligopoly games which differ only with respect to the

Table 8.1 *Experimental literature on horizontal mergers*

	Asset dimension	
Time dimension	Pseudo-merger	Real mergers
Static	Huck *et al.* (2004) Dufwenberg and Gneezy (2000)	Isaac and Reynolds (2002)
Dynamic	Huck *et al.* (2007)	Davis and Holt (1994) Davis and Wilson (2000)

number of firms. In principle, comparison of such games with different numbers of players can help us to understand the effects of mergers, with large numbers of players corresponding to pre-merger situations and small numbers to post-merger situations. However, there is a severe disadvantage of such a procedure: players are not clearly in the role of insiders or outsiders to a merger, so that there are limits to what we can learn from these papers.

Fortunately, there is a small group of papers that does not suffer from this deficiency: They consider experiments where an oligopoly game is played for a certain number of periods, after which a merger, or, in our terminology, a pseudo-merger takes place.[1] The oligopoly game is then continued with the reduced number of players. In such a setting, players have clearly defined roles as insiders and outsiders, so that the effects of the merger on the different groups of players can be addressed more directly.

Thus, we can categorize different approaches to merger analysis as in Table 8.1, which classifies existing experimental research on horizontal mergers.[2]

Except for some comments towards the end of the chapter, we shall not discuss whether there are fundamental reasons to distrust laboratory experiments as a means of understanding the strategic role of firms. Rather, we shall give the benefit of doubt to the experimenters,

---

[1] In the lab, the "merger" is typically implemented by randomly selecting two players, designating one of them as a decision maker for the new firm and sending the other player away or letting him act as an "advisor" to the decision maker.

[2] Vertical and conglomerate mergers typically belong to the right column, as both types of mergers change the set of goods that the firms produce.

asking merely whether the particular experiments chosen are suitable to analyze the policy issues arising in merger policy.

Our chapter is organized as follows. Section 2 surveys experiments that are relevant to horizontal mergers. Section 3 discusses to what extent these experiments can help to answer the policy questions discussed above. In Sections 4 and 5, we discuss vertical and conglomerate mergers respectively. The concluding Section 6 will argue that the relatively small impact of the experimental literature on merger policy analysis is justified in view of the fairly limited contributions that this literature has made so far: Some useful individual contributions notwithstanding, there does not seem to be a research program that matches the needs of competition policy. We will also argue, however, that, in spite of some intrinsic limitations, experiments can potentially play a useful role in informing merger policy.

2. Horizontal mergers

This section summarizes the experimental research on horizontal mergers, embedding it into the context of existing theoretical research on competition policy. We analyze each column of Table 8.1 in turn.

2.1. Pseudo-mergers

2.1.1. Static approaches
We first discuss the theoretical and experimental results that can be obtained for pseudo-mergers in a static setting, by comparing oligopolies with different numbers of firms.

Most of this research deals with the standard linear Cournot oligopoly model with homogeneous firms: the analysis compares the performance of markets with n firms with identical marginal costs with otherwise identical markets with n-1 of these firms. The n-firm market is interpreted as "pre-merger" and the (n-1)-firm market as "post-merger". Thus, neither are there any initial differences in market shares nor does the merger create such differences.

Several theoretical predictions in this setting are rather plausible.

Proposition 1 In the homogeneous linear Cournot model, a pseudo-merger between two firms: (i) increases prices; (ii) reduces total output; (iii) increases the output of each individual firm.

More controversial, however, is an implication pointed out by SSR. They compared the profits of two of the n firms in the pre-merger situation with those of one of the n-1 firms in the post-merger situation, interpreting the former quantity as the joint profits of the merger insiders and the latter as the post-merger profits of the new firm. They arrived at the following conclusion.

Proposition 2 In the homogeneous linear Cournot model, the parties to a pseudo-merger have higher total stand-alone profits than the new entity has as joint profits except when $n = 2$.

Therefore, from the point of view of their owners, firms should not merge in the first place. Unlike the insiders, the outside firms unambiguously benefit from the merger, because it relaxes competition, leading to higher equilibrium prices and per-firm profits. Thus, there are positive merger externalities. Both consumers and merging parties are worse off. Also, total welfare, measured as the sum of consumer surplus and producer surplus, falls. Though total profits are higher, this cannot compensate for the lower consumer surplus.

The solution to the "paradox" that the merging parties lose out is quite simple: SSR use a framework where mergers are not really mergers: In fact, they are equivalent to the disappearance of one of the two firms involved. The merged entity cannot be distinguished from its competitors, as it is not "bigger" in any meaningful way. It does not have more assets, a larger product spectrum or a better technology. It does not have greater internal coordination problems, and it does not suffer from clashes of organizational cultures either. It is just like everybody else. Thus, while the new firm has higher profits than each of its constituent parts used to have, it is not better off than any outsider. Its profit is just the typical profit a firm in an (n-1)-firm market. The total stand-alone profits of the two parties before the merger were twice the typical profit of a firm in an n-firm market.

With one exception to be discussed below, laboratory analysis has not dealt directly with the "merger paradox". Much effort, however, has been devoted to the underlying comparative statics with respect to prices and quantities, that is, to Proposition 1.

The design of the prototypical experiment in this category is as follows. Subjects were given instructions on the game to be played. They receive a profit table that relates their choice of output and the output of all others to profits. Subjects are then asked to answer control questions, ensuring that they understood the instructions and ensuring that they know that all other participants understood the instructions, too. The typical experiment is one where individuals play the Cournot game repeatedly (typically, for twenty to thirty times), facing the same competitors in each round. After each round, the subjects receive feedback: they are informed how much they have earned and of the choices of their competitors (which is sufficient to figure out how much their competitors earned).

In most of the experimental designs with Cournot competition, the Nash equilibrium predicts the outcomes rather well. In particular, the expected comparative-statics prediction holds.

Experimental result 1 Reducing the number of firms in a static pseudo-merger setting lowers total output, much like the theory predicts.

With the exception of Huck *et al.* (2004), few papers formally compare how the number of firms affects outcomes in these experiments. In particular, is there a systematic tendency towards more collusive outcomes when the number of firms is small? In a meta analysis of roughly comparable experiments that differ in the number of firms, there is a weak relationship between the distance of the outcome to the equilibrium and the number of firms (see Huck *et al.*).[3] In their own experiments, Huck *et al.* find that outputs in markets with only two firms are on average 10% below the equilibrium quantity. Outputs in markets with five firms are on average 7% above. This might lead one to conclude that the collusion-enhancing effects of mergers are larger than theory would suggest. Whether the effect is large enough to warrant such a conclusion is a matter of taste.[4]

---

[3] In the treatments considered, there is neither communication nor discounting. Also, subjects are matched with the same opponents throughout the experiment and are only informed about aggregate behavior of opponents. Most experiments have symmetric firms.

[4] Dufwenberg and Gneezy (2000) find much clearer effects in this direction in a Bertrand model with a homogenous good. In their treatment with three competitors, behavior slowly converges to the equilibrium prediction. However, in the treatment with only two firms, behavior initially converges to equilibrium, but diverges from equilibrium behavior in the last few periods. The substantial difference between the two- and three-firm treatments seems closely related to the counterintuitive notion that the number of firms has no effect on the equilibrium outcome in Bertrand oligopolies. It is not surprising that the experiments lead to different outcomes than the implausible benchmark equilibrium.

The subjects in a Cournot experiment essentially face a public goods problem: restricting output would be efficient for the industry as a whole, but is not individually rational.[5] Hence, it is interesting to compare the outcomes in Cournot experiments to the large literature on experiments that are explicitly framed as public goods. While, in the typical public goods experiment, convergence to equilibrium is slower, the outcome in the final few periods is very close to the Nash equilibrium (see, e.g., Fehr and Schmidt, 1999).[6] It is not surprising that convergence in public goods experiments is slower. In these experiments, the equilibrium involves zero contributions. Hence, any error the subjects make moves them away from the equilibrium. On the other hand, in Cournot games, unsystematic errors do not move the outcomes systematically away from the equilibrium.[7] It is also instructive to compare the results on the effects of the numbers of players to the research on public goods experiments: there, the number of players has a relatively small effect on the extent of deviation from the Nash prediction (see Isaac, Walker and Arlington, 1994).[8]

An interesting extension of the literature reviewed in this section is Lindqvist and Stennek (2005). Unlike the papers discussed above, they do not merely carry out comparative statics with respect to the number of firms. Rather, following the endogenous merger theory of Kamien and Zang (1993), they explicitly model merger decisions in the laboratory, showing how they depend on the structure of the underlying product market profits. They consider a three-player setting where one player (the buyer) can make merger offers to the two others (the sellers), which they can accept or reject.[9] If both sellers

---

[5] Choosing a low output in the Cournot model increases the equilibrium price, which is beneficial for all competitors. Thus, like supplying a public good, restricting output involves positive externalities on the other players.

[6] There are institutions under which public goods experiments do not converge, and they are important. However, they are not relevant to our context here. See Fehr and Gaechter (2000) for a discussion.

[7] In public goods experiments with an interior equilibrium as in Cournot games, equilibrium is reached very quickly. See, e.g., Falkinger *et al.* (2000).

[8] A recent meta-analysis of 349 primary sources (Zelmer, 2003) confirms this impression.

[9] The authors consider both treatments where the two offers are made simultaneously and the two acceptance decisions are made simultaneously, as well as sequential settings.

accept, there is a merger to monopoly, whereas if only one seller consents a merger to duopoly takes place. The authors test how the decision to merge depends on the size of duopoly profits when they leave monopoly and triopoly profits constant. As one would expect, a *ceteris paribus* increase in the size of the duopoly profit significantly reduces the number of mergers to monopoly: intuitively, a higher duopoly profit corresponds to high outside options of the sellers. The paper constitutes an interesting step into the direction of analyzing endogenous mergers in the lab; it remains to be seen whether further analysis will follow.

2.1.2. Dynamic setting

Next, we move to the lower left corner of Table 8.1. Theoretical analysis that treats the effects of a merger by distinguishing explicitly between pre-merger and post-merger behavior is very rare. Levin (1990) takes such an approach. He supposes that, before the merger, firms act as Cournot players, whereas after the merger the new firm may adopt a different role. For instance, it may act as a Stackelberg leader to which the competitors adapt their behavior. As a result, outputs and profits of the new firm may be higher than for the competitors, even when firms are symmetric ex ante and the merger does not affect technology.

Inspired by Levin's paper, Huck, Konrad, Müller and Normann (2007), henceforth HKMN, explore the idea that a merger might have psychological effects distinguishing the behavior of the new firms from the competitors. They consider a fifty-period experiment. In a typical treatment, an initial number of n firms plays a symmetric homogeneous linear Cournot ("pre-merger") oligopoly game for the first twenty-five periods. Then, two of the players are randomly chosen as parties to a merger. One of them is assigned the role of a decision maker; the other one can act as an "advisor" by suggesting output decisions. The post-merger game continues for another twenty-five periods, without any changes in the underlying technology. Thus, using the terminology of Section 1, the authors are considering a pseudo-merger.

The experimental results suggest that the new firm's behavior indeed differs from the competitors', even though the only difference between the merged entity and the remaining competitors is that it originates from formerly separated firms.

Experimental result 2 In HKMN, the firm that originated from the merger produces more than the symmetric Cournot quantity; the competitors produce less. Profits of merging firms tend to increase in the short term and are roughly like the joint pre-merger profit in the long term (with details depending on the initial number of firms).

Thus, the firm that originates from a merger behaves differently, even though it does not differ from the competitors with respect to the assets it owns. HKMN propose the following psychological mechanism behind their result: each of the two merging firms has an aspiration level in mind that is shaped by previous play. Falling below the aspiration level feels like a loss.[10] In the post-merger period, the newly merged firm aggressively increases output to avoid falling behind the reference profit. The other firms anticipate this and decrease their output somewhat. Thus, even though two firms out of a pool of perfectly symmetric firms merged, the merger alone creates an asymmetry, because after the merger, one of the firms has a much higher reference profit than the others. As the experimental results show, this is enough to substantially change the distribution of output levels between firms. Thus, there is a slight movement towards Stackelberg behavior, even though the post-merger decisions are made simultaneously.

This result is potentially relevant for competition policy: it suggests that even in instances where two out of a pool of symmetric firms merge, the outcome need not be symmetric. If the two merged firms each have a reference profit in mind, the merger produces a new entity where the reference outcome is the sum of the two reference profits, and hence creates an asymmetry, and may even change the market structure from Cournot to Stackelberg.

More tentatively, the results also suggest that the type of merger may matter for the subsequent outcome. The effect in HKMN can only arise in cases where both previous decision makers are still involved in the post-merger firm.[11] Thus, the result does not apply to situations where one firm simply buys all the stock of the other firm,

---

[10] The argument is closely related to research in psychology showing that falling short of a reference outcome by one unit is distinctly more painful than exceeding it by one is pleasurable, and that the prospect of a loss can have a strong influence on behavior (Tversky and Kahneman, 1981).

[11] In fact, the authors show that the effect is no longer present when one of the parties to the merger is sent away with a compensation that does not depend on the performance of the merged entity.

and the previous owners are not involved in the management subsequently.

Finally, unlike some of the experiments discussed earlier, the HKMN analysis generates outcomes that do not just confirm the predictions of standard theory.

2.2. Real mergers

2.2.1. Introduction
Real-world discussions of mergers hinge in an important way on the change in asset ownership that goes along with a merger. In the theoretical or experimental papers mentioned so far, however, there is no role for assets.

We therefore now move towards treatments of real mergers in which the merged entity differs from its component parts in some objective way. The theoretical literature has considered a number of examples:

1. *Rationalization mergers* between sufficiently heterogeneous firms where the new entity works with the technology of the more efficient constituent part (Farrell and Shapiro, 1990; Barros, 1998).
2. *Synergy mergers* where the new entity works more efficiently than either of the inside firms (Farrell and Shapiro, 1990).
3. *Capacity mergers* where the merger combines the production capacities of the constituent parts, so that the firm indeed has more assets (Perry and Porter, 1985).
4. *Variety mergers* where the new firm produces a larger product spectrum than before (Deneckere and Davidson, 1984; Aydemir and Schmutzler, 2008).

We do not delve deeply into the welfare analysis of real mergers.[12] Rather, we just sketch why such mergers can potentially be beneficial for the insiders, though the details differ. In cases (1) and (2), the driving force of the profit increase is the cost reduction. In case (3), if the new firm has a high capacity relative to its competitors, then it has some scope for setting high prices without having to worry that the competitors can then supply the entire market by undercutting them.

---

[12] The most useful source is still Farrell and Shapiro (1990).

In case (4), the merged entity benefits not only from selling a larger number of products, but also indirectly from controlling the prices of a larger number of products. Either way, unlike in the pseudo-merger case, the profits of the merged entity may well be higher than for the joint profits of the inside firm.

For real mergers, the effects on competitors and customers may also differ from the pseudo-merger case. This is most easily seen for synergy mergers: with sufficiently strong synergy effects, if the marginal costs of the merging firms are considerably lower than the costs of its constituent parts, the new firm will set lower prices in equilibrium. Thus, competitors suffer from "negative merger externalities" in spite of the reduction in the number of firms, whereas customers benefit from the lower prices. When synergies are small, however, the anti-competitive effects familiar from the pseudo-merger case dominate, giving rise to "positive merger externalities" for competitors and detrimental effects on consumer surplus.

The analysis so far suggests:

- Whether a real merger is beneficial for customers depends on the details of the situation, in particular, on the size of synergies.
- Mergers tend to be beneficial for customers when they are bad for outside firms.

Laboratory experiments are well-suited to investigate real mergers, because costs, capacities and product spectrum can easily be controlled by the experimenter. Relevant experiments have been carried out both in the comparative-static setting (corresponding to the upper-right corner in Table 8.1) and in the dynamic setting (corresponding to the lower-right corner).

2.2.2. Static case

We start with the static case. Isaac and Reynolds (2002) is the only example we are aware of. Before outlining their approach, it is important to note that their objective was not primarily to analyze mergers. Rather, they belong to a large group of papers searching for the "magic number of firms" at which a market becomes competitive. Nevertheless, comparing their treatments can be potentially informative of the impact of mergers, as we will see below. They use a two-by-two design where they vary the number of firms and their capacity in such a way that the impact of the number of these

Table 8.2 *The design and the main results from Isaac and Reynolds (2002)*

	Capacity	
Number of firms	Low	High
2	Prices are near the Cournot equilibrium	Prices are near the upper range of the competitive equilibrium
4	Prices are near the upper range of the competitive equilibrium	Prices are near to the lower bound of the competitive equilibrium

parameters on market outcomes can be examined. Firms post prices to computer-simulated buyers who fully reveal trades.[13] Importantly, demand is not known to the sellers. The demand functions resulting in this way are step functions so that there exists an entire range of prices that is compatible with the competitive equilibrium. Their treatments and basic results are summarized in Table 8.2.

Three results are noteworthy. First, market prices never exceed the Cournot prices. Second, the results suggest a consistent impact of excess capacity on market outcomes: greater capacity leads to more efficient outcomes. Third, in this setting, there appears to be a number effect: the lower the number of firms, the less competitive the outcomes.

The first result differs from the results one obtains in Cournot settings without explicit capacity constraints: the most likely explanation appears to be that demand uncertainty might make sellers cautious in their demands.

Additional interpretations might be possible if the treatment of the buyers in the experiment was clearer. Suppose, as some formulations suggest, sellers thought that the buyers were real players. Intuitively, having to present price offers to real buyers rather than "producing" to satisfy a computer-simulated demand puts competitive pressure on firms (see, e.g., chapter 5 in Kagel and Roth, 1995). Other research in

---

[13] The description of the demand side in this (preliminary) paper is not entirely clear at the present stage. Specifically, some formulations suggest that the buyers are experimental subjects themselves.

experimental economics (Kahneman *et al.* 1986) suggests that fairness considerations on behalf of the buyers might contribute to this outcome. There is evidence that buyers reject trades with a positive profit for them if the price is so high that it creates a very unequal split of the surplus between the firm and the buyer.[14] Thus, the differences between Isaac and Reynolds (2002) and the Cournot examples without capacity constraint appear to be related to the presence of "real" buyers as opposed to a computer-simulated demand curve used in most other experiments we discuss here.[15] A better understanding of how the presence of "real" buyers changes the way mergers affect market outcomes appears to us as one of the areas where experiments could contribute to competition policy.

2.2.3. Dynamic case

Finally, we deal with real mergers in a dynamic setting. All the experiments we consider have a common set-up. For a certain number of periods (typically thirty), the firms play one oligopoly game. Then there is a change in the rules of the game which usually involves a reallocation of assets between different firms. This may involve a fully fledged merger, but it may also just be a capacity reallocation leading to growth of some firms at the expense of others. After this exogenous shock, the modified game is played until the end of the session.

Davis and Holt (1994) is an early example of such a paper. Their experiments were designed to disentangle the effects of capacity reallocation and of changes in the number of firms on market power. In each period, the players were confronted with one of three designs: "No-Power – Five Sellers", "Power – Five Sellers" and "Power – Three Sellers".

---

[14] The results in Fehr *et al.* (1993) rely on exactly this mechanism, though in a different context.

[15] As an aside, fairness concerns can be relevant for competition policy because they affect the price elasticity. When a firm raises prices because of increased market power, this would alter the distribution of surplus. If customers refuse to buy at the new "unfair" price, the price elasticity might be quite large and the firm might, in fact, have very little pricing power. On the contrary, if firms raise prices because costs have increased, this price increase does not necessarily redistribute surplus towards the firm, and no fairness effect is expected. Thus, if one uses variation in costs to estimate the price elasticity, this estimate may significantly overstate market power.

In the "No-Power" design, there are three large sellers, each with three capacity units, and two small sellers, with one unit each.[16] In the "Power – Five Sellers" design, a capacity reallocation takes place. As a result, there are two remaining large firms, each with four capacity units, and three small firms with one unit each. Thus, the change in market structure corresponds to a situation where two of the three large firms each buy one-third of the assets of the third one, rather than to a fully fledged merger. In the "Three Sellers" design, the three small firms from the "Power – Five Sellers" design merge. The crucial result of the paper is the following.

Experimental result 3 In the Davis and Holt experiment, the shift from the "No-Power – Five Sellers" design to the "Power – Five Sellers" design has much greater impact on prices than the actual merger, that is, the shift from "Power – Five Sellers" to "Power – Three Sellers".

To understand this result, it is important to consider the nature of the demand function with which the subjects are confronted. For each of the first eight units, the willingness-to-pay of the (simulated) buyers is r, which is substantially above the high marginal production costs. For the last three units the willingness-to-pay is only slightly above marginal costs.

As a result, it makes an enormous difference for the pricing incentives of sellers whether they have three or four units of capacity. In the former case, competitors supply eight units to the market, which corresponds exactly to the number of units which can be sold at a high price. In the latter case, the competitors only have seven units, so that the seller can be sure to sell at least one unit as long as he prices below r. Thus, the large sellers in the Power treatment have considerably stronger incentives to set high prices than the larger sellers in the No-Power treatments. The reallocation of capacity which falls short of being a merger should thus be expected to lead to higher prices on theoretical grounds. This idea is formalized by Davis and Holt, and it is also confirmed in the lab. It turns out that the capacity reallocation has price effects that come close to what one would expect from a concentration-increasing merger. The additional movement to the three-firm treatment has a comparatively small effect. Thus, a

---

[16] For a precise argument, it is important that these units have different marginal costs but, for the purpose of brevity, we ignore this.

"merger-like" capacity reallocation by which two of the three largest firms become larger at the expense of the third one has stronger effects on market prices than the following merger between the three smallest firms. Very roughly, this corresponds to the familiar idea that mergers involving industry leaders should be viewed with greater caution than mergers involving laggards. Before jumping to general conclusions, however, one should take the very special nature of the demand function into account.[17]

Davis and Wilson (2000) is an interesting paper pertaining to merger policy. Like Davis and Holt (1994), the authors do not explicitly model a merger, but consider the effect of capacity reallocations that fall short of describing an actual merger. Nevertheless, the paper provides some insights for the discussion of merger-related synergies. The standard problem facing authorities is to weigh the expected increases in market power against potential efficiency effects. We argued above that sufficiently high efficiency gains justify the merger not only from the insiders' perspective, but also from a social welfare point of view. The argument was implicitly based on an assumption of constant marginal costs. In a setting with increasing marginal costs which appears more appropriate for certain industries (e.g. electricity), the potential positive effects of cost savings on consumer surplus are less obvious. Indeed, the following observation arises naturally.

Experimental result 4 In the Davis and Wilson experiment, capacity reallocations that are accompanied by cost reductions do not necessarily lead to lower prices than capacity reallocations that are not.

The authors argue theoretically how this effect comes about; they then show that the theory is borne out in the lab. Intuitively, the idea depends on the difference between efficiency increases concerning marginal units and efficiency increases concerning inframarginal units. While the former typically tend to reduce market power, this is not true for the latter.

More precisely, the authors consider four treatments: N, P, NS and PS. The N-treatment is similar to the "No-Power" treatment in Davis

---

[17] A second reason why the result should not be overstated is that the experiment again, like much of the literature, uses simulated buyers. As pointed out before, this may matter critically: in light of the previous evidence, it is not clear whether this result survives in an experiment with real buyers.

and Holt (1994) except that there are only three firms, two of which are large. Each of the large firms has one low-cost (C_L) unit of capacity and one high-cost (C_H) unit. The small firm has one low-cost unit. Also as in Davis and Holt, moving to P corresponds to a market-power increasing reallocation of capacity: one of the large firms (firm 1) now has both high-cost units, whereas the other large firm only keeps its low-cost unit. Finally, the demand structure is similar to Davis and Holt, with willingness to pay for the first three units being r which is much higher than C_H and only slightly above C_L for the remaining two units. As before, therefore firm 1 has market power because it can be sure to sell at least one unit at a high price; and the experiment shows that prices are considerably higher in the P-treatment.

The additional treatments allow for "synergies". NS is like P, except that the cost of producing the high-cost units (C_H) drops to C_L. PS is like P, except that the costs for producing those units remains at C_H. However, the costs of producing one of the low-cost units drop even further (to C_{LL}).

The results from the experiment are as follows: First, prices in the no-power treatment converge to the competitive equilibrium, irrespective of the cost of the infra-marginal unit. Second, market power increases prices. Third, moving from N to NS or from P to PS does not affect mean prices. The first statement says that a change of costs for marginal units neutralizes an increase in market power — increasing capacity reallocations. The second statement says that cost changes on inframarginal units do not affect mean prices.[18]

3. Horizontal mergers: what have we learnt?

In the introduction, we raised four sets of questions that come up in merger policy. We now discuss how the existing experimental literature has contributed to answering these questions, and which contributions are conceivable in the future. Much of the discussion will focus on the first question concerning the effects of mergers on profits and welfare.

---

[18] At the risk of repeating ourselves, it should be pointed out that the buyers were simulated in this experiment. In particular, having real buyers that are informed about the changes in the market could have an interesting effect: Based on the previous evidence, we would expect buyers to lose power when cost savings on infra-marginal units are introduced.

3.1. Welfare effects of mergers

Existing merger policy literature (e.g. Neven *et al.*, 1993; Motta, 2004) has identified a long list of factors that might influence whether the welfare effects of mergers are likely to be positive or negative. These factors include: 1. market concentration; 2. synergies; 3. the likelihood of entry; 4. productive capacities; 5. demand variables; 6. the intensity of competition; 7. buyer power.

3.1.1. Market concentration

The most important parameters in the practical evaluation of mergers are related to concentration. There is a broad consensus that, other things being equal, the problematic effects of mergers dominate when (i) the initial concentration is large and (ii) the expected increase in concentration resulting from the merger is strong. Most of the experimental literature that is related to this issue concerns the case of symmetric firms. Moreover, it typically relates to pseudo-mergers where the firms remain symmetric even after the merger. For these cases, the literature surveyed by Huck *et al.* (2004) suggests that reductions from three to two firms have substantial price effects and similarly for reductions from four to three firms, whereas mergers with larger initial firm numbers are not problematic. In other words, as long as the post-merger Herfindahl-Hirschmann Index (HHI) is 2500 or less, there is no reason to worry.[19] Taking this result literally would suggest that existing merger policy might be slightly too restrictive.[20]

Unfortunately, the much more common scenario that firms are initially asymmetric has not received much attention in the experimental literature. Thus, existing experiments have relatively little to say about who should be allowed to merge with whom for some given initial concentration level. Roughly speaking, common practice is to take a more hostile view towards mergers involving leaders than

---

[19] The HHI is defined as the sum of the squares of the market shares of all firms (in percent), so it is $2500 = 4 \times 25^2$ for four identical firms.

[20] The US merger guidelines recommend waving through a merger unconditionally if the expected post-merger HHI is below 1000. If the expected post-merger concentration is higher, the merger is challenged unless the expected increase in the HHI is small, that is, below 100 if the expected HHI is below 1800 or below 50 otherwise (Motta 2004).

towards mergers involving laggards. Experiments are very well-suited to check whether such rules of thumb make sense in principle.

Some very preliminary evidence in support of this practice can be obtained from the study by Davis and Holt (1994). As discussed earlier, the transition from the treatment "Five Sellers – No Power" to "Five Sellers – Power" has much in common with mergers by which two of the leaders get larger. The transition from "Five Sellers – Power" to "Three Sellers – Power", however, is literally a merger between laggards. To recall, the increase in power was much stronger in the former case than in the latter. This might be interpreted casually as suggesting that mergers between laggards are less problematic than mergers between leaders. However, one should be careful not to overemphasize the point. At the very least, the peculiar demand structure of the Davis and Holt experiments should be kept in mind: it would appear to be quite possible to construct demand functions where theory predicts that mergers between laggards increase prices more than mergers between leaders, and where experiments would come to the same conclusion. This points to a limitation of experiments that is less a matter of principle than a consequence of budgetary limitations. Often, even in fairly simple theoretical models, the comparative-statics prediction about one parameter (e.g., the number of firms) may depend strongly on the remaining parameters (e.g., of the demand function), which may take infinitely many different values. Observing how subjects react to changes of one parameter in one or even a few of the infinitely many conceivable parameter constellations is better than observing nothing at all, but it is arguably not enough to draw far-reaching conclusions.

3.1.2. Synergies

There seems to be very little debate that the more a merger contributes to reducing costs, the more likely it is to be welfare-increasing. For fairly general situations, such a statement is hardly arguable on theoretical grounds. Indeed, it seems so self-evident that an experiment confirming it would hardly receive much attention. It is thus not surprising that the only experimental paper we mentioned on the issues of synergies is one that cautions against the notion that synergies must necessarily make mergers more desirable. Davis and Wilson (2000) deserve credit for pointing this out. However, as interesting as their example may be, without further evidence it provides no cause for rethinking the simple rule of thumb that substantial synergies make the merger desirable not only for the insiders, but also for consumers. After all, the example relies not only on a relatively special type of synergy, but also on a very special case of demand function. It is also worth pointing out that the experimental evidence of Davis and Holt is quite consistent with theory. In fact, the authors derived it from standard game-theoretical reasoning.

3.1.3. Entry

The undesired effect of a merger on market power may well be mitigated by potential entry. Thus, mergers in markets where sunk costs play a limited role are generally seen as less problematic than in industries with high sunk costs. While we are not aware of any experiments that deal directly with the influence of sunk costs on merger policy, there is a related literature comparing the behavior of monopolists in settings with and without entry barriers. While the evidence for a very strong disciplining role of potential competition is mixed, there is some support for the idea that such a role is more likely when sunk costs are low.[21]

3.1.4. Productive capacities

Whether a merger causes competitive harm may well depend on the outside firm's productive capacities. If the competitors have excess capacities initially, the merger does not necessarily increase the market power of the merging parties very much as they must take into account that competitors can easily supply the market as a response to a price increase. To our knowledge, this idea has not yet been tested directly in the laboratory. However, the experiment of Isaac and Reynolds suggests this conjecture may be true. At least for given firm numbers, excess capacity of some firms increased competitiveness.[22]

---

[21] See Coursey *et al.* (1984), Harrison and McKee (1985), Harrison *et al.* (1989), and Millner *et al.* (1990). This literature is framed as a test of the contestable markets hypotheses of Baumol *et al.* (1982), which has been criticized by Tirole (1988) and others.

[22] Recently, Fonseca and Normann (2008) have pointed out that the distribution of the capacity plays an important role. Keeping excess capacity constant, their experiments show that asymmetries hinder collusion.

3.1.5. Demand variables
It is well known that high demand elasticity can discipline the price-setting behavior of firms. The elasticities of market demand are therefore also important to estimate the potential negative effects of mergers on market power. Again, there seems to have been no direct attempt to assess the role of demand for mergers in the lab by comparing treatments where everything else is fixed. Davis and Holt (1994) and Davis and Wilson (2000), however, have exploited the effect of demand elasticity in their experiments. There, if the merger reduces the elasticity of (firm) demand substantially, the observed market power tends to rise, which is consistent with the theoretical prediction.

3.1.6. Intensity of competition
Often, there are some firms in the pre-merger market who compete more vigorously with each other than with the remaining firms. Specifically, this will be true when they are producing closer substitutes. A merger between such firms who are initially intense competitors should have stronger price effects than a merger between firms who are not competing vigorously even before the merger. Again, we are not aware of any experiments comparing the effects of mergers under different assumptions about pre-merger competition (except when intensity of competition is identified with the number of firms).

3.1.7. Buyer power
In many important merger cases, the firms face buyers who operate in imperfectly competitive markets themselves. In such cases, buyer power may constrain the market power of the merged firm.[23] Even though we are not aware of any existing experiment investigating the effects of buyer power on merger performance, such an analysis is clearly possible. The literature above typically dealt with simulated demand, which corresponds to low buyer power. If, instead, the buyer side was modeled with a small number of real buyers, it would presumably be possible to understand the role of buyer power better. The chapter by Ruffle in this volume is a useful starting point in this

---

[23] Neven *et al.* (1993) argue that buyer power was important in at least three European merger cases (*Alcatel/Telettra*, *Viag/Continental Can* and *Alcatel/ AEG Kabel*).

direction, even though it is only concerned with buyer power, not with its relation to merger performance.

3.2. Circumstances fostering merger activity

Actual competition policy is mainly concerned with the effects of mergers. Understanding their causes may appear to be merely of an academic interest at first glance. However, understanding which circumstances lead to mergers is essential in judging how they should be viewed from a competition policy perspective. If we knew that firms want to merge precisely when this has positive welfare effects, there would be no rationale for merger policy.

In some ways, such an alignment of interests does not seem so far-fetched: for instance, when there are strong synergies, firm owners and consumers should both benefit from mergers. In other ways, however, the private and the public interest are likely to diverge. For instance, mergers between firms that already have high market shares may be particularly attractive to the firms, but particularly undesirable for consumers. In the extreme case of the homogeneous, linear Cournot model without synergies, mergers between duopolists are the only profitable ones, and they clearly have a very negative welfare effect. Similarly, mergers between firms that are initially more competitive than others appear particularly profitable and particularly likely at the same time. More generally, Farrell and Shapiro (1990) have provided a theoretical analysis of the relation between merger profitability and welfare effects.

Experiments do not seem to have addressed these issues. It would seem quite possible to confront subjects with the decision whether they want to merge in different experimental settings where some mergers are desirable from a social point of view and others are not, and then investigate how the decision to merge is correlated with its social desirability.

3.3. Rules of thumb

In theoretical models, the welfare effects of mergers are judged on the basis of information that is typically not readily available for competition policy authorities, at least not within the time frame that is necessary to judge whether a merger should be allowed or not. Most obviously, this information includes demand and cost functions. More fundamentally, the standard welfare analysis of mergers proceeds as though there was a clearly defined product market. It is well known, however, that in most actual merger cases, it is not entirely obvious what the relevant market is. Practical merger policy uses rules of thumb to deal with these problems.

A common practice to find the relevant market is the SSNIP Test (Motta, 2004), which asks whether a "small but significant non-transitory increase in prices" in the market under consideration would be profitable for a hypothetical monopolist. If the answer is affirmative, then the possibility for substituting the goods in the market by using outside goods is limited, and there is no need to move to a wider market. In implementing the SSNIP test, own- and cross-price elasticities play an important role, with high elasticities suggesting low price effects of mergers. While experiments are clearly of no help in estimating real-world demand elasticities which are used to define the relevant markets, we have already argued that they could be designed to better understand the relation between elasticities and merger effects, precisely because the demand functions are controlled by the experimenter.[24]

Once the relevant market is defined, the standard approach in the US to screen out unproblematic mergers is to use the pre-merger HHI as a measure of concentration and calculate the expected post-merger HHI under the assumption that the new firm's market share is the sum of shares of the inside firms (see endnote 20). In principle, one could design experiments to analyze the relation between post-merger HHI and merger price effects in different environments. Though the evidence from the pseudo-merger experiments suggests otherwise, such an analysis might reveal that the relation between post-merger HHI, its increase and the price effects is not sufficiently close to justify relying on it as a rule of thumb.

If the analysis of concentration reveals a potential problem, additional information will be looked at to clear the merger, including

---

[24] Of course, the choice of demand functions and, in particular, elasticities could be guided by real-world data (see Hong and Plott, 1982, for such an approach in a different setting). Also note that the direct control of the experimenter only relates to market demand, not to the perceived demand of each firm which also depends on competitor reactions (see Neven *et al.* 1993).

buyer power, potential entry, synergies and so on. For instance, an efficiency defense might be applied if the parties involved can convince the authorities of substantial synergies from the merger. Davis and Wilson (2000) motivate their paper by arguing that US procedures to assess whether cost synergies might justify a merger are problematic. To determine whether consumers are likely to benefit from whatever efficiency gains a merger might generate, historical pass-through rates are sometimes considered, the idea being that if cost reductions were passed through to the consumers in the past, this should also be true in the future. One implication of the Davis and Wilson paper is that this is hardly true in general.

A related issue concerns the usage of simulation models to estimate merger effects. The US Department of Justice uses an Antitrust Logit Model (ALM) to screen mergers. This model requires relative little information, which makes it easy to apply.[25] It also relies on very specific assumptions, however. Davis (2002) uses laboratory experiments to compare the performance of the model in a setting which comes close to the ALM set-up with the ALM predictions. It also checks for the robustness of the behavior to violations of the ALM assumptions.

The evidence suggests that:

- the ALM predictions are not correct in general, but
- screen out nonproblematic mergers quite well.

Summing up, though relatively little has been done in this respect, experiments are potentially useful for evaluating rules of thumb.

4. Vertical mergers

As indicated above, there has been much discussion about the precise welfare effects of horizontal mergers. However, most debates concern the question of which types of mergers are detrimental to welfare. There is not much disagreement that horizontal mergers can have negative effects in principle. Accordingly, regulation of horizontal mergers is firmly established. The policy towards vertical merger is much less

---

[25] The model uses information on prices, market shares, demand elasticity and substitutability to infer the industry cost structure, which is then used to predict post-merger performance.

uniform. In the US, for instance, periods of hostility towards mergers were followed by periods where the antitrust authorities took a more lenient view (e.g., Kwoka and White, 1998).

In a similar vein, industrial organization theory has not come to a definite conclusion about the effects of vertical mergers. The disputed issues do not concern vertical integration per se. For instance, mergers between upstream and downstream firms in a bilateral monopoly are usually seen as efficiency enhancing. Similarly, there is relatively little concern that oligopolies where all firms are vertically integrated are less desirable than oligopolies where all firms are separated.[26] However, the welfare discussion of asymmetric vertical integration in successive oligopolies is not settled. The debate circles around two main issues. First, if there is an asymmetric vertical structure, does it matter? Proponents of unconstrained integration emphasize its efficiency effects: because of technical reasons (economies of scope) or because of the elimination of a double mark-up, integration is believed to reduce marginal costs of the integrating firms. Opponents highlight the potential foreclosure effects: integration is seen as a commitment not to serve downstream rivals, which is likely to result in higher production costs for these competitors and thus in reduced outputs. The theoretical literature is ambiguous about whether integration will lead to foreclosure effects and whether they will dominate over the efficiency effects. The answer depends on such details as the number of upstream and downstream firms, the demand functions and the type of contracts between suppliers and downstream firms that are allowed (Salinger, 1988; Rey and Tirole, 2007). Second, even in situations where the potential negative foreclosure effects of asymmetric vertical integration exist and dominate over the welfare gains from higher efficiency of the integrated firm, is there reason to believe that asymmetric vertical integration is likely to occur? The Chicago School (Bork, 1978) has argued that asymmetric vertical integration is likely to create a bandwagon effect, with non-integrated firms following their integrated counterparts. Meanwhile, however, many authors have used game-theoretic reasoning to explain why asymmetric integration may well be an equilibrium outcome in fairly general circumstances (Ordover *et al.*,

---

[26] Therefore, an experiment of Mason and Phillips (2000) demonstrating that a vertically integrated industry produces higher output than its separated counterpart does not quite get to the heart of the problem.

1990; Jansen, 2003; Bühler and Schmutzler, 2005). This is also consistent with empirical evidence. Even so, the debate is far from settled. In principle, therefore, experiments might contribute to answering the open questions.

Martin, Normann and Snyder (2001), henceforth MNS, is presumably the best-developed contribution to the subject.[27] These authors design their experiment to come close to the setting of Rey and Tirole. In their design, an upstream sector produces an essential input for the downstream sector. In one group of scenarios (separation), one firm is exclusively active on the upstream market, and there are two downstream firms. In a second scenario (integration), the upstream firm merges with one of the downstream firms. In all treatments, the upstream firms offer a contract to each downstream firm, specifying the amount of input they are prepared to deliver and a payment they expect in return. Downstream firms decide whether to accept or reject. Upstream firms also decide how much to produce themselves. Essentially, the authors ask how the vertical merger affects market performance, that is, output prices and firm profits. The results provide some support for foreclosure theories.

Experimental result 5 In the integration treatment of MNS, total quantities are lower and upstream profits are higher than in the various separated treatments.

This is consistent with the idea that the integrated firm finds it easier to commit to an output restriction in the integrated case than in the separated case.

Though the argument that vertical integration can be problematic comes across quite convincingly, there are several caveats. First, as the authors themselves note, not all the theoretical predictions of Rey and Tirole are confirmed.[28] Second, the set-up of MNS has been chosen in a way that is highly conducive to foreclosure. In particular, because there is only one upstream firm, competitors cannot step in to supply separated downstream firms when they are foreclosed by the upstream firm. While there are very important cases, where an upstream

---

[27] Other vaguely related contributions are Elliot *et al.* (2003), and Mason and Phillips (2000).

[28] Specifically, the effect of the types of contracts allowed on performance differs from the predictions.

monopoly faces several downstream competitors, in particular network industries, many industries are better described as sequential
oligopolies. In these industries, it is much more controversial whether
foreclosure can be successful. Third, the analysis has nothing to say
about bandwagoning issues. As the vertical industry structure is fixed,
the authors cannot clarify whether firms will respond to vertical integration by integrating themselves. Thus, they say nothing about
whether asymmetric vertical integration is likely to arise. Obviously,
answering this question would not only require endogenous integration decisions, but also more than one upstream competitor.

In spite of these qualifications, the analysis of MNS is clearly
promising. To repeat, however, at this stage, it is premature to draw
far-reaching conclusions about the effects of integration: theory suggests that the effects of vertical integration depend in a subtle and not
very transparent way on such details as demand functions, the number
of upstream and downstream firms and the type of contracts that are
allowed. We should therefore be reluctant to put too much weight on
the outcomes of a small series of experiments: it may well be that
familiar ambiguities from theory would also show up in experimental
research if sufficiently many design variations were considered.

5. Conglomerate mergers

Unlike horizontal or even vertical mergers, conglomerate mergers
receive relatively little attention by competition policy authorities.
Though it has often been debated whether excessive diversification is
healthy for the firms involved, there is little worry that, by expanding
into unrelated markets, a firm might be able to exercise more market
power. Nevertheless, conglomerate mergers could potentially be
problematic from a joint dominance perspective. This stance was
already taken by Edwards (1955) who conjectures that "the prospect
of advantage from vigorous competition in one market may be
weighted against the danger of retaliatory forays by the competitor in
other markets" (Phillips and Mason 1992: 395). A more recent paper
by Bernheim and Whinston (1990) uses a game-theoretic setting to
investigate whether multi-market contact might foster collusive
behavior. Their argument why this might be true formalizes the simple
idea that for firms who meet in several markets, the costs of deviating
from collusive behavior are high, because a breakdown of collusion

will lead to losses in more than one market. However, they also highlight that the argument is not quite as straightforward as it seems, because the potential gains from deviation are also higher under multi-market interaction. Thus, the effects of multi-market interaction are typically ambiguous. Roughly speaking, collusion decreases on the relatively collusive market and increases on the less collusive market.

These ideas pertain to such conglomerate mergers that, before the merger, some other firms are already active in at least two of the markets under consideration: then the merger creates multi-market contact where there was none before.

A small number of experiments have been carried out to check whether multi-market contact indeed has a positive effect on collusion. For instance, Phillips and Mason (1992) conduct a series of experiments to analyze how multi-market contact affects pricing. The underlying two individual markets are chosen so that in one of them collusion is easier to sustain than in the other one in the absence of multi-market contact. The authors compare output decisions in each individual market with output in an experiment where each firm operates in both markets. The results basically confirm theory.

Experimental result 6 In the Phillips and Mason experiment, multi-market contact increases prices on the less collusive markets and decreases them on the more collusive market.

6. Conclusions

In this chapter, we surveyed experimental work that relates to merger policy analysis. In the remainder of this chapter, we shall argue that, although these experiments have generated some interesting results, the analysis has not yet produced insights into merger policy that would either give more confidence into the conventional wisdom on merger policy or, to the contrary, suggest a fundamental rethinking of familiar ideas. However, we shall also argue that, to some extent these limitations can be overcome.

A large body of experimental research deals quite directly with the relation between market structure and performance. Some of this work is applicable to merger policy in a very broad sense. For instance, many papers support the notion that reductions in the number of firms tend to induce higher prices, which is the basis for merger policy. A much smaller number of papers discuss experiments that were specifically designed to address mergers. For instance, some authors ask how mergers affect different parties. Others attempt to clarify whether certain practices that are used in merger policy are reasonable. By and large, these papers come to reasonable conclusions, either confirming standard intuition or suggesting in a plausible way why such intuition may be flawed. There are some interrelated limitations, however.

First, and most importantly, it is hard to discern a clear research agenda. Each paper appears to attack a fairly isolated issue, and there is no clear sense of direction. Second, only a small fraction of the large number of potentially interesting questions in the area has been addressed. Third, arguably, one might complain that those results that have been obtained so far are relatively unspectacular. On the one hand, we have not seen a robust-looking corroboration of any truly contested idea: competition-policy authorities cannot appeal to existing experiments to judge if and how efficiency defenses, buyer power or potential entry should be weighed in merger cases. On the other hand, there seems to be no example where any undisputed idea has been refuted in a convincing manner: for instance, the experiments do not give us a reason to advise against the use of concentration measures as a useful first step in judging the desirability of mergers. However, we should emphasize that there is also a scientific value to experiments that simply confirm what most people would have expected anyway.

Some of the problems just sketched can be overcome quite easily, at least in principle. The simplest step is to carry out a more extensive discussion about which kind of topics relating to merger policy should be addressed with experiments. Some of the comments in this chapter point in this direction, but they clearly fall short of a full-fledged research agenda. In addition, a "simple" way to improve the output of experimental research on competition policy would be to invest more resources. In particular, robust insights on such issues as to which factors make mergers less problematic might be obtained by carrying out many similar experiments with small modifications.

There are also a number of other limitations: many potentially interesting questions in the area relate to comparative-statics results which might depend in a very subtle way on those parameters that are kept fixed in the comparative-statics exercise. As each experiment only corresponds to one specific realization of these fixed parameters, even obtaining clear comparative-statics observations in a small number of experiments may not convince us fully of the generality of such a statement.

Further, many of the decisive issues in merger policy depend on specific knowledge of the particular case. In principle, one might design experiments that fit the particular case to inform policy makers. Unfortunately, given the usual time frames of merger policy, this appears very difficult.

Finally, even for authors who are sympathetic to experimental research it is not obvious that the lab is ideally suited to test theories on problems involving very large timescales: in the real world, the impact of mergers only becomes entirely clear after many months or even years of adjustment. At the very least, therefore, the external validity of merger experiments should be discussed with a healthy dose of skepticism.

References

Andreoni, J. (1995), Cooperation in Public-Goods Experiments: Kindness or Confusion, *American Economic Review* 85, 891–904.

Aydemir, Z. and A. Schmutzler (2008), Small Scale Entry vs. Acquisitions of Small Firms: Is Concentration Self-reinforcing? *Journal of Economic Behavior and Organization*, 65, 133–146.

Barros, P. P. (1998), Endogenous Mergers and Size Asymmetry of Merger Participants, *Economics Letters* 60, 113–119.

Baumol, W., J. Panzar and R. Willig (1982), *Contestable Markets and the Theory of Industrial Structure*; New York, Harcourt, Brace, Jovanovich.

Bernheim, B. D. and M. D. Whinston (1990), Multimarket Contact and Collusive Behavior, *Rand Journal of Economics* 21, 1–26.

Bork, R. (1978), *The Antitrust Paradox*; New York, Basic Books.

Bühler, S. and A. Schmutzler (2005), Asymmetric Vertical Integration, *The B. E. Journal of Theoretical Economics* (Advances) 5, Article 1.

Coursey, Don, R. Mark Isaac, Margaret Luke, and Vernon L. Smith (1984), Market contestability in the presence of sunk (entry) costs, *Rand Journal of Economics* 15, 69–84.

Davis, Douglas D. (2002), Strategic Interactions, Market Information and Predicting the Effects of Mergers in Differentiated Product Markets, *International Journal of Industrial Organization* 20, 1277–1312.

Davis, Douglas D., and Charles A. Holt (1994), Market Power and Mergers in Laboratory Markets with Posted Prices, *Rand Journal of Economics* 25, 467–487.

Davis, Douglas D. and B. J. Wilson (2000), Firm-specific Cost Savings and Market Power, *Economic Theory* 16, 545–565.

Deneckere and Davidson (1984), Horizontal Mergers and Collusive Behavior, *International Journal of Industrial Organization* 2, 117–132.

Dufwenberg, M., and U. Gneezy (2000), Price Competition and Market Concentration: An Experimental Study, *International Journal of Industrial Organization* 18, 7–22.

Edwards, C. (1955), Conglomerate Bigness as a Source of Power; in National Bureau of Economic Research, *Business Concentration and Price Policy*, Princeton, N.J., Princeton University Press.

Elliott, S. R., R. Godby and J. Brown-Kruse (2003), An Experimental Examination of Vertical Control and Cost Predation, *International Journal of Industrial Organization* 21, 253–281.

Falkinger, J., E. Fehr, S. Gaechter and R. Winter-Ebmer (2000), A Simple Mechanism for the Efficient Provision of Public Goods: Experimental Evidence, *American Economic Review* 90, 247–264.

Farrell, J., and C. Shapiro (1990), Horizontal Mergers: An Equilibrium Analysis, *American Economic Review* 80, 107–126.

Fehr, E., and S. Gaechter (2000), Cooperation and Punishment in Public Goods Experiments, *American Economic Review* 90(4), 980–994.

Fehr, E. and S. Gächter (2002), Altruistic Punishment in Humans, *NATURE* 415, 137–140

Fehr, E., G. Kirchsteiger and A. Riedl (1993), Does Fairness Prevent Market Clearing?, *Quarterly Journal of Economics* 108, 437–460.

Fehr, E. and K. Schmidt (1999), A Theory of Fairness, Competition, and Cooperation, *Quarterly Journal of Economics* 114, 817–868.

Fonseca, M. A. and H-T. Normann (2008), Mergers, Asymmetries and Collusion: Experimental Evidence, *Economic Journal* 118, 387–400.

Harrison, G.W., and M. McKee (1985), Monopoly Behavior, Decentralized Regulations and Contestable Markets: An Experimental Evaluation, *Rand Journal of Economics* 16, 51–69.

Harrison, G.W., M. McKee, and E.E. Rutstrom (1989), Experimental Evaluation of Institutions of Monopoly Restraint, in *Advances in Behavioral Economics*, Vol. II, L. Green and J. Kagel (eds), Norwood, N.J., Aplex Press, 54–94.

Hong, J., and C.R. Plott (1982), Rate Filing Policies for Inland Water Transportation: An Experimental Approach, *Bell Journal of Economics* 13, 1–19.

Huck, S., K. Konrad, W. Müller, and H.-T. Normann (2007): The Merger Paradox and why Aspiration Levels Let it Fail in the Laboratory, *Economic Journal* 117, 1073–1095.

Huck, S., H.-T. Normann, and J. Oechssler (2004), Two are Few and Four are Many, Number Effects in Experimental Oligopolies, *Journal of Economic Behavior and Organization* 53, 435–446.

Isaac, M., J. Walker, and A. Williams (1994), Group Size and the Voluntary Contribution of Public Goods: Experimental Evidence Utilizing Large Groups, *Journal of Public Economics* 54, 1–36.

Isaac, M., and S. S. Reynolds (2002), Two or Four Firms: Does it Matter?, in C.A. Holt and M. Isaac (eds.), *Research in Experimental Economics, Vol. IX: Experiments Investigating Market Power*, Amsterdam, Elsevier Publishers.

Jansen, J. (2003), Coexistence of Strategic Vertical Separation and Integration, *International Journal of Industrial Organization* 21, 699–716.

Kagel, J. and A. Roth (eds.) (1995), *The Handbook of Experimental Economics*, Princeton, NJ, Princeton University Press.

Kamien, M.I., and I. Zang (1993), Monopolization by Sequential Acquisition, *Journal of Law, Economics, & Organization*, 9(2), 205–229.

Levin, D. (1990), Horizontal Mergers: The 50-Percent Benchmark, *American Economic Review* 80, 1238–1245.

Lindqvist, T., and J. Stennek (2005), The Insider's Dilemma: An Experiment on Merger Formation, *Experimental Economics* 8, 267–284.

Kahneman, D., J. Knetsch, and R. Thaler (1986), Fairness as a Constraint on Profit Seeking: Entitlements in the Market, *American Economic Review* 76, 728–741.

Kwoka, J.E. Jr., and L.J. White (1998), *The Antitrust Revolution*, New York, Oxford University Press.

Martin, S., H.T. Normann, and Ch. M. Snyder (2001), Vertical Foreclosure in Experimental Markets, *RAND Journal of Economics*, 32, 466–496.

Mason, Ch. R., and O. R. Phillips (2000), Vertical Integration and Collusive Incentives: an Experimental Analysis, *International Journal of Industrial Organization* 18, 471–496.

Millner, Edward L., Michael D. Pratt, and Robert J. Reilly (1990), Contestability in Real-Time Experimental Flow Markets, *RAND Journal of Economics* 21, 584–99.

Motta M. (2004), *Competition Policy, Theory and Practice*, Cambridge, Cambridge University Press.

Neven, D., Nuttal, R., and Seabright, P., (1993), *Merger in Daylight: The Economics and Politics of European Merger Control*, London, Centre for Economic Policy Research.

Ordover, J. A., G. Saloner, and S. C. Salop (1990), Equilibrium Vertical Foreclosure, *American Economic Review* 80, 127–142.

Perry, M.K., and R.H. Porter (1985), Oligopoly and the Incentive for Horizontal Merger, *American Economic Review* 75, 219–227.

Phillips, O. R., and C. F. Mason (1992), Mutual Forbearance in Experimental Conglomerate Markets, *RAND Journal of Economics*, 23, 395–414.

Rey, P., and J. Tirole (2007): *A Primer on Foreclosure*, in Armstrong, M., and Porter, R. H. (eds.): *Handbook of Industrial Organization*, Vol. III, Amsterdam, North-Holland.

Salinger, M. A. (1988), Vertical Mergers and Market Foreclosure, *Quarterly Journal of Economics* 103, 345–356.

Salant, S., S. Switzer, and R. Reynolds (1983), Losses from Horizontal Merger: The Effects of an Exogenous Change in Industry Structure on Cournot–Nash Equilibrium, *Quarterly Journal of Economics* 98, 185–199.

Tirole, J. (1988), *The Theory of Industrial Organization*, Cambridge, MIT Press.

Tversky, A., and D. Kahneman (1981), The Framing of Decisions and the Psychology of Choice, *Science* 211, 453–458.

Zelmer, J. (2003), Linear Public Goods Experiments: A Meta-Analysis, *Experimental Economics* 6(3), 299–310.

9 | Mergers in Stackelberg markets: an experimental study

STEFFEN HUCK[*]

We implement bilateral mergers in experimental Stackelberg markets with initially three firms: one leader and two followers. Mergers are either between one leader and one follower or between two followers. Post-merger predictions are identical for both treatments and imply increasing profits for the merging firms. This prediction is not borne out in the laboratory. Mergers leave insiders' profits unchanged but do benefit outsiders. These results are compared to experimental findings on mergers in Cournot markets.

1. Introduction

In Cournot markets bilateral mergers can harm the merging firms. Postmerger profits of the merged firm may be smaller than the joint profits of the two merging firms prior to the merger. This is known as the "merger paradox," first pointed out by Salant, Switzer and Reynolds (1983). In ordinary Cournot markets the paradox always holds with linear demand and cost[1] – but not so in Stackelberg markets. Recognized first by Huck, Konrad and Müller (2001), mergers in Stackelberg markets can be profitable despite the absence of "synergy effects." This illuminates the importance of the underlying market structure and the role of strategic power for a comprehensive merger analysis. More specifically, Huck, Konrad and Müller analyze a

[*] I gratefully acknowledge financial support from the ESRC via ELSE and the Leverhulme Trust.
[1] If mergers generate significant cost advantages (for example, because costs are highly convex and production in two plants is more efficient) the paradox can, of course, be overcome. However, such assumptions on cost savings appear problematic and it is perhaps more interesting to observe that the paradox can also disappear in institutionally richer markets where, for example, export subsidies or strategic delegation matters, even when demand and costs are linear. For an overview on profitable mergers without cost advantages, see Huck, Konrad, and Müller (2005).

framework with a number of Stackelberg leaders (all of whom decide simultaneously) and a number of Stackelberg followers (who also decide simultaneously, knowing the total output of all Stackelberg leaders) and show that a merger between two different firms, i.e., a merger between a Stackelberg leader and a Stackelberg follower, is always profitable[2] while a merger between two equal firms is only profitable if there are exactly two of them prior to the merger. With respect to consequences for outsiders, consumers and overall welfare, Stackelberg mergers are similar to Cournot mergers: in all cases, outsiders gain, consumers lose and overall welfare is reduced.

In this chapter I experimentally investigate Stackelberg mergers. More specifically, I analyze markets that have initially three firms: one leader and two followers. In the two main treatments these markets operate for thirty periods before an exogenously imposed merger is implemented. In treatment LF, the leader merges with a randomly chosen follower; in treatment FF the two followers merge. Both mergers result into ordinary Stackelberg duopolies with one leader and one follower that now operate for another thirty periods. Additionally, there is a duopoly control treatment (DUO) where one leader and one follower play for thirty periods.

Equilibrium predictions for treatments LF and FF are identical both pre and post merger. Moreover, the post-merger predictions for LF and FF are identical to the predictions for treatment DUO. While the two merger treatments allow us to perform direct tests of the equilibrium predictions which, in this case, imply the profitability of mergers, a comparison of the two merger treatments with treatment DUO will allow us to test, in addition, whether market outcomes are indeed independent of market histories as predicted by orthodox theory. Previous research on mergers in Cournot markets has indicated that this may not be the case due to the role of history-induced aspiration levels (see Huck, Konrad, Müller and Normann, 2007, henceforth HKMN).

The main findings are that both types of mergers do not, contrary to what theory predicts, increase joint profits. Instead joint profits basically stay where they are. Mergers neither benefit nor harm the merging firms. All other theoretical predictions are, however, qualitatively

---

[2] Interestingly, the leader simply "swallows" the follower in this case without increasing output. This is equivalent to buying a competing firm and shutting it down.

correct. Outsiders do gain significantly and substantially and total output drops significantly and substantially (which, since the market is linear, shows not only that consumers are harmed by the merger but also that overall welfare drops). There are also no significant history effects.

It is interesting to compare these results with experimental findings on Cournot mergers. HKMN investigate bilateral mergers in linear Cournot markets with initially three or four firms. They, too, find that the merging firms basically maintain pre-merger profits while outsiders gain and total output is reduced.

This similarity appears surprising since the deviations from theory go in opposite directions in the two experiments. Experimental Cournot mergers are more profitable than predicted while experimental Stackelberg mergers are less profitable than predicted. This apparent contradiction is resolved when it turns out that behavior in the experimental Stackelberg markets is actually far closer to the Cournot simultaneous-move equilibrium prediction than to the (subgame perfect) sequential-move Stackelberg equilibrium prediction. This corroborates earlier findings by Huck, Müller and Normann (2001) who compare experimental Cournot and Stackelberg duopolies with random and fixed-pair matching and find outcomes very close to Cournot in fixed-pair Stackelberg duopolies.

This pattern is related to the other fundamental difference between HKMN and what I find here. While HKMN report strong history effects there is nothing comparable in the present data. This difference is easily explained when one considers that history matters in HKMN because, for some subjects, the merger implies decreasing profits. HKMN study several control treatments to conclude that subjects who are predicted to make losses "fight back" due to aspiration levels. In the experiments reported here everybody is supposed to gain and the aspiration level prediction has no bite.

2. Experimental design and procedures

In all markets linear inverse demand is given by

$$P = 100 - Q \tag{1}$$

where P is the market price and Q is total output. The cost function is

$$C(q_i) = 4q_i \tag{2}$$

Table 9.1 *Predictions for the treatments. Notice that post-merger predictions for LF and FF coincide with predictions of DUO*

Treatment	LF	FF	DUO
Pre-merger leader output	48	48	48
Pre-merger follower output	16	16	24
Pre-merger total output	80	80	72
Pre-merger leader profit	768	768	1152
Pre-merger follower profit	256	256	576
Insider's gain through merger	128	64	n/a
Outsider's gain through merger	320	320	n/a
Cournot output per firm	24	24	32
Total Cournot output	72	72	64

where q_i is firm i's output. In the two main treatments there are initially three firms: one Stackelberg leader and two Stackelberg followers. In the unique subgame perfect equilibrium of the one-period two-stage game the leader chooses $q_1 = 48$ and the two followers react with $q_2 = q_3 = 16$. The resulting price is 20. In a finitely repeated game these outcomes are predicted (by a unique subgame perfect equilibrium) for each round of play.

In a duopoly with the same market parameters the output of the Stackelberg leader remains unchanged. The follower's output is 24. These predictions hold, of course, regardless of whether this duopoly has resulted from a merger or not. Table 9.1 above summarizes equilibrium predictions, including equilibrium profits and gains through merger. The table also includes in its last line the seemingly irrelevant simultaneous-move Cournot outputs that, as I mentioned earlier, will play a role.

In both main treatments, LF and FF, one leader and two followers play for thirty periods. Between periods feedback is given about own output, others total output, market price, and own profit. After the thirtieth period an exogenous merger is implemented. Subjects know that the experiment will have two phases with thirty periods each, but when the first phase begins they only know the rules for this phase and have no information about what is to come in the second.

In treatment LF, the Stackelberg leader merges with a randomly chosen follower. In treatment FF the two followers merge. In both cases, one of the subjects becomes "sole manager" of the firm and takes all decisions in the thirty periods of the post-merger market. In treatment LF this is always the subject who played the leader firm prior to the merger (to make sure that leader firms post-merger can make use of their experience as leaders prior to the merger). In treatment FF one of the two follower subjects is randomly chosen to become the decision maker of the merged follower firm. The subject that is not chosen to manage the merged firm stays in the laboratory and gets a share of the profit of the merged firm. The share they receive is based on the equilibrium share of total profits prior to the merger. That is, in treatment LF the passive subject (who used to be a follower and has merged with a leader) receives a quarter of the profits, while in treatment FF the passive subject (an ex-follower merged with another follower) receives a half. In both treatments passive subjects also receive feedback information between rounds.

The experiments were conducted at the ELSE laboratory in spring 2005. For all treatments we conducted six markets. Subjects were recruited from a large subject data base and were UCL students from all fields. In all sessions there were at least three groups of subjects present to make sure that subjects could not infer with whom they were playing. Role allocation was random and subjects received written instructions prior to learning their roles. Interactions were fully computerized using Tomlinson's (2005) Expecon. On average, experiments lasted an hour and payments were £27 which included a £5 show-up fee.

3. Results

Table 9.2 shows average outputs across treatments, based on data from the last third of each phase of the experiment, i.e., based on rounds 21–30 and 51–60 in treatments LF and FF, and on rounds 21–30 in treatment DUO.[3]

---

[3] Remarkably, there were no significant end-game effects. For this reason, I did not exclude any rounds towards the very end. Otherwise this procedure mirrors HKMN. Results are robust to changing the size of the window. For example, all key results that I am going to show still hold when I take the last halves instead of the last thirds of the experiment.

222

Steffen Huck

Table 9.2 *Output data for last third of both phases. Data for exogenous duopolies from treatment DUO (where no merger took place) shown in comparison to post-merger duopolies from treatments LF and FF. Standard deviations (based on market averages) shown in parentheses*

Treatment	LF	FF	DUO
Pre-merger leader output	26.8 (11.4)	29.4 (13.5)	
Pre-merger follower output	22.4 (4.6)	21.9 (4.4)	
Pre-merger total output	71.5 (18.8)	73.2 (14.1)	
Post-merger leader output	32.1 (5.6)	31.5 (10.2)	27.5 (3.9)
Post-merger follower output	25.7 (5.8)	32.2 (1.7)	30.9 (6.1)
Post-merger total output	57.7 (7.1)	63.7 (9.8)	58.4 (9.81)

A number of observations can be easily made:[4]

1) Total outputs are remarkably close to the theoretically irrelevant simultaneous-move Cournot outputs, in particular in treatments LF and FF prior to the merger, i.e., in markets with three firms, where they are almost spot on. In the six duopolies total output is also much closer to Cournot than to Stackelberg. In fact, output is even slightly below the Cournot prediction of 64. While one should have expected that there are no significant differences between LF and FF prior to merger (where subjects played actually identical games), this is less self-evident post merger. But also there the difference is not statistically significant, nor are the differences between LF and FF on the one hand and DUO on the other.
2) The mergers are clearly anti-competitive. The output reduction in treatment LF is significant at $p = 0.02$ and in treatment FF at $p = 0.04$ (one-sided Wilcoxon matched pairs tests).
3) Somewhat oddly, followers in treatment DUO produce more than leaders. The difference is small but highly significant ($p = 0.03$, two-sided Wilcoxon). We will find out why this is the case further below. In all other treatments and phases there are no significant differences between leader and follower outputs.

[4] All tests will be based on group averages, i.e., we shall take each market as one independent observation.

Table 9.3 *Estimated response functions*

Treatment	Phase	a	b	R^2	N
LF	pre merger	20.07*** (5.49)	0.09 (0.16)	0.02	120
FF	pre merger	26.00*** (3.48)	−0.14 (0.09)	0.07	120
LF	post merger	29.77*** (3.43)	−0.12 (0.09)	0.04	60
FF	post merger	34.18*** (2.10)	−0.06 (0.05)	0.01	60
DUO	n/a	20.45* (9.18)	0.38 (0.29)	0.10	60

While the deviations form the subgame perfect equilibrium predictions that we observe are fairly systematic, we need some further investigation to find out what is driving these deviations. For that purpose we estimate followers' response functions.

The subgame perfect equilibrium strategies of followers in the pre-merger phase treatments LF and FF are

$$q_2(q_1) = q_3(q_1) = (96 - q_1)/3 \tag{3}$$

and in the Stackelberg duopolies

$$q_2(q_1) = (96 - q_1)/2. \tag{4}$$

We estimate linear response functions of the type

$$q_2(q_1) = a - bq_1 + \varepsilon \tag{5}$$

with robust standard errors (clustering at the market level and taking again just the last third of each phase). The estimation results are shown in Table 9.3.

First of all, we find that in both treatments with mergers all response functions are essentially flat. Basically, it appears that followers choose quantities very close to the Cournot quantities regardless of what leaders are doing. Given such behavior it is, of course, optimal for leaders to play Cournot, too. A slightly different picture emerges in treatment DUO where the intercept is much smaller than in phase 2 of treatments LF and FF. Moreover, in this treatment the estimated slope of the reaction function is positive, although not significantly so. This is due to rather large variance in individual responses that are also reflected in very small R^2s. This tendency to increase own outputs when leaders produce more is in line with the

Table 9.4 *Average profits*

Treatment	LF	FF	DUO
Pre-merger leader profit	487.4 (207.7)	513.2 (139.0)	
Pre-merger follower profit	469.5 (286.2)	481.2 (228.5)	
Post-merger leader profit	1114.8 (230.4)	927.3 (107.7)	980.4 (172.0)
Post-merger follower profit	946.3 (190.3)	1011.2 (365.5)	1090.9 (125.1)
Insider's gain	157.9	48.8	
Outsider's gain	476.8	481.2	

observation that followers, on average, produce significantly more than leaders in this treatment.[5]

Overall, we find very strong evidence that followers are not willing to reduce their own output in response to increased outputs by leaders. Instead, they seem to "educate" leaders to play Cournot.[6]

How does this affect profits (the ultimate question from the firm perspective)? Table 9.4 shows pre- and post-merger profit levels and indicates gains and losses (based on the averages shown in the table).

Table 9.4 shows that, on average, all firms benefit from the mergers we study but the average gain of the insider is much smaller than the average gain of an outsider and fails to be significant while outsiders do earn significantly more post merger than before ($p = 0.01$, one-tailed Wilcoxon).

4. Conclusion

We find that mergers in Stackelberg markets that are predicted to be profitable, despite the absence of cost savings, fail to generate significant increases in profits. On the other hand, outsiders gain enormously. Total industry profits rise due to a substantial contraction of

---

[5] Huck, Müller, and Normann (2001) report very similar findings on the followers' response functions in their Stackelberg duopolies. In particular, they find with fixed-pair matching as it is employed here a significantly positive slope of the response function. They discuss this as a reward-for-cooperation and punishment-for-exploitation scheme.

[6] This striking attraction of the Cournot outcome where it is not predicted is also found in Fonseca, Huck, and Normann (2004) who study experimental endogenous timing games that predict the emergence of Stackelberg leadership with asymmetric cost.

total industry output. As a consequence consumers are much worse off post merger and overall welfare is substantially reduced.

These results are remarkably similar to the findings in HKMN who analyze mergers in Cournot markets (where merging firms are able to avoid predicted losses). There, too, mergers do not affect the merging firms but benefit outsiders and reduce welfare. HKMN offer as an explanation for this effect that behavior is guided by aspiration levels. Merged firms produce more than they should according to theory because they want to maintain their pre-merger profit levels. (HKMN test this explanation against a number of competing explanations by running diverse control treatment. The data confirm the aspiration level hypothesis in each instance.) Outsiders are willing to accept unequal market shares because their profit rises anyway. In the merger treatments reported here the merging firms appear to be happy to maintain their earlier income level and the rising industry profits are completely absorbed by outsiders. Since nobody's profits are predicted to fall, the aspiration levels hypothesis of HKMN has no bite.

Theoretically, Stackelberg mergers should be more likely to occur than Cournot mergers since they can be profitable under cost conditions that render Cournot mergers unprofitable. The experimental evidence presented here, however, suggests that it is difficult to exploit the gains from mergers predicted in the Stackelberg model. If this also holds outside the laboratory it could bias empirical estimates that take equilibrium behavior as given.

Appendix: Instructions

Phase 1

Welcome to our experiment!
Please be quiet during the entire experiment. Do not talk to your neighbors and do not try to look at their screens. Simply concentrate on what you have to do.

If you have any questions, please raise your hand. We will come to you and answer them privately.

In this experiment you will act as one of three firms, A, B and C, that sell a product in a market. You will be randomly matched with two other participants who will act as the other firms. For example, if you are firm A, then you will be matched with a participant acting as firm B and another participant acting as firm C. You will stay together with the two other participants in the same market for 30 rounds. In each round, all firms make a decision about their output, i.e., how many items they want to sell. For your output, you can choose any whole number from zero to 100.

For each item you produce you have to pay the production costs. The production costs are 4 ECU (Experimental Currency Units) per item. Once all firms have decided how much to produce, the market price (the amount of money you get for selling each unit you produce) adjusts accordingly. The higher the total number of items produced, the lower the market price. Specifically, the market price will be calculated as follows:

Market Price $= 100 -$ Total Output

where Total Output is the sum of your output and the two other firms' outputs. Note that the market price cannot fall below zero. If the total output exceeds 100, the market price will be zero regardless of how much the total output is above 100.

Accordingly, your profit in each round can be calculated as

Your Profit $=$ Your Output $\times$ Market Price $-$ Your Production Costs

where your production costs are simply $4 \times$ Your Output.

The procedure in each round is as follows. First, firm A makes its output decision. This decision is then communicated to firms B and C who then decide simultaneously about their output. Thus, when firms B and C decide about their output, they do so knowing firm A's output in this period. Once firms B and C have made their output decision, all firms receive information about this period's market outcome. This means you will be reminded about your own output, and you will also see the other firms' outputs, the resulting market price and your own profit. Then we move on to the next period where you will interact with the same participants again. This continues for 30 periods and constitutes Phase 1 of this experiment. Once Phase 1 is over, you will receive new instructions detailing what will happen in Phase 2.

The roles of firms A, B and C will be randomly assigned by the computer at the start of the experiment. You will keep your role for the entire experiment.

The total amount of money you will earn in this experiment will be calculated from your total ECU profits from both phases of the experiment. In Phase 1 your total is simply the sum of ECU profits from all 30 periods. At the end of the experiment, ECU will be exchanged to Pound Sterling using a rate of £1 for every 1500 ECU.

Finally, be assured that we ask you for your name and email address for purely administrative reasons. All data will be processed in a way that assures you full anonymity. You will also stay anonymous to other participants, i.e., you will not find out with whom you were matched.

Phase 2

There has now been a merger of firms A and B. This new firm is called firm AB and it is managed by participant A. However, the profits of the new firm AB are shared between the two participants A and B according to the following rule: A will receive 75% from all profits and B will receive 25%. Firm C remains independent.

Participant B is passive in this second phase but receives the same information about market outcomes as does participant A. In particular, participant B still needs to click on the "Continue" button after each screen.

The new market that comprises only two firms is otherwise identical to the previous market. Costs, prices and profits are calculated in the same way as before.

The timing in each period is now as follows: Firm AB decides first. Its output decision is communicated to C who then decides about his own output knowing AB's output.

As before, there will be 30 periods. The ECU profits from Phase 2 will be the sum of ECU profits from all 30 periods. Your total ECU profit is your total from both Phase 1 and Phase 2. At the end of the experiment, ECU will be exchanged to Pound Sterling using a rate of £1 for every 1500 ECU.

Bibliography

Fonseca, M., S. Huck, and H.-T. Normann (2004), Playing Cournot Although They Shouldn't: Endogenous Timing in Duopoly with Asymmetric Cost, *Economic Theory* 25, 669–677.

Huck, S., K. Konrad, and W. Müller (2001), Big Fish Eat Small Fish: On merger in Stackelberg markets, *Economics Letters* 73, 213–217.

(2005), Profitable Mergers Without Cost Advantages, in: Wayne Dale Collins (ed.), *Issues in Competition Law and Policy*, American Bar Association Book Series.

Huck, S., K. Konrad, W. Müller, and H.-T. Normann (2007), The Merger Paradox and Why Aspiration Levels Let it Fail in the Laboratory, *Economic Journal* 117, 1073–1095.

Huck, S., W. Müller, and H.-T. Normann (2001), Stackelberg Beats Cournot – On Collusion and Efficiency in Experimental Markets, *Economic Journal* 111, 113–125.

Salant, S. W., S. Switzer, and R. J. Reynolds (1983), Losses From Horizontal Mergers: The Effects of an Exogenous Change in Industry Structure on Cournot–Nash Equilibrium, *Quarterly Journal of Economics* 98, 185–99.

Tomlinson, C. (2005), Expecon: A Flexible Architecture for Building Networked Experiments, *Technical Report*, ELSE/University College London.

PART IV

10 | Making uncompetitive auctions competitive: a survey of experiments

THEO OFFERMAN AND
SANDER ONDERSTAL*

In the past fifteen years, governments around the world have often used auctions to sell scarce licenses to operate in markets. In many of these auctions, the number of interested competitors is relatively small compared to the number of available licenses. Auction design is crucial in such uncompetitive circumstances. Details of the design affect participants' decisions to compete seriously or not. Such decisions are important for the industry structure and the efficiency of the aftermarket as well as for the revenue raised in the auction. This chapter provides a survey of emerging experimental work on the question of how competition can be stimulated in uncompetitive license auctions. We consider papers that deal with the performance of standard auctions (such as the simultaneous ascending auction and the discriminative auction) in uncompetitive circumstances. We also discuss papers that investigate the performance of some less-known auctions (such as the Anglo-Dutch auction, the Amsterdam auction, and Right-To-Choose auctions) that actively seek to foster competition among bidders who would not compete in standard auctions.

1. Introduction

In the years 2000 and 2001, several European governments auctioned licenses for third-generation mobile telecommunication (UMTS). Governments raised an incredible amount of more than €100 billion in these auctions.[1] Although the auctions in the different countries

* The research of Offerman has been made possible by a fellowship of the Royal Netherlands Academy of Arts and Sciences. Onderstal gratefully acknowledges financial support from the Dutch National Science Foundation (NWO-VICI 453.03.606).
[1] The European UMTS auctions are not the only license auctions that took place in the recent past. In the past fifteen years, governments all over the world have used auctions to sell scarce licenses to operate in markets. For instance, before the European governments decided to auction their spectrum, the Federal

may have been very similar to a layperson's eye, they differed in small but crucial details. In uncompetitive circumstances, where the number of competitors is small compared to the number of licenses for sale, such details may have a profound effect on the auction outcome. A good example is offered by the UMTS auction in the Netherlands and the UK. While both countries offered five licenses in a simultaneous ascending auction, the Netherlands auction witnessed only one entrant besides the five incumbents and a revenue of €170 per capita was collected, while thirteen competitors participated in the UK auction which raised more than €650 per capita. What was the cause of this substantial difference in auction outcomes?

One difference between the Netherlands and the UK was that in the Netherlands, five firms were already active in the market for second-generation mobile telecommunication, while in the UK this number was four. Incumbents have some important competitive advantages compared to newcomers, as they already have a network of base stations and a customer base. Furthermore, their willingness to pay may be larger for preemptive reasons as they prefer to keep out entrants to protect their profits in related markets. As both governments auctioned five licenses, it is quite possible that potential entrants in the UK were perceived to have a much larger probability to win a license than in the Netherlands. Another difference was that the auction in the Netherlands was run after the auction in the UK. The sky-high prices in the UK may have deterred potential entrants in the Netherlands' auction. A third difference is that the Netherlands is a much smaller country than the UK, and the opportunities to make money are fewer in the Netherlands. Finally, it can also not be excluded that part of the difference is just explained by luck.

Ideally, one would like to run a controlled field experiment to see which factor is responsible for differences in auction outcomes. In practice this is impossible. A good alternative option is to run a series of controlled laboratory experiments, in each of which a couple of auctions are compared that differ in one aspect only. Notice that laboratory experiments also offer the important possibility of

Communications Commission (FCC) had allocated licenses for second generation mobile telecommunication in a series of auctions. Other examples are auctions for commercial radio, petrol stations, wireless local loop, and passenger railway services.

replication, which clarifies a potential role of luck. With sufficiently repeated observations in identical circumstances, the researcher has the possibility to draw statistically meaningful conclusions. Notice that within the field of industrial organization, the application of experiments to auctions is very fruitful, because it is straightforward to introduce the institutional details of the auction in an experiment.

An objection raised against laboratory experiments is that the subjects in the lab (usually undergraduate students) are not representative of the decision makers in the field. Notice, however, that the subject pool of the experiment is a choice of the experimenter, and the experiment can be run with decision makers in the field. The question of whether students and decision makers in the field behave similarly is an empirical one that has been investigated. Most often the differences between students and professionals are small or absent (see Friedman and Sunder, 1994: 39–43 and Abbink and Rockenbach, 2006 for references to this kind of work). For instance, Dyer *et al.* (1989) observe in an auction experiment that experienced business executives in the construction contract industry perform qualitatively similarly as inexperienced undergraduate students. We would welcome more experiments of this kind, though, and think that this remains an important avenue for future research.

In this chapter, we offer an overview of experimental work that investigates the performance of auctions in uncompetitive circumstances. We consider papers that deal with the performance of standard auctions (such as the simultaneous ascending auction and the discriminatory auction) in uncompetitive circumstances. Questions that are addressed in those papers are: How vulnerable is an auction design to revenue-reducing strategies? How likely is the auction to attract entry? Is the allocation of the auction efficient? How does the auction design affect competition in the market? How much revenue does the auction raise? We also discuss papers that investigate the performance of some less-known auctions that actively seek to foster competition among bidders who would not compete in standard auctions: the Anglo-Dutch auction, the Dutch-Anglo auction, premium auctions and right-to-choose auctions.[2]

---

[2] We focus on situations where there are no strong synergies between licenses. Therefore we do not deal with combinatorial auctions in this chapter.

Before we discuss these auctions, it is good to stress that the competition law alone is not sufficient to induce competition, neither in the auction, nor in the aftermarket. Of course, one may also turn to competition law to prevent undesirable practices like collusion. For instance, "bidding rings" in which bidders make agreements about who wins the license at which price, are considered illegal under Article 81 of the EC Treaty. However, in both auctions and product markets, it is quite difficult to prove tacit collusion to be a violation of competition law. A well-designed auction may discourage (tacit) collusion, so that the government does not have to rely on competition law in the first place. Indeed, Motta (2004) argues in his book on competition policy that "it is better to try to create an environment that discourages collusion in the first place than trying to prove unlawful behavior afterwards. A clear advantage of auction markets is that the environment can be affected directly, since the rules of the game are specified at the beginning by the auctioneer." Motta's advice also applies to the market for which the licenses are auctioned: a well-designed auction encourages entry into the market so that (tacit) collusion in the market becomes more difficult. One of the central questions of our survey is: which auction formats are more successful in encouraging competition, both in the auction and in the aftermarket?

The set-up of this chapter is as follows. In Section 2, we discuss the goals that governments may pursue when they design license auctions. In Section 3, we briefly discuss some basic notions of auction theory. Section 4 contains an overview of laboratory experiments on standard auctions, while in Sections 5 and 6, we focus on hybrid auctions and right-to-choose auctions respectively. Section 7 concludes with the main lessons and some policy advice.

2. Objectives of license auctions

Usually governments pursue a hybrid of objectives, some of which relate to efficiency while others relate to revenue. We first deal with issues related to the efficiency of a license auction. The concept of efficiency is defined differently in the sale of licenses than in the sale of say a painting. In an auction of a painting, the result is efficient if the painting is won by the person who attaches the highest value to it. In a license auction, efficiency results if the stream of future surpluses in the aftermarket are as high as possible. The surplus in the aftermarket consists of a consumer part (the difference between consumers' willingness to pay for the product that is traded in the aftermarket and the price that they pay) and a producer part (roughly the difference between the price for the product and the costs of the product). Because it is quite impossible to directly measure the efficiency level of a real license auction, it is useful to identify a number of targets that correlate with efficiency:

- *Entry by newcomers.* Entry is an important target, since according to mainstream theory, more competition leads to lower prices, better quality, and more innovation, and thus to a higher level of efficiency in the aftermarket. Notice also that newcomers may be useful to stir up a collusive product market.
- *Make sure that the licenses end up in the hands of the firms that can serve the market most efficiently.* Cost efficiency is one of the contributors to producer surplus and welfare, so it is important that inefficient firms are unlikely to win licenses. Note that this target could be in conflict with the first, as an incumbent could be the more efficient producer in the market, while in some situations it may be better to have a somewhat less cost-efficient firm enter the market to stir up competition.
- *Make sure that firms use licenses to produce services that are valued by consumers.* Sometimes incumbent firms face preemptive reasons to bid high. They want to overbid potential entrants in order to maintain their attractive powerful position in the market (Gilbert and Newbery, 1982, and Hoppe *et al.*, 2006). Once having obtained the license, they use it in an inferior way than an entrant would have used it. To pursue efficiency, licenses have to be assigned to firms that use them for the right reason, that is, to make consumers happy. Notice that this target may conflict with the second target, as it may be the case that an incumbent firm is cost efficient but plans to use the license in a preemptive way only.

Other objectives of governments usually relate to revenue. Many sellers of commodities in the private market relentlessly pursue as high an expected revenue as possible. Quite often governments pursue a more sophisticated goal when it comes to revenue. In particular, many governments refrain from setting the considerable reserve prices that would correspond to expected revenue maximizing auctions. Considerable reserve prices lead to the possibility that some licenses go unsold. Policy makers tend to dislike this outcome, probably both because it harms efficiency and because unsold licenses make them look bad in the eyes of the public. Also, governments often explicitly state that they want to prevent the *winner's curse*, i.e., a situation in which a firm pays so much that it makes a loss. Although a high revenue may be served by a winner's curse, governments usually want to avoid it for the fear that winning firms go bankrupt or want to renegotiate the deal in court. Policy makers also dislike the opposite outcome where firms keep auction prices low and receive windfall profits. In other words, policy makers prefer to avoid auction formats with a high variance of revenue. Therefore, for policy makers it is usually important to know about both an auction format's expected revenue and its variance.

Revenue and efficiency are not independent targets. A high auction revenue implies that governments can levy less distortionary taxes. Indeed, Ballard *et al.* (1985) estimate deadweight losses of raising taxes to lie between 17 and 56 cents for every extra $1 raised. On the other hand, the experiment by Offerman and Potters (2006) suggests that auctioning licenses increases consumer prices in the aftermarket as firms become more willing to pursue collusion after they pay a high price to enter a market. A related theoretical argument is provided by Janssen (2006) who argues that the high revenue raised in an auction serves as a forward-induction device that helps firms coordinate on the most collusive equilibrium of the oligopoly game. High consumer prices in the aftermarket harm efficiency and counteract society's gain resulting from the decrease in distortionary taxes in other domains. Note also that realizing much revenue can easily conflict with pursuing efficiency. In some situations, the government could generate a very high revenue if it gives one firm the right to operate as a monopolist in the market rather than sell licenses to several firms, a solution that would clearly harm efficiency in the aftermarket.

Of course, governments have other means available besides varying the auction format. For instance, governments could give an advantage to weak bidders when they pursue a high revenue. One way to favor a weak bidder is to give her a bidding credit, i.e., give her a discount on her bid. In one of the FCC auctions, companies owned by minorities or women only had to pay 80% of their bid when they won a license. Another possibility is to reserve licenses for weak bidders. For instance, in the UMTS auction in the UK, incumbent parties were not allowed to bid on one of the licenses. Still, favoring weak bidders has some disadvantages. First, it is not clear whether favoring one group of bidders over another is in conflict with anti-discrimination law, such as Article 87(1) of the EC Treaty. Second, it is not so easy to get the details of the auction right. To which extent should weak bidders be favored? For instance, if the government wishes to maximize the revenue of the auction then the optimal bidding credit largely depends on the environment, such as the underlying distribution of signals or the utility functions of the bidders (Myerson, 1981). For these reasons, we only consider "detail free" auctions, i.e., auctions that are context independent in the sense that "the rules of the game" do not depend on the parameters of the environment.[3]

3. Some theoretical notions

We first discuss the basics of auction theory, so that we have a framework in which the results of the experiments can be placed.[4] The most commonly studied auctions of a single object are the English, the Dutch, the first-price sealed-bid, and the second-price sealed-bid or Vickrey auction (the 'standard auctions'). In the English auction, the price is raised successively until one bidder remains. This bidder wins the object at the final price. The price can be raised by the auctioneer, or by having bidders call the bids themselves. In the Dutch auction, the auctioneer begins with a very high price, and successively lowers it, until one bidder announces that she is willing to accept the current price. This bidder wins the object at that price. In the first-price sealed-bid auction, bidders independently submit sealed bids. The object is sold to the highest bidder at her own price. The Vickrey auction has the same rules as the first-price sealed-bid auction, except that the price the winner pays is not her own bid, but the second highest bid.

In his seminal theoretical work on auctions, Vickrey (1961) studies bidding behavior in standard auctions in the symmetric independent private values model. In this model, one indivisible object is sold to one of a set of bidders who draw their value for the object independently from the same value distribution function. Vickrey proves

---

[3] Wilson (1987) promotes the use of detail-fee mechanisms. See also Krishna (2002: 75).
[4] For excellent overviews of auction theory and its relation to practice see the books by Krishna (2002) and Klemperer (2004).

two important 'equivalence' theorems: (1) all standard auctions are efficient, and (2) the (expected) revenue from all standard auctions is the same. This finding suggests that the seller does not have to worry much about the auction design, as many auctions generate the same outcome. Early laboratory experiments mainly tested the outcomes of Vickrey's model. Kagel (1995), in an excellent overview, observes that these experiments confirm quite a few of the predictions of Vickrey's theory. The main deviation is that first-price auctions raise more revenue than the other auctions.

Later theoretical research reveals that Vickrey's equivalence results rely on several crucial assumptions: (1) independent private values, (2) symmetric bidders, (3) no externalities and (4) only one object is sold. The equivalence results may break down if at least one of these assumptions is violated. Let us shortly discuss alternative models in which deviations from the symmetric independent private values model are studied. More specifically, we compare first-price auctions (the first-price sealed-bid auction and the Dutch auction) and second-price auctions (the English auction and the Vickrey auction). In first-price auctions, the winner pays a price equal to her own bid, while in second-price auction, it is the runner-up's bid that determines how much the winner pays.[5]

- *Independent private values.* Vickrey assumes that all bidders draw their value for the object independent from the same distribution function. Milgrom and Weber (1982) show that in an environment in which values are correlated, the English auction and to a lesser extent the Vickrey auction yield more revenue than the first-price auction. The reason is that in the English auction, information is revealed while the price increases: active bidders observe who steps out at which price. This information may be useful to update a bidder's belief about the true value of the object, so that she is less prone to the winner's curse, and is hence willing to bid higher than in a first-price auction in which no information is released. This is one of the reasons why the simultaneous ascending auction was advocated to sell licenses, as this auction is a generalization of the English auction to multi-object environments.

---

[5] In some formats of the English auction, strictly speaking, the winner pays her own bid. However, in equilibrium, this bid is just above the highest losing bid.

- *Symmetric bidders.* The assumption that bidders are symmetric means that all bidders draw their value for the auctioned object from the same distribution function. Bulow *et al.* (1999) and Klemperer (1998) show that first-price auctions may yield (far) more revenue than second-price auctions if only a slight asymmetry is introduced. However, Plum (1992) and Maskin and Riley (2000) show in a more general model that the revenue ranking of first-price and second-price auctions is ambiguous. Moreover, the first-price auction turns out to be inefficient in the sense that the object does not always end up in the hands of the bidder that attaches the highest value to it, in contrast to second-price auctions. These models are very relevant, as they apply to situations in which 'strong' bidders (e.g. an incumbent) compete in the auction against 'weak' bidders (e.g. a potential entrant).
- *No externalities.* Vickrey assumes that the winning bidder imposes no externality on the losers. This assumption may be violated in license auctions. For instance, if an entrant wins a license, an incumbent may experience a negative externality as more competition in the market may induce the price, and hence his profit, to be lower. The incumbent may then bid more than his value for the object, i.e., bid preemptively in order to prevent entry (Gilbert and Newbery, 1982 and Hoppe *et al.*, 2006). First-price and second-price auctions may perform quite differently in these environments (Jehiel *et al.*, 1996, 1999; Jehiel and Moldovanu, 2000; Das Varma, 2002; and Goeree *et al.*, 2004a).
- *Single unit.* Vickrey studies a model in which only one unit is sold. However, in many license auctions, the government simultaneously sells several licenses. In multi-object auctions, the discriminatory auction and the simultaneous ascending auction may be considered as multi-unit extensions of the first-price and second-price single-unit auctions respectively. In a discriminatory auction, the bidders submit sealed bids on the objects, and the winner of each object pays a price equal to their own bid. The simultaneous ascending auction is the auction format that has been used most frequently to assign licenses in markets.[6] The following rules apply to this auction.

[6] It was very often used in the American FCC auctions (see Plott, 1997, Roth, 2002) and in several UMTS auctions (Binmore and Klemperer, 2002, Abbink *et al.*, 2005).

Multiple units are sold simultaneously and bidding occurs in a series of rounds. In each round, those bidders who are eligible to bid make sealed bids for as many objects as they want or are allowed. At the end of each round, the auctioneer announces the standing high bid for each object along with the minimum bids for the next round, which is computed by adding a pre-determined bid increment such as 5% or 10% to the standing high bids. A standing high bid remains valid until it is overbid. The auction concludes when no new bids are submitted. The standing high bids are then declared winning bids, and each winner pays an amount equal to the standing high bid. One difference between a discriminatory auction and a simultaneous ascending auction is that the latter is more prone to tacit collusion, and may hence generate less revenue than a discriminatory auction. The following example illustrates why this is the case. Suppose two bidders, 1 and 2, bid for two licenses, A and B. Each bidder attaches value 100 to each license. The bidders may tacitly agree to divide the market such that 1 gets A and 2 gets B. The bidders may do so, by bidding 0 on 'their' license. In the simultaneous ascending auction, such agreement is stable. Imagine that bidder 1 deviates from the agreement, and overbids bidder 2 on license B. Then bidder 2 can immediately 'punish' bidder 1 by placing a bid on license A. These punishment strategies are not available in a discriminatory auction. In other words, the simultaneous ascending auction is prone to 'demand reduction', which may imply that revenues are low and that the allocation of the licenses is inefficient (Noussair, 1995; Engelbrecht-Wiggans and Kahn, 1998; Ausubel and Cramton, 2002; and Goeree *et al.*, 2004a).

In the remainder of this chapter we will see to what extent these theoretical considerations play a role in practical auctions.

4. Standard auctions

In this section, we compare standard auctions (including the simultaneous ascending auction and the discriminatory auction) in uncompetitive circumstances. Klemperer (2002b) conjectures that in such situations, first-price auctions perform better than second-price auctions. The main question that is answered in this section is: do first-price auctions indeed outperform second-price auctions in thin markets? In Section 4.1, this question is answered for auctions in which only a single object is sold, while in Sections 4.2 and 4.3 we focus on multi-object auctions, looking at homogeneous objects and heterogeneous objects respectively. Section 4.4 contains a summary of the main findings.

4.1. Single object auctions

In the previous section, we noted that in theory, the ranking of first-price and second-price auctions is ambiguous if bidders are asymmetric, for instance when an incumbent and a potential entrant in a market compete to get a license which gives them additional capacity to operate in that market. Does this theoretical result carry over to the lab? Pezanis-Christou (2002) and Güth *et al.* (2005) conduct experiments in asymmetric environments in order to study the efficiency and the revenue generating properties of the first-price sealed-bid auction and the Vickrey auction. More precisely, they study an environment in which one object is auctioned to one out of two bidders. Let bidder 1 be the weak bidder and bidder 2 the strong one, and let v_i denote the value for the object to bidder i, $i = 1, 2$.

In both studies, it is assumed that the values for the object are independently drawn from uniform distributions. More precisely, Güth *et al.* (2005) consider an environment in which $v_1 \sim U[50, 150]$ and $v_2 \sim U[50, 200]$. Pezanis-Christou (2002) conducts two series of experiments. In his first (second) parametrization, he assumes $v_1 \sim U[-100, 100]$ ($v_1 \sim U[-300, 100]$) and $v_2 \sim U[0, 100]$.

The theoretical predictions are the following. According to Maskin and Riley (2000), the Vickrey auction is always efficient, in contrast to the first-price sealed-bid auction. Moreover the revenue ranking of the first-price sealed-bid auction and the Vickrey auction is ambiguous for risk-neutral bidders. Observe that in Güth *et al.*'s (2005) setting, the weak bidder's distribution function is "stretched out" over a longer interval in order to obtain the distribution function of the strong bidder. Maskin and Riley show that in these type of environments, first-price auctions generate more revenue than second-price auctions. In contrast, in the model of Pezanis-Christou (2002), the weak bidder obtains his distribution function by shifting some mass of the strong bidder's distribution function to the point zero (as bidders with a negative valuation for the object behave as if their value is zero).

Maskin and Riley prove that these types of distribution shifts imply that the Vickrey auction dominates the first-price auction in terms of revenue, in contrast to Güth *et al.*'s (2005) framework. The predicted revenue differences are the following. In Güth *et al.*'s set-up, the first-price sealed-bid auction generates slightly more revenue than the Vickrey auction (about 2%). In Pezanis-Christou's (2002) first (second) parametrization, the seller's expected revenue in the first-price sealed-bid auction is 10% (33%) less than in the Vickrey auction.

Güth *et al.* (2005) observe the following in their experiment. First, the Vickrey auction is slightly more efficient than the first-price sealed-bid auction (99% versus 98%).[7] The difference is statistically significant but small. The average revenue of the first-price (Vickrey) auction was more than 10% higher than (about the same as) what theory predicted, so that the first-price auction clearly dominated the Vickrey auction. Finally, the variance of the revenues was substantially smaller for the first-price auction compared to the Vickrey auction.

Pezanis-Christou (2002) finds qualitatively similar results as Güth *et al.* The efficiency levels for both the Vickrey auction and the first-price sealed-bid auction are very high (97% and 95% respectively for the first parametrization and 99% and 96% for the second), and are not statistically significantly different. Moreover, the first-price auction generates more revenue than the Vickrey auction as bidders bid substantially more than in the risk-neutral equilibrium, while in the Vickrey auction, bids are very close to the theoretical prediction. The variance of the revenues in the first-price auction is smaller than in the Vickrey auction.

To summarize, both Güth *et al.* (2005) and Pezanis-Christou (2002) observe that the first-price sealed-bid auction outperforms the Vickrey auction in asymmetric environments. The first-price auction yields substantially more revenue than the Vickrey auction, while the theory indicates that in Güth *et al.*'s environment this difference would be much less substantial, and that in Pezanis-Christou's environment the revenue ranking would be reversed. Moreover, the variance of the revenue is smaller for the first-price auction than for the Vickrey

---

[7] Efficiency is defined as follows. Let the surplus of an allocation be the sum of the values the winners realize. The efficiency e of the auction outcome is the actual surplus (S^{act}) as a fraction of the maximal surplus (S^{max}): $e = S^{ac}/S^{max}$.

auction. Finally, the efficiency differences between the two auctions are negligible, although the theory indicates that the Vickrey auction is more efficient than the first-price auction. These observations support Klemperer's (2002b) conjecture that in thin markets, first-price auctions perform better than second-price auctions, in contrast to what the theory sometimes suggests.

4.2. Auctions of multiple homogeneous objects

Sometimes governments auction multiple homogeneous objects while they allow bidders to acquire more than one object. The UMTS auctions in Germany and Austria provide clear examples that fit this setup. Both countries made use of the simultaneous ascending auction to sell their UMTS licenses. In Germany as well as in Austria, twelve blocks of spectrum were sold from which bidders could buy two or three blocks. Thus the industry structure was determined by the auction itself. One salient outcome is that four bidders each buy three blocks, while another focal outcome is the one where six bidders each buy two blocks. Some observers noted that this design exploits preemptive motives of incumbent firms, as it allows them to coordinate and keep price-fighting entrants out of the aftermarket. In such a preemptive process incumbent firms win the available spectrum and drive up the revenue. Others commented that this design could easily lead to the opposite outcome where six bidders choose to reduce demand and be satisfied with two blocks each to ensure that auction prices stay low. In fact, the German outcome was in between these two extremes. Deutsche Telecom continued pushing up the price when the market could have been divided among six bidders, but then ended the auction before working one or two of the participating newcomers out of the market. In Austria the auction outcome was in line with the strategic demand reduction prediction, as six bidders were satisfied with two blocks each after only a few rounds of bidding. These two outcomes suggest that a high variance may exist in the outcomes of a simultaneous ascending auction in this kind of setup, but two observations are of course way to few to draw statistically meaningful conclusions.

In a series of experiments, Goeree, Offerman and Sloof (2004a) investigate which outcome prevails in the simultaneous ascending auction in this kind of setup. Another goal of this study is to compare the performance of the simultaneous ascending auction with the discriminatory auction, that is easily defined in this environment. In the discriminatory auction, bidders may simultaneously submit multiple sealed bids. The seller awards the identical objects to the highest bids at prices equal to the bids. In theory, the discriminatory auction supports neither the strategic demand equilibrium nor the preemptive equilibrium of the simultaneous ascending auction. Thus, a comparison of the auction formats depends on the equilibrium that tends to be selected in the simultaneous ascending auction.

In particular, Goeree *et al.* (2004a) consider the following situation. Two incumbents compete with one entrant for six identical objects. To keep the theoretical model tractable and the experimental procedure simple, bidders have flat demand for the objects offered for sale, which means that each bidder draws one private value that is valid for each object acquired. Each bidder can only buy up to three objects. If the entrant acquires one or more objects, a negative external effect is inflicted upon the incumbents. The incumbents can only avoid the negative external effect if they manage to keep the entrant completely out of the market. Subjects either participate in the discriminatory auction or in the simultaneous ascending auction. Each auction format is run through three different regimes, one where the negative external effect is absent, another one where a mild negative external effect exists and a final one with a strong negative external effect.

In the experiments, demand reduction in the simultaneous ascending auction is widespread. For each level of external effect, demand reduction is observed more frequently (60.4%, 25.5% and 30.3% for the no, low and high negative external effect, respectively) than the preemptive bidding outcome (7.2%, 14.8% and 20.4% for the no, low and high negative external effect, respectively).[8] As a consequence, the ascending auction raises substantially lower revenue at a higher variance than the discriminatory auction: with no (mild) [strong] external effect, it raises 26.0% (51.0%) [51.9%] of the revenue of the discriminatory auction. Although equilibrium predictions

---

[8] There are also cases in practice where firms successfully "divided the market" (see Cramton and Schwartz, 2000 for the FCC auctions and Jehiel and Moldovanu, 2001, and Grimm *et al.*, 2003 for the auction for second-generation mobile telecommunication licenses in Germany).

track the observed revenues of the discriminatory auctions quite well, subjects' bidding behavior departs from predicted bidding in several ways. Perhaps the most striking departure is that subjects, unlike theory predicts, submit different bids for identical objects. This feature of actual bidding is the main reason why the discriminatory auction leads to higher entry than predicted in the equilibrium. Similar high levels of entry characterize the simultaneous ascending auction, because there incumbents and entrants tend to peacefully divide the supplied objects. From this perspective the two auction formats lead to similar levels of efficiency. However, the discriminatory auction does a better job in assigning the objects to the bidders with the higher private values, as in the demand reduction of equilibrium of the ascending auction each bidder receives two objects independently of her private value. In this sense, the discriminatory auction yields higher efficiency levels than the simultaneous ascending auction. This result contrasts strongly with the rhetorics of some popular texts on this topic, that advocate the simultaneous ascending auction as a useful tool to "put the licenses in the hands of the firms who value them most."

The bidding data of the simultaneous ascending auction reveal an empirical selection device. It turns out that incumbents only pursue the preemptive equilibrium when they have high private values. With low private values incumbents figure out that there is not much chance to keep the entrant out of the market. If one incumbent settles for demand reduction, the other bidders often reduce their demand quickly. An intuitive empirical finding is that with a stronger negative external effect the threshold value above which incumbents tend to pursue preemption decreases.

A sizable minority of the outcomes of the simultaneous ascending auction is characterized as a cheap preemptive attempt (8.1%, 22.1% and 18.9% for the no, low and high negative external effect respectively). As in the German auction, in quite a few auctions the incumbents try to work the entrant out of the market, but if this attempt is not successful at moderate prices one incumbent chooses to reduce demand and the other incumbent and the entrant follow swiftly. In the regime with a mild negative external effect, the experimental auctions that are characterized as cheap preemptive attempts even outnumber the auctions characterized as true preemptive attempts (where incumbents are willing to bid their value or more on all three objects).

The study by Goeree *et al.* (2004a) complements previous experimental studies that investigate the phenomenon of demand reduction in situations without negative external effects. Alsemgeest *et al.* (1998) compare the ascending auction and a sealed-bid auction where the price equals the lowest accepted bid. They consider two regimes, one where bidders only demand one unit and another where bidders demand two units. The sealed-bid mechanism raises higher revenue than the ascending auction in both regimes. Alsemgeest *et al.* observe some demand reduction in the ascending auctions where bidders have demand for two units. In a field experiment, List and Lucking-Reiley (2000) observe some demand reduction when they sell sports cards in a uniform-price auction (the auction where all winning bidders pay a price equal to the highest rejected bid). Nevertheless, the uniform-price auction does not raise less revenue than the Vickrey auction because bidders tend to bid too high on their first units.[9] Kagel and Levin (2001) have a human bidder with two units demand participate against a computer in a uniform-price auction, an ascending auction and the Vickrey/Ausubel auction. The ascending auction produces a higher level of demand reduction than the uniform-price auction, even though a substantial level of demand reduction is observed in the latter auction. Engelmann and Grimm (2004) run five auction formats: the uniform-price, the ascending, the discriminatory, the Vickrey and the Ausubel auction. They observe a higher level of demand reduction in the ascending auction than in the uniform-price auction. The discriminatory auction outperforms the other auctions in terms of raising revenue.

Pooling across studies, the conclusion is that demand reduction is a real danger in uniform-price auctions and even more so in simultaneous ascending auctions. Surprisingly, demand reduction is even more likely than preemptive bidding in situations where entrants inflict negative externalities upon incumbents. In the setting where bidders may buy multiple homogeneous objects, the discriminatory auction performs better than the simultaneous ascending auction.

---

[9] In an m-object Vickrey auction bidders submit as many individual unit bids as they like. The top m bids are declared winning bids. For the kth unit won by a bidder, she pays a price equal to the kth highest of the rejected bids submitted by others. Demand reduction is not supported as an equilibrium phenomenon in a Vickrey auction. The Ausubel auction is a continuous version of the Vickrey auction.

4.3. *Auctions of multiple heterogeneous objects*

Quite often governments consider auctions to assign heterogeneous licenses with the restriction that each bidder can obtain at most one license. The results reported in the previous section cannot directly be extrapolated to this case. Most importantly, the rules of the discriminatory auction need to be adapted when the licenses are heterogeneous and bidders are restricted to one license each. In a discriminatory auction with heterogeneous licenses, it may occur that one and the same bidder has the highest bid on more than one license. In that case it may be true that the revenue for the seller is larger when this bidder is awarded her second highest instead of her highest bid. For instance, assume that there are two bidders and two licenses. Bidder 1 bids 20 on license A and 18 on license B, while bidder 2 bids 10 on license A and 1 on license B. If license A (B) is awarded to bidder 1 (2), the revenue is 21, whereas the other allocation where bidder 1 wins license B raises a revenue of 28. Still, even if it is not straightforward to incorporate a first-price element in the auction, the evidence obtained for other cases suggests that it may be worthwhile to search for ways to introduce one.

Goeree *et al.* (2006) compare the standard simultaneous ascending auction with three versions of a discriminatory auction. The first version of the discriminatory auction is the so-called "simultaneous first-price auction." In this format, each bidder simultaneously submits (at most) one bid for each license for sale. The seller collects all the bids and assigns the licenses such that the revenue is as high as possible and each bidder is assigned at most one license. In the sequential first-price version the licenses are sold sequentially one after the other. In a sequential auction the seller has to decide whether she wants to put up the best license first ("best foot forward") or whether she keeps the best licenses for last ("best for last"). In the simultaneous descending auction, for each license a clock starts moving down from a very high price. The first bidder who stops the clock of a license buys the license and pays a price equal to the level of the clock. The clocks of the other licenses move further down until one is stopped by a second bidder. This bidder buys the license at a price equal to the level where she stopped the clock. This process continues until all available licenses are sold.[10]

---

[10] The authors do not consider a right-to-choose auction, which could be an interesting alternative in environments with heterogeneous objects (see Section 6).

The sale of licenses in the thin Dutch FM-radio market was taken as the motivating example for the study of Goeree *et al.* (2006), and the experiments were designed accordingly. That is, in each auction four bidders competed for three licenses. Subjects participated in one auction format only. They were run through different environments with increasing complexity. In the first environment, subjects drew a separate private value for each of the licenses. In this setting, there were differences in the quality of the licenses but bidders were symmetric (i.e., distributions that were used to draw the values varied across licenses but not across bidders). In the second environment asymmetries between the bidders were introduced. In these auctions, three "strong" bidders competed against one "weak" bidder (the support of the distributions of the private values of the weak bidder started below the support of the strong bidders and partly overlapped the support of the strong bidders). The third environment differed from the second in the sense that the private values of the bidders were multiplied by an unknown common value component (that reflected unknown developments in the demand of the product market). Each bidder received a private estimate of this common value component. In the final environment, an additional layer of realism was added to the experiment. Here, prior to the auction subjects sequentially made the decision whether or not to enter the auction at an opportunity cost.

Although this type of auction is intractable from a theoretical point of view, it is a useful test-bed for some of the intuitions of auction experts. As said, Klemperer (2002b) pointed out that in uncompetitive circumstances, first-price auctions may be more attractive to entrants since they offer the possibility of surprise. In a first-price auction, an incumbent firm may be too optimistic about the profit margin in its bid such that there is scope for a weak entrant to submit a higher bid. Another intuition of auction experts is that in a sequential auction with common value uncertainty, it is better to save the best licenses for last. The idea is that in the sale of the first licenses information about the common value component is released. With less uncertainty bidders can bid more aggressively later in the auction. From this perspective, it is better to sell the good licenses last, because then the most aggressive bidding is observed on the superior licenses. In agreement with this intuition, in March 2000 the Swiss auctioned three nationwide wireless-local-loop licenses in increasing order of value. Surprisingly, the first two identical licenses were sold for 121 and 134 million francs respectively, while the third superior license sold for only 55 million francs. This result suggests that it may be wiser to sell the good licenses first when all interested bidders are present to drive up the price, although again it is hard to generalize from one observation only.

The experimental results of Goeree *et al.* (2006) underline the strength of first-price auctions when it comes to raising high revenue at low variance. From the revenue perspective all first-price auctions perform better than the simultaneous ascending auction. In line with the Swiss experience, the sequential first-price auction where the seller uses the best-foot-forward strategy provides the most promising way to incorporate a first-price element when the goal is to generate high revenue: pooled across all environments, it raises 15% more revenue than the simultaneous ascending auction. The high revenues of the first-price auctions come at a price for efficiency though. The simultaneous ascending auction is the superior mechanism when the goal is to assign the licenses to the bidders with the highest private values. Notice that here the simultaneous ascending auction is not hindered by the possibility of demand reduction, because each bidder is restricted to one license.

The experimental results suggest a refinement of the idea that first-price auctions are conducive to entry of weak bidders. In fact, with an exogenous number of bidders, the first-price auctions promise less profits to the winners of the auction. As expected, first-price auctions increase the prospects for weak bidders to win a license relative to second-price auctions. At the same time, however, the amount that winners win is less than in the simultaneous ascending since first-price auctions elicit more aggressive bidding. As a result, Goeree *et al.* do not observe more entry by weak bidders in first-price auctions than in the simultaneous ascending auction. In fact, with endogenous entry the differences in the auctions' performances tend to diminish.

Finally, the simultaneous ascending auction shows the highest incidence of winner's curse outcomes and the highest variance in per-license profits. These facts may cause feelings of injustice and may result in bankruptcies or costly lawsuits after the auction.

4.4. Summary

In this section, we have observed that laboratory experiments confirm Klemperer's (2002b) conjecture that first-price auctions perform better than second-price auctions in uncompetitive environments. First-price auctions raise more revenue at a lower variance than second-price auctions. The results regarding efficiency depend on the setting. If the possibility of demand reduction exists, the simultaneous ascending auction may achieve a lower level of efficiency. If bidders are restricted to one license each, second-price auctions and the simultaneous ascending auction are more efficient than first-price auctions, but often the differences are small, and sometimes not even statistically significant.

5. Hybrid auctions

In the previous section, we concluded that in thin markets, first-price auctions often outperform second-price auctions. One disadvantage of first-price auctions relative to second-price auctions could be that in second-price auctions, bidders can take into account information that is released by the bidding strategies of other bidders. This feature is even more prominent in the English auction, as bidders observe when others leave the auction. In order to combine the best of both worlds, Klemperer (1998) proposes the Anglo-Dutch auction as an alternative auction format that could work well in uncompetitive markets. The Anglo-Dutch auction is a hybrid auction that combines features of first-price and second-price auctions. We discuss this auction in Section 5.1. Other hybrid auctions that are tested in the lab are the Dutch-Anglo auction and premium auctions, which are the topics of Sections 5.2 and 5.3. Section 5.4 summarizes the main findings in these experiments.

5.1. Anglo-Dutch auction

The Anglo-Dutch auction has the following rules for k identical licenses and the restriction of one license per bidder. The auction consists of two stages:

1. The auctioneer raises the price round by round. In each round, each bidder can decide to leave or stay in the auction. If a bidder leaves the auction, she cannot re-enter. This round ends as soon as no more than $k+1$ bidders are left.
2. The $k+1$ remaining bidders submit a sealed bid, which should at least be equal to their highest first-stage bid. The highest k bidders

win a license. The amount they pay depends on the format. In the discriminatory Anglo-Dutch auction, each winner pays her bid. In the uniform Anglo-Dutch auction, each winner pays the kth highest bid.

Note that this auction is a hybrid between two types of standard auctions. Klemperer (1998) conjectures that the Anglo-Dutch format combines the best of both worlds. The first-price element (stage 2) makes the auction attractive for weak bidders, as they are better able to compete against the strong ones. Moreover, in the ascending phase (stage 1), bidders can deduce valuable information from the other bidders' behavior, which could increase the efficiency of the auction and the seller's revenue, as bidders are less likely to be prone to the winner's curse. To our knowledge, this claim has not been proved yet in a formal model.

In an experiment, Abbink *et al.* (2005) explore a design that resembles the UK UMTS auction as closely as possible. They study the situation that was prevalent two years before the actual auction, when the British Radiocommunication Agency (BRA) intended to sell four almost identical licenses (instead of five as in the actual auction). As the number of incumbents was also four, BRA's advisors feared that a simultaneous ascending auction would hardly attract entry, as they expected entrants to have little chance to win a license in this format (Binmore and Klemperer, 2002). Abbink and his coauthors compare the performance of the discriminatory Anglo-Dutch auction, the uniform Anglo-Dutch auction and the English auction.

They study a situation with eight bidders: four incumbents (denoted by INC) and four potential new entrants (NEW). The value of a license to bidder i is the sum of a private value component v_i (which may differ between bidders) and a common value component c (which is the same for all bidders). Each bidder i draws v_i from the set $\{-100, -99, \ldots, +100\}$. INC-type (NEW-type) bidders draw their value with 80% (20%) probability independently and uniformly from the set $\{0, 1, \ldots, 100\}$ and with the remaining 20% (80%) probability from $\{-100, -99, \ldots, 0\}$. The common value c is randomly drawn from the set $C \equiv \{1000, 1001, \ldots, 1500\}$. The bidders were not informed about c or C, but each bidder i received a signal s_i which was commonly known to be independently and uniformly drawn from the set $D(c) \equiv \{c-200, c-199, \ldots, c+200\}$.

Table 10.1 *Efficiency, entry and revenue in Abbink et al.'s (2005) experiment*

Auction	Efficiency	Entry	Revenue
Discriminatory Anglo-Dutch	74.9%	1.5	93.8%
Uniform Anglo-Dutch	69.8%	1.7	95.1%
English	69.4%	1.9	94.7%
Efficient	100%	1.1	

In a closely related setting, Goeree and Offerman (2002) show both theoretically and experimentally that an efficient outcome is not always reached. The reason is that an efficient allocation can only be realized if bidders condition their bids only on their private information. But, naturally, the equilibrium bids are strictly increasing in a bidder's signal on the common value. Inefficient allocations arise as in equilibrium, bidders with a high signal on the common value and a low private value could outbid bidders with a low signal on the common value and a high private value.

Abbink *et al.* compare the auctions on several dimensions. They define the surplus of an allocation as the sum of the values the winners realize. The efficiency *e* of the auction outcome is the difference between the actual surplus (S^{act}) and the minimal surplus (S^{min}) as a fraction of the difference between the maximal surplus (S^{max}) and the minimal surplus:

$$e = \frac{S^{act} - S^{min}}{S^{max} - S^{min}}.$$

They also look at entry, i.e., the number of NEW-type bidders that win a license. Moreover, they measure revenue as standardized revenue, i.e., total revenue as fraction of S^{max}. Table 10.1 summarizes the outcomes of the three auction formats relative to the efficient outcome.

The experiment of Abbink *et al.* shows that the nice properties of first-price auctions in thin markets, relative to second-price auctions, do not carry over to the Anglo-Dutch auction, even though this auction is expected to combine the best of first-price and second-price auctions. The Anglo-Dutch formats that are considered do not outperform the English auction in any of three dimensions: efficiency, entry and revenue.

Binmore and Klemperer (2002) criticize Abbink *et al.*'s design in the sense that potential newcomers were relatively strong: on average, one entrant has a higher value than at least one incumbent. It may be more realistic that all incumbents have higher values than all entrants, and that this is common knowledge to all bidders. Moreover, entry into the auction was costless, while in practice, bidders do have to make some costs to enter. Although these costs may be negligible relative to the total value of a license, if a bidder expects not to win a license, she will not enter. Therefore, it remains interesting for future research to see how Anglo-Dutch auctions perform in other circumstances.

5.2. Dutch-Anglo auction

The Dutch-Anglo auction is another hybrid auction that is sometimes used in practice to sell a single indivisible object. The auction consists of the following two stages:

1. All bidders submit a sealed bid. The highest bidder wins and pays her bid if the difference between her bid and the second highest bid is at least equal to some $z \in (0, \infty)$. Otherwise, all bidders for whom the difference between the highest bid and their own bid is smaller than z, enter stage 2.
2. The remaining bidders then play the English auction with a reserve price equal to the highest bid in the first stage.

This auction format was used by the Brazilian government in the partial privatization of the telecommunications firm Telebras (Dutra and Menezes, 2001). Dutra and Menezes study an auction in the lab that is closely related to the Dutch-Anglo auction: the Dutch-Vickrey auction. The Dutch-Vickrey auction has the same rules as the Dutch-Anglo auction with the exception that in the second stage, the Vickrey auction is played instead of the English auction. Dutra and Menezes make the following additional assumptions:

- Three bidders compete for the object.
- Each bidder draws her private value for the object independently from the set $\{0,3,6\}$, where the first (second, third) element has probability 0.4 (0.3).

Dutra and Menezes (2002) solve for the equilibrium of this auction, and show that for risk-neutral bidders, the Dutch-Vickrey auction's revenue dominates the first-price sealed-bid auction.[11] Moreover, both auction formats are efficient in the sense that the winner of the auction is the bidder who attaches the highest value to the object.

In their experiment, Dutra and Menezes (2001) compare the first-price sealed-bid auction with two instances of the Dutch-Vickrey auction, with $z = 1$ and $z = 3/2$. They do so using a within-subject design. In the first six rounds, the object was sold in the first-price sealed-bid auction. In rounds 7–12 (13–18), the Dutch-Vickrey auction with $z = 1$ ($z = 3/2$) was used to sell the object.

Dutra and Menezes' (2001) experiment partly confirms the theory. They find that both auction formats are highly efficient. However, they cannot reject the hypothesis that the three auctions yield the same expected revenue. Most observations are higher than the risk-neutral equilibrium, but none of the auction format's revenue dominates the others.

Still, Dutra and Menezes' experiment leaves several questions open for further research. Would a between-subject treatment induce the same results as the within-subjects treatment that the researchers choose? How does the Dutch-Vickrey auction perform relative to the English auction? How does the Dutch-Vickrey auction perform in thin markets?

5.3. Premium auctions

In practice, hybrid auctions often offer a premium to the highest losing bidder. Premium auctions have been employed in Belgium and the Netherlands since the Middle Ages (Sikkel, 2001). These auctions are used to sell houses, land, boats, machinery and equipment. Many Belgian and Dutch cities claim that their own variant is unique in the world. Although actual premium auctions differ in the institutional details, they all share the feature of offering a premium to the highest losing bidder in order to stir up competition. Goeree and Offerman (2004) consider a stylized premium auction that captures the essential features of a premium auction. They refer to this format as the Amsterdam auction, since Amsterdam has a particular prominent history of premium auctions.

---

[11] The theoretical revenue result may be an artefact of the chosen design. When bidders draw their private values from the same continuous distribution, the revenue equivalence theorem seems to apply.

Goeree and Offerman investigate the situation where a seller sells a single object in an Amsterdam auction. Like the Anglo-Dutch and the Dutch-Anglo auction, the Amsterdam auction consist of two phases:

1. The price level rises until all but two bidders have dropped out. Both bidders enter phase 2.
2. The level at which the last bidder dropped out of the first phase is the reserve price for the second phase. The two remaining bidders submit a sealed bid in the second phase that must be at least as high as the reserve price of the first phase. The highest bidder wins the object for sale and pays a price equal to their own bid in the first-price Amsterdam auction and a price equal to the other finalist's sealed bid in the second-price Amsterdam auction. Both finalists receive a premium proportional to the difference of the lowest sealed bid in the second phase and the reserve price.[12]

In a symmetric private value model, the Amsterdam auction is revenue equivalent with standard auctions like the English auction or the first-price auction (the outcome is efficient and with more than two bidders, the bidder with the lowest possible value expects to earn a zero profit like in standard auctions). However, actual real-estate auctions tend to be characterized by asymmetries between bidders. Usually genuinely interested buyers compete with speculators out for a bargain. Premium auctions may provide an effective tool to exploit asymmetries between bidders. The premium stimulates weak bidders (speculators) to set an endogenous reserve price for the strong bidders (the genuinely interested buyers). Competition between weak bidders dissipates the premium that they can earn. For the single unit case, the optimal auction is well known (Myerson, 1981) and can easily be used as a benchmark.

In a series of experiments, Goeree and Offerman compare the performance of the two Amsterdam auctions, the first-price auction, the English auction and the optimal auction under varying degrees of

---

[12] Notice that it is quite straightforward to design a k-identical objects Amsterdam auction. One possibility is that in the first phase the price rises until $k + 1$ bidders are left. These bidders submit a sealed bid in the second phase, the highest k bids win an object and bidders in the second phase receive a premium proportional to the difference of the lowest sealed bid and the reserve price. Other implementations also seem plausible and future work should identify the best way to generalize the Amsterdam auction to the multi-unit case.

asymmetry. They vary the auction format across sessions and the degree of asymmetry within sessions. First, four subjects compete in a symmetric environment where all draw an independent private value from a uniform U[0,60] distribution. Then mild asymmetries are introduced as one strong bidder who receives a private value from a U[40,100] distribution competes against three weak bidders who continue to draw their values independently from a U[0,60] distribution. The final part makes use of strong asymmetries where the distributions of the strong buyer U[70,100] and the weak buyers U[0,60] do not overlap anymore. In the premium auctions the two finalists receive a premium of 30% of the difference of the lowest sealed bid and the reserve price.

In the symmetric environment, the two versions of the Amsterdam auction raise a roughly equal revenue to the English auction, as theory predicts. As usual, the English auction is outperformed by the first-price auction when bidders are symmetric. The first-price auction raises about 10% more revenue at a lower variance. With mild asymmetries, the first-price auction, the first-price Amsterdam auction and the optimal auction all generate roughly 20% more than the English auction. With strong asymmetries, the second-price Amsterdam auction and the optimal auction raise about 15% more revenue than the first-price auction, and about 45% more revenue than the English auction. Interestingly, the optimal auction hardly ever outperforms the Amsterdam auction.

The English auction performs better in assigning the object to the bidder with the highest private value, although the efficiency differences with the first-price auction are surprisingly small (98.5% for the English auction versus 96.7% for the first-price auction, pooled across all environments). Raising revenue through an Amsterdam auction comes at a cost of reducing efficiency (efficiency levels drop to 94.0% in the first-price Amsterdam auction, 90.3% in the second-price Amsterdam auction and 91.2% in the optimal auction). On the other hand, the Amsterdam auctions stimulate serious participation by bidders with low private values. In contrast to the English auction, weak bidders are more inclined to participate in the Amsterdam auctions as asymmetries grow. In fact, with strong asymmetries 39.1% of the bids in the English auction are almost zero, while in the Amsterdam auctions only 4.2% (first-price Amsterdam) and 6.5% (second-price Amsterdam) of the bids are almost zero. As such, the

Amsterdam auction may be an attractive format to pursue efficiency if a government wants to stimulate entry into a collusive industry.

5.4. Summary

Among the hybrid auctions (Anglo-Dutch, Dutch-Anglo and Amsterdam), the results for the Amsterdam auction seem most promising. In the environments that are investigated, both the Anglo-Dutch auction and the Dutch-Anglo auction do not outperform standard auctions. This is in sharp contrast to the Amsterdam auction in which the seller stirs up competition by offering a premium to the highest losing bidder. In environments with asymmetries between bidders, the Amsterdam auction raises substantially more revenue than a standard ascending auction. Moreover, it occurs relatively more often that a newcomer wins a license even if it is less cost-effective than an incumbent firm.

6. Selling the right to choose

In this section, we consider the case in which a seller sells multiple heterogeneous objects of comparable value. When auctioneers fear that there is little demand for each object separately, they often switch to using so-called "right-to-choose auctions" or "pooled auction". In these auctions, the auctioneer gives the winners the opportunity to choose their most favorite object. In Sections 6.1 and 6.2, we focus on right-to-choose auctions and pooled auctions respectively. Section 6.3 includes a summary.

6.1. Right-to-choose auctions

In a right-to-choose auction (also known as "bidder's choice auctions" or "choice selling"), bidding proceeds in multiple rounds. The highest bidder of the first round selects the object that she likes best. This item is deleted from the list and the remaining objects are offered in the second round. Again the highest bidder of this round selects her preferred object which is then deleted from the list of objects, and so on, until all objects are sold. This is a common method to sell real-estate and condominiums in the US (Ashenfelter and Genesove, 1992). It is also frequently employed to sell jewelry, movie posters, lamps, watches, pottery, glassware and militaria. In 2004, the Dutch government used a right-to-choose auction to assign scarce phone numbers to businesses.

Auctioneers sometimes switch to using this auction format because they believe that there are situations where right-to-choose auctions are the superior revenue-raising mechanism. Auction law attorney Steve Proffitt describes this belief as follows:

> Choice selling sometimes has the ability to generate higher selling prices than straight item-by-item offerings. Auctioneers often don't know who has the most interest in what piece and how much that bidder might be willing to pay to own it. The auctioneer wants to push that bidder as far as he can (and he should), so long as it's done legally and ethically. One way to do this is to force bidders to compete who would not otherwise do so, and choice selling does that. (*www.maineantiquedigest.com/articles/feb04/ethi0204.htm*)

Burguet (2005, 2007) provides a theoretical investigation of right-to-choose auctions when a seller sells two items and each bidder's private values for the two items can be summarized by a single parameter. When bidders are risk neutral, the right-to-choose auction is revenue equivalent to standard good-by-good auctions (like a sequential Vickrey auction and a simultaneous ascending auction). With risk-averse bidders, right-to-choose auctions generate higher revenues than the sequential Vickrey auction or the simultaneous ascending auction: the intuition is that risk-averse bidders dislike the uncertainty arising from not winning the first round – the winner of the first round might pick their most preferred good – and as a consequence they are willing to raise their bids in the first round.[13] Eliaz *et al.* (2008) extend the theoretical analysis to the case where the seller sells $k>2$ objects and where there are $n>k$ interested bidders for each object. Again, revenue equivalence results for the case where bidders are risk neutral. Eliaz *et al.* identify an interesting trick that a seller may use in a right-to-choose auction. By selling rights to choose instead of heterogeneous objects, the seller artificially creates monopoly power. As a consequence, the seller may raise more revenue by restricting the number of rights to choose offered for sale. Selling fewer rights than available goods enhances the expected revenue of the seller.

---

[13] Burguet also explains why prices decline in successive rounds of a right-to-choose auction, a phenomenon observed by Ashenfelter and Genesove (1992).

Experimental tests of right-to-choose auctions are provided by Goeree, Plott and Wooders (2004b) and Eliaz *et al.* (2008). Goeree *et al.* (2004b) consider the case where a seller sells two heterogeneous goods to four buyers through either an ascending right-to-choose auction or a simultaneous ascending auction. In both auctions, bidders who do not have the current highest bid have the possibility to submit a higher bid than the current highest bid. Bidding stops if in a given time interval no new bid is submitted. Bidders can buy at most one good. The experimental results confirm the revenue-raising virtues of the ascending right-to-choose auction: the right-to-choose auction raises almost 20% more revenue than the simultaneous ascending auction. Maximum likelihood estimation shows that a utility function of $u(x) = x^{0.39}$ matches the data well. Thus, consistent with Burguet, the authors are able to explain their data with risk aversion. Interestingly, the increase in revenue hardly affects the efficiency level of the auctions: the right-to-choose auction achieves an efficiency level of 98.4%, only slightly below the efficiency level of the simultaneous ascending auction (100.0%).

In their experiment, Eliaz *et al.* (2008) use a tougher benchmark to judge the performance of the second-price right-to-choose auction. They compare how this auction performs in comparison to the theoretically optimal auction. For completeness, they also consider a standard Vickrey good-by-good auction. All auctions are implemented via the second-price format, which means that the highest bidder wins and pays a price equal to the second highest bid. In particular, Eliaz *et al.* focus on the setup where a seller has four heterogeneous goods for sale while each good only attracts two interested buyers. They also investigate the possibility of reducing quantity via a right-to-choose auction, by having a treatment where the seller offers three rights to choose from the four available goods. The right-to-choose auction strongly outperforms the standard good-by-good auction in terms of raising revenue: the seller collects 40% more revenue in the right-to-choose auction. Like in Goeree *et al.*, the right-to-choose auction achieves an efficiency level close to the one of the good-by-good auction (98.2% for the right-to-choose auction versus 98.3% for the good-by-good auction).

Surprisingly, the right-to-choose auction even raises more revenue than the theoretically optimal auction. Indeed, the bids in the right-to-choose auction are so competitive that it is not possible to explain them with reasonable degrees of risk-aversion. Instead, the authors argue that the right-to-choose auction induces a competitive mindset such that only bidders with very high private values dare to submit bids below value in early phases as all are supposed to do. Given the staggering amounts raised in the right-to-choose auction, there is hardly room for improvement when the seller reduces quantity. Therefore, it is not surprising that with quantity reduction the seller raises a roughly similar revenue as without quantity reduction. Nevertheless, a right-to-choose auction with quantity reduction is still an interesting option because it is the format with the smallest variance in revenue.

6.2. Pooled auctions

A related type of auction is the so-called "pooled auction." In this auction, $n>2$ bidders simultaneously submit one sealed bid for k heterogeneous objects, $n>k>1$. The highest bidder chooses her preferred object and pays a price equal to her own bid. The second highest bidder then chooses from the list of remaining objects and pays a price equal to his own bid. This procedure continues until all objects are sold. Menezes and Monteiro (1998) characterize the risk-neutral equilibrium of the pooled auction. Salmon and Iachini (2007) test the pooled auction in an experiment, and compare its performance with that of a simultaneous ascending auction. Like the right-to-choose auctions, pooled auctions elicit competitive bidding and thereby raise higher revenue than the simultaneous ascending auction. The disadvantage of a pooled auction is that bidders often experience losses, when they have to pay a high bid while their preferred objects have already been chosen by others. In practice, these losses may lead to bankruptcy or costly renegotiation by bidders who prefer to get out of the deal.

6.3. Summary

Both right-to-choose auctions and pooled auctions induce more competitive bidding in thin markets with heterogeneous objects relative to standard auctions. In the lab, both auctions are found to raise considerably more revenue than standard auctions, while achieving an almost equal level of efficiency as the simultaneous ascending auction.

For pooled auctions, these advantages may come at the cost of over-bidding.

7. Conclusions

Auction design matters in thin markets. Experiments demonstrate that if the number of bidders is small compared to the number of objects for sale, details of the auction may have a tremendous effect on the outcome. For standard auctions, the most robust results pertain to the revenue-raising qualities of the mechanisms. First-price auctions consistently raise higher revenue than the simultaneous ascending auction and they do so at a lower variance. This is even true for cases where standard theory predicts the opposite result.

The results for efficiency are more delicate and depend in more detail on the specific situation of the auction. For instance, when a government sells multiple licenses and each bidder can buy more than one license, experiments show that the theoretical possibility of demand reduction in the simultaneous ascending auction is indeed a real practical danger. With demand reduction, each bidder gets part of the cake at a low price irrespective of its cost effectiveness. Therefore, against the popular wisdom, the simultaneous ascending auction may not succeed in putting the licenses in the hands of the firms that value them most. In fact, in such a situation a discriminatory auction does a much better job in fulfilling that goal. Interestingly, demand reduction also leads to the rejection of another popular wisdom, which says that the simultaneous ascending auction discourages entry because it facilitates the process by which incumbent firms can keep newcomer firms out of the market. If newcomers anticipate a demand reduction outcome, the ascending auction may be very attractive to them because it gives them a foothold in the industry for a very low price. In fact, the experimental study by Goeree *et al.* (2004a) demonstrates that the two opposite forces approximately balance each other, and that newcomers enter at a similar pace in a discriminatory auction as they do in a simultaneous ascending auction.

If, on the other hand, each bidder is restricted to one license only, demand reduction is excluded by design. In such situations, simul-taneous ascending auctions usually do the better job in assigning the licenses to the cost-effective firms, although differences in efficiency levels between auction formats are often not that large. However,

Goeree *et al.* (2006), in an experiment that endogenizes the entry
decision, do not find support that first-price auctions attract more
entries than the simultaneous ascending auction. It is indeed the case
that in first-price auctions, a newcomer has a higher chance to win a
license, but it is also true that the amount that they win tends to be less
due to aggressive bidding. In the aggregate, the two opposite effects
tend to cancel.

The experimental literature has also identified some promising
exotic auctions. Among the hybrid auctions that are held in two
phases (Anglo-Dutch, Dutch-Anglo, Amsterdam) the results for the
Amsterdam auction seem most promising. By offering a premium to
the highest losing bidder, the seller stirs up competitive bidding by
weak bidders. In environments with asymmetries between bidders, the
Amsterdam auction raises substantially more revenue than a standard
ascending auction. In an Amsterdam auction, it occurs relatively more
often that a newcomer wins a license even if it is less cost-effective
than an incumbent firm. Such outcomes may be desirable if governments want to shake up a collusive industry by selling a license to a
newcomer.

Another interesting format that is often used in practice is a right-
to-choose auction. In this format bidders bid for the right to choose
between heterogeneous objects. This mechanism makes bidders
compete who are interested in different objects and who would not
compete otherwise. In thin markets where there is little interest per
license, a right-to-choose auction may raise considerably more revenue than a standard ascending auction, while it achieves an almost
equal level of efficiency as the simultaneous ascending auction does.
As such, this auction, like the Amsterdam auction, is a prime candidate for practical mechanism design.

There is still a lot to be done.[14] A shortcoming of all studies mentioned in this chapter is that they aim to say something about efficiency in the aftermarket without actually modeling the aftermarket.
In current experimental work, the aftermarket is reduced to a set of
private values. This is not optimal for a couple of reasons. First, it

[14] If you plan to do an experiment yourself it is interesting to surf to Jacob
Goeree's webpage; he is currently developing software that can be used for
laboratory experiments on auctions. See www.hss.caltech.edu/126jkg/
jAuctions.html.

blurs issues that relate to consumer surplus in the aftermarket. Second, Offerman and Potters (2006), the only experimental study that explicitly models the auction together with the aftermarket, shows that auctioning licenses may affect how firms behave in the subsequent market. In particular, in an oligopoly setting, the prices that firms pay to obtain a license enhance the prices that firms charge to consumers in the aftermarket. The explanation offered by Offerman and Potters is that auctions enhance the firms' willingness to embark on a risky but profitable collusive price path. In agreement with this hypothesis, they do not find a price-enhancing effect of auctioning a monopoly license, where collusion is excluded by design. The message of their study is that new insights can be gained if the interaction of firms in license auctions and aftermarkets is not reduced to a simple auction game. In our view, this opens an interesting avenue for future experimental research. The challenge is to design richer games that explicitly model the license auction together with the important processes before and after the auction.

References

Abbink, K., B. Irlenbusch, P. Pezanis-Christou, B. Rockenbach, A. Sadrieh, and R. Selten (2005), An Experimental Test of Design Alternatives for the British 3G/UMTS Auction, *European Economic Review* 49, 505–530.

Abbink, K. and B. Rockenbach (2006), Option Pricing by Students and Professional Traders: A Behavioural Investigation, *Managerial and Decision Economics* 27, 497–510.

Alsemgeest, P., C. Noussair, and M. Olson (1998), Experimental Comparisons of Auctions under Single- and Multi-unit Demand, *Economic Inquiry* 36, 87–97.

Ashenfelter, O. and D. Genesove (1992), Testing for Price Anomalies in Real-Estate Auctions, *American Economic Review* 60, 501–505.

Ausubel, L. M. and P. Cramton (2002), Demand Reduction and Inefficiency in Multi-Unit Auctions, Working paper, University of Maryland.

Ballard, C. L., J. B. Shoven, and J. Whalley (1985), General Equilibrium Computations of the Marginal Welfare Costs of Taxes in the United States, *American Economic Review* 75, 128–38.

Binmore, K. and P. Klemperer (2002), The Biggest Auction Ever: the Sale of the British 3G Telecom Licences, *Economic Journal* 112, C74-C96.

Bulow, J., M. Huang, and P. Klemperer (1999), Toeholds and Takeovers, *Journal of Political Economy* 107, 427–454.

Burguet, R. (2005), The Condominium Problem; Auctions for Substitutes, *Review of Economic Design* 9, 73–90.

(2007), Right-to-choose in Oral Auctions, *Economics Letters* 95, 167–173.

Cramton, P. and J. Schwartz (2000), Collusive Bidding: Lessons from the FCC Spectrum Auctions, *Journal of Regulatory Economics* 17, 229–252.

Das Varma, G. (2002), Standard Auctions with Identity-dependent Externalities, *RAND Journal of Economics* 33, 689–708.

Dutra, J. C. and F. Menezes (2001), Hybrid Auctions II: Experimental Evidence, Working Paper, Australian National University.

(2002), Hybrid Auctions, *Economics Letters* 77, 301–307.

Dyer, D., J. H. Kagel, and D. Levin (1989), A Comparison of Naive and Experienced Bidders in Common Value Offer Auctions: A Laboratory Analysis, *Economic Journal* 99, 108–115.

Eliaz, K., T. Offerman, and A. Schotter (2008), Creating Competition Out of Thin Air: An Experimental Study of Right-to-Choose Auctions, *Games and Economic Behavior* 62, 383–416.

Engelbrecht-Wiggans, R. and C. Kahn (1998), Multi-unit Auctions with Uniform Prices, *Economic Theory* 12, 227–258.

Engelmann, D. and V. Grimm (2004), Bidding Behavior in Multi-unit Auctions: An Experimental Investigation, *Economic Journal*, in press.

Friedman, D. and S. Sunder (1994), *Experimental Methods – A Primer for Economists*, Cambridge University Press.

Gilbert, R. and D. Newbery (1982), Preemptive Patenting and the Persistence of Monopoly, *American Economic Review* 72, 514–526.

Goeree, J. K. and T. Offerman (2002), Efficiency in Auctions with Private and Common Values: An Experimental Study, *American Economic Review* 92, 625–643.

(2004), The Amsterdam Auction, *Econometrica* 72, 281–294.

Goeree, J. K., T. Offerman, and R. Sloof (2004a), Demand Reduction and Preemptive Bidding in Multi-Unit License Auctions, Working paper, University of Amsterdam.

Goeree, J., C. Plott, and J. Wooders (2004b), Bidders' Choice Auctions: Raising Revenues Through the Right to Choose, *Journal of the European Economic Association* 2, 504–515.

Goeree, J. K., T. Offerman, and A. Schram (2006), Using First-Price Auctions to Sell Heterogeneous Licenses, *International Journal of Industrial Organization* 24, 555–581.

Grimm, V., F. Riedel and E. Wolfstetter (2003), Low Price Equilibrium in Multi-Unit Auctions: The GSM Spectrum Auction in Germany, *International Journal of Industrial Organization* 21, 1557–1569.

Güth, W., R. Ivanova-Stenzel, and E. Wolfstetter (2005), Bidding Behavior in Asymmetric Auctions, *European Economic Review* 49, 1891–1913.

Hoppe, H., P. Jehiel, and B. Moldovanu (2006), License Auctions and Market Structure, *Journal of Economics and Management Strategy* 15, 371–396.

Janssen, M. C. W. (2006), Auctions as Coordination Devices, *European Economic Review* 50, 517–532.

Jehiel, P. and B. Moldovanu (2000), Auctions with Downstream Interaction among Buyers, *RAND Journal of Economics* 31, 768–791.

(2001), The European UMTS/IMT-2000 License Auctions, Working paper, University College London.

Jehiel, P., B. Moldovanu, and E. Stacchetti (1996), How (Not) to Sell Nuclear Weapons, *American Economic Review* 86, 814–829.

(1999), Multidimensional Mechanism Design for Auctions with Externalities, *Journal of Economic Theory* 85(2), 258–294.

Kagel, J. and D. Levin (2001), Behavior in Multi-unit Demand Auctions: Experiments with Uniform Price and Dynamic Auctions, *Econometrica* 69, 413–454.

Kagel, J. H. (1995), Auctions: A Survey of Experimental Research, in: J. H. Kagel and A. E. Roth (eds.), *The Handbook of Experimental Economics*, Princeton, NJ, Princeton University Press, 501–585.

Klemperer, P. (1998), Auctions with Almost Common Values: The "Wallet Game" and Its Applications, *European Economic Review* 42, 757–769.

(2002a), How (Not) to Run Auctions: the European 3G Telecom Auctions, *European Economic Review* 46, 829–845.

(2002b), What Really Matters in Auction Design, *Journal of Economic Perspectives* 16, 169–189.

(2004), *Auctions: Theory and Practice*, Princeton University Press.

Krishna, V., (2002), *Auction Theory*, Academic Press.

List, J. and D. Lucking-Reiley (2000), Demand Reduction in Multiunit Auctions: Evidence from a Sportscard Field Experiment, *American Economic Review* 90, 961–972.

Maskin, E. S. and J. G. Riley (2000), Asymmetric Auctions, *Review of Economic Studies* 67, 413–438.

McMillan, J. (1994), Selling Spectrum Rights, *Journal of Economic Perspectives* 8, 145–162.

Menezes, F. and P. Monteiro (1998), Simultaneous Pooled Auctions, *Journal of Real Estate Finance and Economics* 17, 219–232.

Milgrom, P. R. and R. J. Weber (1982), A Theory of Auctions and Competitive Bidding, *Econometrica* 50, 1089–1122.

Motta, M. (2004), *Competition Policy*, Cambridge University Press.

Myerson, R. B. (1981), Optimal Auction Design, *Mathematics of Operations Research* 6, 58–73.

Noussair, C. (1995), Equilibria in a Multi-object Uniform-price Sealed Bid Auction with Multi-unit Demands, *Economic Theory* 5, 337–351.

Offerman, T. and J. Potters (2006), Does Auctioning of Entry Licenses Induce Collusion? An Experimental Study, *Review of Economic Studies* 73, 769–791.

Pezanis-Christou, P. (2002), On the Impact of Low-balling: Experimental Results in Asymmetric Auctions, *International Journal of Game Theory* 31, 69–89.

Plott, C. R. (1997), Laboratory Experimental Testbeds: Applications to the PCS Auction, *Journal of Economics and Management Strategy* 6, 605–638.

Plum, M. (1992), Characterization and Computation of Nash-equilibria for Auctions with Incomplete Information, *International Journal of Game Theory* 20, 393–418.

Roth, A. E. (2002), The Economist as Engineer: Game Theory, Experimental Economics and Computation as Tools of Design Economics, *Econometrica* 70, 1341–1378.

Salmon, T. and M. Iachini (2007), Continuous Ascending vs Pooled Multiple Unit Auctions, *Games and Economic Behavior* 61, 67–85.

Sikkel, M. (2001), Plokken en Mijnen, *Parool* (Dutch newspaper), April 3.

Van Damme, E. (2002), The European UMTS Auctions, *European Economic Review* 46, 846–858.

Vickrey, W. (1961), Counterspeculation, Auctions, and Competitive Sealed Tenders, *Journal of Finance* 16, 8–37.

Wilson, R. B. (1987), Game-Theoretic Approaches to Trading Processess, in: T. Bewley (ed.), *Advances in Economic Theory*: Fifth World Congress, Cambridge University Press.

11 | Investment incentives in auctions: an experiment

VERONIKA GRIMM, FRIEDERIKE MENGEL,
GIOVANNI PONTI AND
LARI ARTHUR VIIANTO *

We experimentally analyze first- and second-price procurement auctions where one bidder can achieve a comparative cost advantage by investment prior to the auction. Theory predicts that bidders invest more often prior to second-price auctions than prior to first-price auctions, which is clearly confirmed by our experimental data. Bidding in the auction (after investment) is more aggressive than the equilibrium prediction in both auction formats.

1. Introduction

Different market institutions provide different incentives for firms to engage in activities that affect their competitive positions. For example, prior to a procurement auction investments can be made either to reduce a firm's own cost of production, or even to raise the cost of possible competitors. Empirical evidence indicates that companies make use of this possibility extensively.[1] Thus, both auction rules *and* investment incentives have to be accounted for when it comes to comparing revenue and efficiency of selling (or buying) institutions.

A number of papers theoretically analyze investment incentives in procurement auctions. Most of them assume that investment decisions are not observable prior to a competition.[2] Then, a typical finding is that

---

* We thank Aitor Calo Blanco, Thyge Benned Jensen, Jaromir Kovárik and Ricardo Martinez for valuable research assistance. We also wish to thank seminar participants in Alicante, Istanbul (SCW 2006), Jena, Sevilla (SMYE 2006) and Valencia (EARIE 2007) for helpful comments. Financial support by the Deutsche Forschungsgemeinschaft and the Instituto Valenciano de Investigaciones Económicas (IVIE) is gratefully acknowledged.
[1] De Silva, Dunne and Kosmopolou (2003).
[2] See Tan (1992), Piccone and Tan (1996), and Bag (1997).

investment is symmetric so that revenue equivalence between market
institutions is preserved also in a model that allows for investment.
This is not necessarily true if investment is observable. If firms strategically react to the decisions made at the investment stage, it is not
immediately clear whether ex ante symmetry implies symmetric
investment. For the case that only one firm has the possibility to invest,
first- and second-price auctions with observable investment have been
analyzed by Arozamena and Cantillon (2004). They show that equilibrium investment is lower prior to first-price auctions than prior to
second-price auctions. The reason is that, in a first-price auction, a
bidder's investment in his own comparative advantage makes his
opponents' bids more aggressive. This strategic effect generally dimin-
ishes benefits from investment; it can even make investment undesirable.

In this chapter we experimentally investigate investment behavior
prior to first- and second-price auction markets in a framework that is
inspired by the model of Arozamena and Cantillon. Throughout the
experiment we ran procurement auctions with two subjects each.
Subjects played a two-stage game. At the first stage, one subject could
invest in order to obtain a superior distribution of cost (not investing
led to symmetry). At stage two, subjects competed in a procurement
auction that was first or second price, depending on the treatment.

As expected, we find that bidding behavior at the auction stage does
not perfectly coincide with equilibrium bidding. In the first-price
auction, bidders bid more aggressively than predicted by the risk-
neutral Nash equilibrium. In the second-price auction, about half of
the bids are close to equilibrium, while a rather large fraction of bids is
below cost. Both observations are standard in the experimental literature on auctions.[3] We find, however, that the relative investment
incentives in the two auction formats are preserved given the observed
behavior at the auction stage. That is, investment incentives given the
actual play are still higher in the second-price than in the first-price
auction, although investment is less profitable than predicted in both
formats. At the investment stage we observe that, in accordance with
the theory, investment is indeed lower prior to first-price auctions than
prior to second-price auctions. Given the actual play in the auctions,
investment is too high in both formats.

---

[3] For surveys, see Kagel (1995) and the chapter by Offerman and Onderstal in this
volume.

To summarize, our experimental evidence clearly shows that participants are aware of the strategic links between the investment and the auction stage. However, observed behavior does not perfectly coincide with the theoretical benchmark. We run two additional treatments to study the potential influence of the (existence of an) investment stage on bidding behavior in the auction more deeply. In our first control treatment we run asymmetric auctions with two players, where the strong player's cost advantage was exogenous. In our second control treatment the opponent's behavior was simulated by a computer algorithm programmed to play the (risk-neutral) symmetric Bayes–Nash equilibrium strategy in both stages. With few exceptions we find no significantly different investment or bidding behavior in either of the two control treatments.

Our chapter is, to the best of our knowledge, the first experimental study on the impact of investment on bidding behavior in procurement auctions. We chose procurement auctions (instead of auctions) since investment in cost reduction is a natural choice to present to participants. There are very few experimental studies of procurement auctions, and, thus, our study (as a byproduct) demonstrates that behavior largely does not depend on the frame. There is, of course, a vast experimental literature on auctions, to which our chapter relates.[4,5] The experimental study which is closest to ours is Güth *et al.* (2005), who study asymmetric first- and second-price auctions (without an investment stage) and afterwards elicit the participants' preferences for the auction format (first- or second-price auction). In this respect, their experimental environment corresponds to our treatment with exogenous investment (with the difference that they deal with a standard auction format) and our findings in this treatment confirm theirs.

The remainder of this chapter is organized as follows. In Section 2 we introduce the theoretical model that was the basis for our experimental design. The experimental design is presented in Section 3, and our hypotheses in Section 4. We report the results in Section 5 and conclude in Section 6. Experimental Instructions and Regression Tables can be found in the Appendices.

---

[4] Kagel (1995).

[5] In this respect, our evidence mostly confirms results from the experimental literature on "standard" auctions (take, for example, more aggressive bidding on behalf of the weak firm).

2. Investment incentives in procurement auctions

2.1. The game

We consider a two-player, two-stage game. At stage one, one of two firms (firm 1) can affect its relative competitive position through an investment in cost reduction. At stage two both firms (1 and 2) compete in a procurement auction. Production costs are privately observed by the firms prior to the procurement auction at stage two. In the following we analyze behavior at both stages for two alternative auction formats: a second-price auction (SPA) and a first-price auction (FPA).

Investment stage

At the investment stage, one of the two firms, say firm 1, can make a decision that affects its production cost at stage two in a probabilistic sense. Investment is a binary choice to realize or not to realize a certain pre-specified reduction of (stage two) production cost. Investment is costly. Investment cost k is observed only by firm 1 prior to its investment decision. Under these assumptions, firm 1's decision can be formalized by an investment function $\delta^f(k)$, where $\delta^f(k) = 1$ ($\delta^f(k) = 0$) denotes the decision (not) to invest when the investment cost is k and the stage two auction format is $f \in \{FPA, SPA\}$. If $\delta^f(k) = 1$ (i.e. firm 1 decides to invest), its production cost at stage two, C_1, is uniformly distributed in $[\underline{c} - w, \overline{c}]$. If $\delta^f(k) = 0$, C_1 is uniformly distributed in $[\underline{c}, \overline{c}]$. In either case, firm 2's production cost, C_2, is drawn uniformly from $[\underline{c}, \overline{c}]$. In other words, if firm 1 decides not to invest, firms are symmetric at stage two. In contrast, if firm 1 invests, its production cost is lower in the sense of first-order stochastic dominance and firms are asymmetric at stage two.[6] In this latter case, we refer to firm 1 (2) as the *strong* (*weak*) bidder.

Auction stage

Prior to bidding in the auction, costs c_1 and c_2 are realized according to the relevant distribution.[7] Each firm observes its own production cost,

---

[6] Note that as we are dealing with procurement auctions, the distribution that is first-order stochastically dominated is advantageous.

[7] We denote random variables by capitals and realizations by the corresponding lower case letters.

but not the other firm's cost. We consider two auction formats: a first-price auction (FPA), and a second-price auction (SPA).

2.2. *Bidding behavior, investment decisions and equilibrium payoffs*

We solve the model by backward induction, starting from stage two. We use the same parameters as in our experimental design, namely $\underline{c} = 300$, $\bar{c} = 400$ and $w = 100$.[8]

Stage two: Equilibrium bid functions
As for SPA, bidding the observed production cost is a weakly dom-inant strategy, independently of whether firm 1 has invested or not. Thus, we have

$$b_i^{SPA}(c_i) = c_i, i = 1, 2, \tag{1}$$

where $b_i^f(c_i)$ *is firm i's bid function under auction format f*, condi-tional on her privately observed production cost c_i.

As for FPA, equilibrium bid functions differ in the symmetric and the asymmetric case. We focus on the risk-neutral symmetric Bayes–Nash equilibrium. In the symmetric case (no investment by firm 1) equilibrium bid functions, for both firms, are

$$b_i^{SPA}(c_i) = \frac{(\bar{c} + c_i)}{2}, i = 1, 2 \tag{2}$$

In the asymmetric case, equilibrium bid-functions are given by

$$b_1^{FPA}(c_1) = \frac{200(6c_1 - 2600 + \sqrt{520000 - 2400c_2 + 3c_1^2})}{3(c_1 - 400)} \tag{3}$$

$$b_2^{FPA}(c_2) = \frac{200(6c_1 - 2200 + \sqrt{2400 + 3c_2^2 - 44000})}{3(c_1 - 400)} \tag{4}$$

---

[8] While we could solve the model also for general values of our parameters, we believe that there is little value added by doing so. Using the parameter configuration of the experiment moreover facilitates interpretation of the data. All our results qualitatively also hold for different parameterizations.

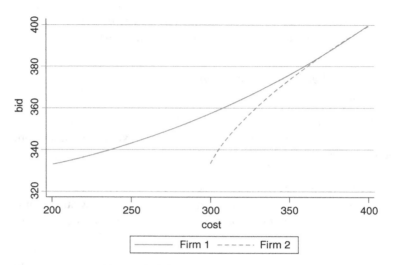

Figure 11.1 Equilibrium bid functions in the asymmetric FPA

Here $b_1^{FPA}(c_1)$ is the bid-function of a firm that has invested and, thus, has the more advantageous cost distribution. See Figure 11.1.

Comparison of (3) and (4) yields that the advantaged bidder should bid point-wisely higher than the disadvantaged bidder, i.e. be less aggressive (recall that we consider a procurement auction). This implies that the ex ante disadvantaged bidder may sometimes win the auction although he observed a higher cost than his opponent. Consequently, the asymmetric first-price auction is inefficient with positive probability.

Stage one: Optimal investment decision

Given the above equilibrium bid functions at stage two, we can calculate the optimal investment decision at stage one. Whether it is beneficial for a firm to invest or not depends on how the firm's competitor reacts. Consequently in order to judge the profitability of an investment, one has to compute the equilibria at stage two for both the asymmetric case (corresponding to $\delta^f(k) = 1$) and the symmetric case (corresponding to $\delta^f(k) = 0$). Investment is profitable whenever investment cost is smaller than the difference between the expected profits obtained in the case of investing ($\delta = 1$) and in the case of not investing ($\delta = 0$). Let $\hat{k}_f$ denote the (equilibrium) investment cost threshold, under auction format $f \in \{FPA, SPA\}$, below which firm 1 should invest.

Optimal investment decision rules, for the two auction formats, are given by

$$
\delta^{SPA}(k) = \begin{cases} 1 & if & k < \hat{k}_{SPA} = 125/3 \\ \{0,1\} & if \ k = \hat{k}_{SPA} \\ 0 & if \ k > \hat{k}_{SPA}. \end{cases} \tag{5}
$$

$$
\delta^{FPA}(k) = \begin{cases} 1 & if & k < \hat{k}_{FPA} = 34 \\ \{0,1\} & if \ k = \hat{k}_{FPA} \\ 0 & if \ k > \hat{k}_{FPA}. \end{cases} \tag{6}
$$

Note that, since $\hat{k}_{FPA} = 34 < \hat{k}_{SPA} = 125/3 \approx 41.67$, in FPA investment is profitable for a smaller range of parameters than in SPA. The reason for this difference is that in the first-price auction investment has a negative strategic effect (through a change in the opponent's bidding behavior), which is not the case in the second-price auction. This can be seen from equations (1) to (4). Investment has no effect on the competitor's bidding behavior in SPA, whereas in FPA it renders the competitor more aggressive in Nash-equilibrium. The reason is that firm 2 (the firm with the "worse" cost distribution) expects tougher competition in the auction than firm 1. Thus, in FPA investment has a drawback, since it makes the opponent relatively more aggressive.

Bidders' equilibrium payoffs

Let us finally present the bidders' equilibrium payoffs in our two auction formats. Payoff here means overall payoff of the entire game, including the investment stage. Obviously this payoff will depend on the cost threshold $\hat{k}_f$, as well as the cost of investment k and the format of the auction. In Table 11.1 we summarize the firms' expected equilibrium payoffs in the first-price and in the second-price auction.

Note that in the symmetric case, both formats yield the same expected payoffs.[9] In the second-price auction, investment by firm 1 decreases firm 2's payoff considerably, whereas in the first-price auction, bidder 2 even benefits from firm 1's investment. This is due to the negative strategic effect of investment.

---

[9] This is due to the revenue equivalence theorem, see e. g. Myerson (1981).

Table 11.1 *Equilibrium payoffs*

| | FPA | | SPA | |
	firm 1	firm 2	firm 1	firm 2
$\delta^f (k) = 1$	50.6 – k	19.4	58.3 – k	8.3
$\delta^f (k) = 0$	16.6	16.6	16.6	16.6

3. The experimental design

The experiment was conducted in seven sessions in May, 2005. A total of 168 students (24 per session) were recruited among the student population of the University of Alicante — mainly undergraduate students from the Economics Department with no (or very little) prior exposure to game theory. All monetary payoffs in the experiment were expressed in Spanish pesetas (€1 is approximately 166 ptas.).[10] Average earnings were about €18.5, for an approximately 90-minute experiment.

Table 11.2 shows our six different treatments. FPA and SPA are the initial treatments with endogenous investment. In treatments EXFPA and EXSPA the asymmetries that could be induced by investment in the first two treatments were exogenously given. In COMPFPA and COMPSPA the opponent of each player was played by a computerized agent.[11]

We ran two sessions each of FPA and SPA and one session each of EXFPA and EXSPA, generating six and three independent observations per treatment, respectively (compare Table 11.2). As for COMPFPA and COMPSPA we ran one session only where twelve participants played each auction format, yielding twelve independent observations.

---

[10] It is standard practice, for all experiments run in Alicante, to use Spanish ptas. as experimental currency. The reason for this design choice is twofold. First, it mitigates integer problems, compared with other currencies (USD or Euros, for example). On the other hand, although Spanish pesetas are no longer in use (substituted by the Euro in the year 2001), Spanish people still use pesetas to express monetary values in their everyday life. In this respect, by using a "real" (as opposed to an artificial) currency, we avoid the problem of framing the incentive structure of the experiment using a scale (e.g. "Experimental Currency") with no cognitive content.

[11] In the treatment with computerized opponents participants were informed that the computer is preprogrammed to play an optimal strategy.

Table 11.2 *The experimental treatments*

	First-price auction	Second-price auction
Stage 1: Investment	FPA	SPA
Stage 2: Auction	(6 indep. observations)	(6 indep. observations)
Exogenous advantage	EXFPA	EXSPA
Asymmetric auction	(3 indep. observations)	(3 indep. observations)
Stage 1: Investment		
Stage 2: Auction against	COMPFPA	COMPSPA
computerized agent	(12 indep. observations)	(12 indep. observations)

The seven experimental sessions were computerized.[12] Written instructions were distributed at the beginning of the experiment and read aloud. At the end of the instructional phase, participants had to answer a set of control questions, to make sure that they had properly understood the key features of the experiment.[13]

In each session, participants played one of the six treatments for a total forty-four rounds. In the first six sessions, participants were divided into three *cohorts* of eight. Participants from different cohorts never interacted with each other throughout the experiment. In each round, participants from a cohort were randomly matched in pairs of two, where each subject played as firm 1 (2) every other round. This was done to enhance the subjects' understanding of strategic effects of investment decisions. Let time interval τ_m be the mth block of eleven rounds such that τ_1 refers to rounds 1–11, τ_2 refers to rounds 12 to 22, and so on. Within each time interval τ_m, participants acting as firm 1 experienced each and every possible investment cost of $k \in \{0, 5, \ldots, 45, 50\}$ ptas. The sequence of costs was randomly selected within each time interval and was different for each cohort and period. After being told the current investment cost k, firm 1 had to decide whether to invest. By this design, we are able to characterize four complete investment functions $\delta^f(k)$, one for each time interval.

---

[12] The experiment was programmed and conducted with the software z-Tree (Fischbacher, 2007).
[13] The instructions for FPA, translated into English, can be found in Appendix B. Instructions for the remaining treatments are available upon request.

Participants participating in the experiment initially received 1,000 ptas. These stakes were chosen to exclude the possibility of bankruptcy. Within each round, each subject received an additional fixed endowment of 10 ptas., while only those who had the opportunity to invest additionally received a fixed payment equivalent to the investment cost k that they had in the current round.[14]

After each of the forty-four rounds, participants were informed of the identity of the stage two auction winner and her own monetary payoffs, as well as all the accumulated monetary payoff so far. The same information was also given in the form of a history table, so that participants could easily review the results of all the rounds that had been played so far.

4. Hypotheses and research questions

The theoretical analysis of Section 2 yields the following working hypotheses for our experiment.

(H1) **Bidding behavior.** Irrespective of the treatments we expect the following bidding behavior at stage two:

    (i) In FPA we expect bidding behavior of strong bidders to be less aggressive than that of weak bidders in the sense that, for any given level of the production cost c, the strong bidder's bid should be higher.

    (ii) In SPA, both strong and weak firms should always bid their production cost c.

(H2) **Payoffs.**

    (i) In treatments FPA, SPA, COMPFPA and COMPSPA, if firm 1 does not invest, firms' payoffs should be the same. This is a consequence of the revenue equivalence theorem, since, in this case, bidders are symmetric.[15]

    (ii) In all treatments, if firm 1 invests, her profits should be higher than firm 2's, and also higher than in the symmetric case.

---

[14] The role of this additional payment is to ensure that a bidder who had invested in FPA (SPA) had the same wealth as a bidder who received the advantage for free in EXFPA (EXSPA). Also the risk of bankruptcy is reduced.

[15] This argument does not apply for EXFPA (EXSPA) where, by construction, all auctions are asymmetric. Also note that revenue equivalence can only be expected *conditional* on the fact that no investment has taken place.

Compared to the symmetric case, firm 2's profits in the asymmetric case are lower (higher) in SPA (FPA). From the auctioneer's point of view, FPA yields a lower procurement cost than SPA (for our particular parametrization).[16]

(H3) **Investment behavior.** Investment incentives are higher in treatments SPA and COMPSPA than in treatments FPA, COMPFPA. This is because, by (5)–(6), firm 1's optimal "threshold" strategy anticipates that, in FPA, firm 2 will bid more aggressively in reaction to firm 1's investment (something that does not happen in SPA).

(H4) **Efficiency.** By (1), the SPA outcome is efficient, independently of whether bidders are asymmetric or not. By contrast, in FPA, the allocation is predicted to be efficient only if firm 1 has not invested (i.e. when bidders face a symmetric auction).

In addition, by comparing treatments FPA and SPA to our four control treatments, we will try to answer the following (more behaviorally oriented) questions:

(HB1) **Does the origin of the comparative advantage matter?** That is, does the existence of the investment stage per se affect behavior at the auction stage?

(HB2) **How does the strategic uncertainty affect participants' behavior?** That is, do participants behave differently in treatments FPA (SPA) and COMPFPA (COMPSPA) because of strategic uncertainty?

5. Experimental results

In this section we report our experimental results. We first test our main hypotheses, H1 to H4, based on the evidence from treatments FPA and SPA in Sections 5.1 to 5.4. Then, in Section 5.5, we report evidence from the remaining four treatments to discuss whether and how the existence of an investment stage affects behavior, apart from what is theoretically predicted.

---

[16] In general, revenues do not compare in an unambiguous way in asymmetric auctions. See Maskin and Riley (2000).

5.1. Bidding behavior (H1)

Bidding behavior in the symmetric auctions (no investment) resembles very much what has been found in the experimental literature so far. In what follows we concentrate on the bidding behavior if the bidders have invested.

FPA

Figures 11.2, 11.3 and 11.4 describe the participants' bidding behavior in FPA. We take three snapshots of the data: in Figure 11.2 (3) we plot a scatter diagram of player 1's (2's) bidding behavior after investment took place in stage one. In Figure 11.4 we report participants' bidding behavior (irrespective of their player position) if investment did not take place.

Figures 11.2 to 11.4 share the same structure. Every point of the scatter diagram corresponds to a cost–bid pair (i.e., an individual observation). The two continuous lines correspond to (i) the equilibrium bid-function derived in Section 2 and (ii) production cost c (which corresponds to the lower bound for any rationalizable bid).

As Figures 11.2 to 11.4 show, participants generally bid above cost, but below the equilibrium prediction, which is in line with most

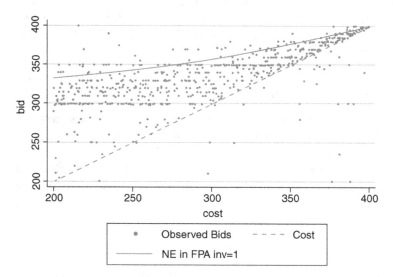

Figure 11.2 Bidding behavior in FPA, firm 1

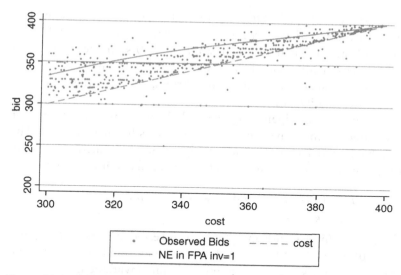

Figure 11.3 Bidding behavior in FPA, firm 2

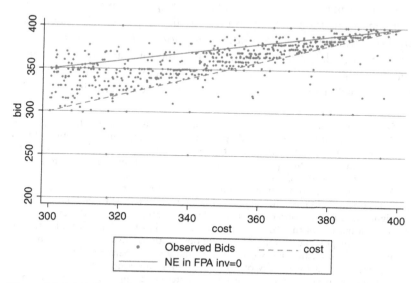

Figure 11.4 Bidding behavior in FPA, symmetric case

experimental findings.[17] After investing at stage one, firm 1 should be aware of the fact that firm 2's cost can never fall below 300. As a matter of fact, as Figure 11.2 shows, $b_1 = 300$ seems to be a "focal bid" for cost realizations below 300.[18] Over time bidders seem to learn to bid somewhat closer to equilibrium, although this (learning) effect is not significant.

To estimate participants' aggregate bid functions, we employ, for all treatments, the same simple random effects linear regression. The underlying model assumes that participants use bid functions that are two-piecewise linear, with a structural break fixed at $c = 300$:

$$b_{it} = a_0 + \beta_0 c_{it} + a_1 \delta_1 + \beta_1 \delta_1 c_{it} + a_2 \delta_1 \delta_{c+} + \beta_2 \delta_1 \delta_{c+} c_{it}$$
$$+ \varepsilon_i + \varepsilon_{it} \tag{7}$$

where $\delta_1 = 1 (\delta_1 = 0)$ if firm 1 has (not) invested at stage one, $\delta_{c+} = 1$ $(\delta_{c+} = 0)$ if $c \geq (<)300$, ε_i is the individual (random) component which describes subject i's unobserved time-invariant heterogeneity and ε_{it} is an idiosyncratic error term.

Table 11A.1 (in Appendix C) reports the estimation results for regression (7) in the case of treatments FPA and SPA.[19, 20] Comparing the estimated bid functions with our theoretical prediction we notice that our estimated bid functions are always (point-wisely) significantly different from their corresponding equilibrium levels. In particular, for both firm 1 and firm 2, bidding behavior *is always more aggressive* than predicted, as the estimated bid functions are always (point-wisely) significantly below equilibrium. Moreover (which is consistent with theory), firm 2 behaves more aggressively than firm 1 in the

---

[17] See, for example, Kagel (1995), or, for asymmetric auctions, Güth *et al.* (2005).

[18] This consideration notwithstanding, we also see a significant proportion of bids below 300 (6.2% of total observations), although these observations mainly correspond to the first periods (i.e. in time interval 4, only 2.7% of total observations were bids below 300).

[19] We also included time dummies for our four time intervals τ_m, $m = 1, \ldots, 4$. The corresponding coefficients (also for interaction terms) turned out not to be significant, i.e., we observe no particular time trends in either direction.

[20] The estimation of the variance–covariance matrix of (7) has been adjusted to control for possible correlation among observations drawn from the same matching group. In other words, our estimations are performed under the assumption that the history of each matching group (and not the history of the eight participants that form each matching group) corresponds to an independent observation.

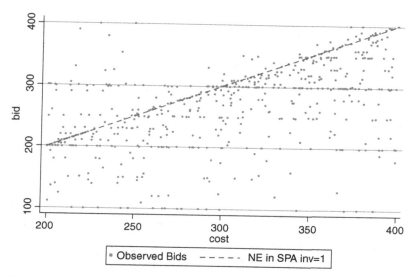

Figure 11.5 Bidding behavior in SPA, firm 1

asymmetric auction. As for firm 1, we observe that bidding behavior is somewhat "closer" to equilibrium when $c<300$, i.e. the difference between theoretical and estimated bids for $c<300$ is much smaller than the corresponding difference for $c \geq 300$ (30.9 versus 42.88). This evidence seems to suggest that, whenever investment yields a dominant position for firm 1 (i.e. production cost $c<300$), firm 1's bidding is comparatively less aggressive than when investment does not yield such a clear cooperative cost advantage.

SPA

Figures 11.5, 11.6 and 11.7 report the same information as Figures 11.2 to 11.4 for the SPA sessions. As Figures 11.5 to 11.7 show, bidding behavior is much noisier in SPA than in FPA, in particular (for both player positions) after firm 1 has invested in stage 1. As a consequence, the fit of our linear regressions in Table 11A.1 (overall $R^2 = 0.5427$ for firm 1 and 0.5127 for firm 2 in FPA, against 0.4294 and 0.1295 in the SPA case, respectively) drops dramatically. This translates into much higher standard errors in the estimated coefficients. This consideration notwithstanding, we see that, once again, participants bid below

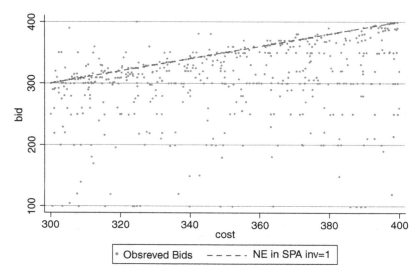

Figure 11.6 Bidding behavior in SPA, firm 2

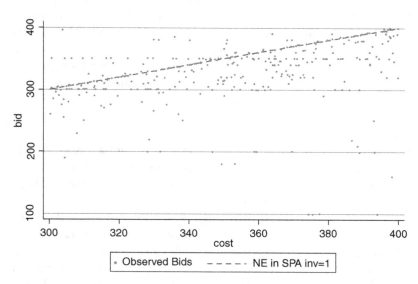

Figure 11.7 Bidding behavior in SPA, symmetric case

Table 11.3 *Proportions of equilibrium bids and over-/underbidding in SPA when* $\delta=1$

	underbidding	equilibrium bidding	overbidding
	< cost – 1 %	= cost +/– 1 %	> cost + 1 %
all periods	49.76 %	41.34 %	8.90 %
time interval 4	46.21 %	47.35 %	6.44 %

equilibrium (i.e. they behave more aggressively than predicted), and this difference is (point-wisely) statistically significant.[21]

Such lower levels of R^2 "between participants", calls for further analysis of our evidence, looking at whether high variance in the data has to be attributed to heterogeneity in our subject pool, rather than heterogeneous responses (of each single individual participating in the experiment) to similar cost levels. As it turns out, participants were indeed quite heterogeneous. Roughly speaking, they can be classified in four types: (i) those who played equilibrium from the very beginning (27%), (ii) those who learned how to play the equilibrium over time (25%), (iii) those who consistently underbid throughout (31%), and (iv) those who alternate over- and underbidding across time (17%).

Table 11.3 summarizes the proportions of bids equal to observed cost +/– 1%, above and below, respectively. As Table 11.3 shows, the percentage of bids close to the theoretical prediction mildly increased over time. Still, more than half of the bidders over- or underbid their cost even in time interval 4, where the vast majority underbid their cost (i.e. run the risk to incur a loss). Over all time intervals, we observe 8.9% of bids below 200, and an additional 24.76% of bids between 200 and 300 that were more than 10% below the corresponding cost. A large proportion of the extremely low bids (below 200 ptas.) were made by three bidders only. In addition, the number of bids below 200 is much higher in the case where player 1 had invested. Then, there are 14.6% firm 1 bids and 6.4% firm 2 bids in this range. In the symmetric case, there are only 3% bids by firm 1 and 3.5% bids by firm 2 below 200.

The observed behavior at the auction stage is in line with the experimental literature. For example, Güth *et al.* (2005) report that

---

[21] This is in line with previous experimental evidence on the second-price auction.

Table 11.4 *Observed and equilibrium payoffs in FPA and SPA*

		FPA		SPA	
		firm 1	firm 2	firm 1	firm 2
$\delta=1$	observed	29.097	2.261	36.007	-3.160
	(std. dev.)	(41.673)	(18.492)	(57.775)	(32.256)
	equilibrium	50.6	19.4	58.3	8.3
$\delta=0$	observed	5.053	6.196	6.693	6.465
	(std. dev.)	(18.337)	(16.940)	(28.143)	(25.844)
	equilibrium	16.6	16.6	16.6	16.6

half of their participants bid approximately truthfully. Underbidding
in their experiment was slightly less prominent. They argue that this is
due to the fact that in their experiments participants had previously
gained experience because they had to participate in several first-price
auctions prior to playing SPA.

Result 1 (bidding behavior)

 (i) In FPA bidding is more aggressive than the equilibrium prediction
     for all types.
(ii) In SPA bidding behavior is highly heterogeneous. While
     approximately half of the subjects bid their cost or learn to do so
     over time, 50% of subjects over- or underbid considerably, where
     underbidding is by far the most prominent pattern.

5.2. Payoffs (H2)

Table 11.4 contains information about average bidder payoffs in FPA
and SPA from the auction at the second stage. Investment costs are not
taken into account. (This is because investment costs are sunk at this
stage and should not affect payoffs in the auction.)

In the symmetric case (i.e. when $\delta = 0$), there are no significant differences between FPA and SPA, as predicted by the revenue equivalence
theorem. In both the symmetric and the asymmetric auctions, however,
participants bid much more aggressively than predicted, with the
consequence that payoffs are lower than their theoretical values.

Table 11.5 *Procurement cost in FPA and SPA*

		FPA	SPA
	observed	327.630	333.024
$\delta=1$	(std. dev.)	(33.819)	(44.620)
	equilibrium	354.1	358.3
	observed	348.074	353.931
$\delta=0$	(std. dev.)	(24.985)	(32.177)
	equilibrium	366.7	366.7

In the asymmetric auctions (i.e. when $\delta = 1$), firm 1's payoff is significantly higher in SPA than in FPA. While, as predicted, firm 2's payoff is significantly higher in FPA than in SPA, also for firm 2 actual payoffs are dramatically lower than their theoretical predictions. In SPA, firm 2's average payoff is even negative (which is due to the excessive underbidding of valuations reported in the previous section). In FPA, firm 2's payoff should theoretically be higher than either firm's payoff in the symmetric case. However, in our experiment the opposite is true. This is presumably due to the extremely aggressive behavior of weak bidders in the FPA format.

Note that comparison of the symmetric and the asymmetric payoffs determines whether investment at stage one is profitable or not. Investment is profitable whenever the investor's additional expected payoff in case of investment is higher than investment cost. The aggregate data (over all time intervals) suggest that investment incentives given the observed behavior are lower than their theoretical prediction. The critical investment cost suggested by aggregate data is 24.044 (theoretical prediction: 34) for FPA and 29.314 (theoretical prediction: 41.667) for SPA. Still, according to the observed payoff differences the relative profitability of investment (which theoretically is higher in the second-price auction) is preserved.

Table 11.5 finally reports the procurement cost in all four auction types together with their theoretical predictions. As expected, procurement cost in both formats is significantly lower if an investment has been made. Revenue equivalence (i.e. the hypothesis that procurement cost in SPA equals procurement cost in FPA) has to be rejected at the 5% level in either case, $\delta = 1$ and $\delta = 0$.

Table 11.6 *Predicted cost thresholds from a logit regression for both FPA and SPA*

	τ_1	τ_2	τ_3	τ_4	prediction
FPA	46.71	39.42	34.93	35.88	34
Threshold given observed bids	15.18	22.78	31.41	26.18	
SPA	50	50	44.20	43.60	41.67
Threshold given observed bids	32.12	26.12	30.22	41.65	

Result 2 (payoffs)

(i) Bidder payoffs are significantly lower than their theoretical predictions, both in the symmetric and the asymmetric auctions. In
the symmetric auctions payoffs do not differ between FPA and
SPA. In the asymmetric auctions bidder payoffs are higher in SPA
than in FPA for firm 1 and vice versa for firm 2.

(ii) Procurement cost is lower in the asymmetric than in the symmetric auction and among the asymmetric auctions lower in FPA.

5.3. Investment behavior (H3)

As theory predicts, our subjects' investment behavior was influenced
by both the investment cost k as well as the auction format (FPA or
SPA), where the probability of investment was significantly higher in
SPA. This seems to suggest that players were able to estimate that the
value of such an investment is higher on average in SPA than in FPA.
In SPA the majority of subjects invested for almost any level of k at the
beginning of the experiment. That is, they invested "too much" both
with respect to equilibrium behavior and expected returns, given
bidding behavior at stage 2. In later rounds they gradually reduced
their propensity to invest, and aggregate behavior became close to the
theoretical prediction.

Table 11.6 reports the predicted cost thresholds as predicted by a
logit regression. Estimated thresholds reported in the table indicate the
maximum cost level for which "not invest" corresponds to the modal
decision.

As Table 11.6 shows, predicted cost thresholds decrease over time
until they reach 35.88 in FPA and 43.60 in SPA. Whereas in the first

twenty-two rounds of FPA and the first thirty-three rounds of SPA it is significantly higher than the threshold bidders should have had, given the actual bidding behavior at stage 2 (see Table 11.6), it is close to this threshold for all other rounds. The two threshold values (i.e. the actual threshold and the optimal threshold given average observed behavior) display a tendency to converge towards the end of the experiment.

Result 3 (investment)

Investment starts out at high levels and over time approaches the theoretical prediction as well as the threshold given the observed behavior.

5.4 Efficiency (H4)

According to the equilibrium prediction, all auctions but the asymmetric FPA should yield an efficient allocation. That is, the bidder with the lower cost should win the auction. Because costs were randomly and independently drawn in our experiment, simply comparing treatments with respect to the achieved production cost would be biased by these random draws. For this reason, we compare the auction formats with respect to three different efficiency measures that are aimed to minimize this bias:

- *Allocative efficiency*: the number of efficiently allocated units (i.e. to the bidder with the lower cost) relative to the total number of units.
- *Relative efficiency loss*: the loss in terms of total production cost relative to the maximum possible efficiency loss.
- *Relative efficiency*: the minimal possible production cost relative to the achieved total production cost.

Allocative efficiency does not reflect the actual magnitude of efficiency losses due to misallocations. If the "wrong" bidder obtains a unit, his cost may be substantially or only slightly above the other bidder's cost, raising production cost either dramatically or only slightly. Our second and third measures take this into account. In Table 11.7 we report for each measure aggregate results over all pairs and time intervals, as well as for time interval 4.

Table 11.7 *Efficiency, measured by allocative efficiency, relative efficiency loss and relative efficiency*

	Periods	Allocative efficiency	Relative efficiency loss	Relative efficiency
FPA	all	85.99 %	8.46%	98.08 %
$\delta=1$	34 – 44 (τ_4)	86.21 %	9.66 %	97.82 %
SPA	all	78.88 %	14.16 %	96.83 %
$\delta=1$	34 – 44 (τ_4)	86.17 %	6.65 %	98.40 %
FPA	all	83.62 %	10.04 %	98.98 %
$\delta=0$	34 – 44 (τ_4)	85.56 %	9.03 %	99.08 %
SPA	all	73.59 %	20.46 %	98.01 %
$\delta=0$	34 – 44 (τ_4)	73.33 %	21.66 %	97.97 %

We observe that allocative efficiency (the percentage of Pareto-efficient allocations) is lower in the asymmetric second-price auction than in the first-price auction. However, the difference disappears if one considers only time interval 4. Thus, while the erratic behavior of many subjects in SPA seems to partly disappear over time, allocative efficiency stays constant in the asymmetric first-price auction, where it coincides with the equilibrium prediction. The effect appears more pronounced if we look at the relative efficiency loss. Here, the efficiency loss increases in FPA, while it decreases remarkably in the asymmetric second-price auction.

The remarkably low efficiency values especially for the symmetric SPA may be due to a small sample size together with a self-selection problem: since in SPA investment was almost always profitable, the group that played the symmetric SPA may have contained a large fraction of subjects that did not understand this. Overall, the efficiency rates are remarkably close to those found by Güth *et al.* (2005), again accounting for the fact that their SPA-players were more experienced than ours.

Result 4 (efficiency)

Efficiency is initially lower in the asymmetric SPA than in the asymmetric FPA. Over the course of the experiment, this result is reversed.

5.5. Robustness of the results

Does the origin of the comparative advantage matter? (HB1)
To answer this question we ran two treatments (EXFPA and EXSPA) where bidders played an asymmetric auction without a preceding investment stage. That is, firm 1 had cost uniformly distributed in [200, 400], while firm 2's cost distribution was uniform in [300, 400]. This is exactly the situation subjects faced in our original treatments in case the investor actually decided to invest. Theoretically, thus, bidders should behave identically in EXFPA (EXSPA) and FPA (SPA). Our data largely confirm the theoretical hypothesis.

Table 11A.2 (in Appendix C) reports estimates of a two-piecewise linear bid function of firm 1 and 2, pooling (in case of investment on behalf of firm 1) observations from FPA (SPA) and EXFPA (EXSPA). We only find a significant (point-wise) difference in the estimated bid functions for firm 1 in SPA when c is sufficiently high ($c > 317$ approx.). In all other cases, subjects do not behave differently in either treatment protocol. In particular, in a first-price auction the existence of an investment stage does not per se affect behavior in the auction.

How does the strategic uncertainty affect subjects' behavior? (HB2)
We address the second question by comparing our results with those coming from treatments COMPFPA and COMPSPA, where subjects bid against computerized agents playing the RNNE strategy described in Section 2 at both stages.

Table 11A.3 (in Appendix C) reports estimates analogous to those of Table 11A.2 only for those observations for which investment took place. Again, we find no significant differences for the first-price auction, while in second-price auctions firm 1 bids significantly less aggressively (i.e. closer to the equilibrium prediction) in COMPSPA than in SPA for sufficiently high cost levels.

Recall, however, that bidders are rather heterogeneous in SPA and, therefore, the bid function of a representative agent might not reflect the behavior of many players. A categorization in bidding types reveals that there are more "rational" players (i.e. types that play equilibrium from the beginning or learn to do so over time) in both control treatments (EXSPA and COMPSPA) than in SPA (see Table 11.8).

This also reflects in the rates of bidders who bid their cost, and over/underbid, respectively (see Table 11.9). Obviously it is not the

Table 11.8 *Bidder types in SPA (EQ: subjects who bid their cost from the beginning, L: those who learned the equilibrium over time, U: those who always underbid, U/O: those who alternated under- and overbidding)*

	EQ	L	U	U/O
SPA	27 %	25 %	31 %	17 %
EXOSPA	37.5 %	29.2 %	20.8 %	12.5 %
COMPSPA	41.6 %	25 %	25 %	8.3 %

Table 11.9 *Proportions of equilibrium bids and over-/underbidding for the three SPA treatments — all periods*

treatment	underbidding	equilibrium bidding	overbidding
	< cost − 1 %	= cost +/− 1 %	> cost + 1 %
SPA	49.76 %	41.34 %	8.90 %
EXSPA	33.62 %	55.68 %	10.70 %
COMPSPA	42.23 %	51.51 %	6.25 %

strategic uncertainty that drives the difference, since in COMPSPA bidders do not bid truthfully more frequently than in EXSPA. A possible explanation could be that players learn the optimal strategy better whenever a) they play against more rational players (as is the case in COMSPA) and b) whenever they face a smaller strategy space and thus a smaller "cognitive load" (as is the case in EXSPA).

6. Conclusion

In this chapter we have experimentally investigated behavior in first- and second-price procurement auctions where one bidder had the possibility to improve his competitive position by investing. Our results are in line with several qualitative predictions of the theory. In particular, we observe that:

- Subjects invest more often prior to SPA than prior to FPA. Over time investment levels approach the theoretical prediction, as well as the optimal threshold given the observed data.

- Procurement cost is lower in the asymmetric FPA than in the asymmetric SPA (and bidder payoffs are also lower in FPA).
- In FPA, weak bidders bid relatively more aggressively than strong bidders.
- In those cases where investment had taken place, efficiency is initially lower in SPA. This turns around in the course of the experiment such that finally efficiency is lower in FPA than in SPA, as predicted.

In line with the experimental literature on auctions, we find that in FPA, bidding is more aggressive than predicted, resulting in very low bidder payoffs and procurement cost. In SPA, bidders are highly heterogeneous with approximately half of them playing close to the equilibrium prediction, while the majority of the remaining subjects underbid. On average this also leads to lower bidder payoffs and procurement cost in SPA.

Our results yield several conclusions for public policy. Obviously, if investment prior to the auction is important or if positive synergies between auctions exist it is not immediately obvious whether first- or second-price auctions are better suited for public procurement. First-price auctions are typically easier understood by the subjects, yield low procurement cost (since bidders bid persistently more aggressively than predicted), and are less susceptible to collusion than second-price auctions. Second-price auctions, on the other hand, imply higher investment incentives. Thus, if improvement of production technologies or process innovations are important, second-price auctions are likely the better choice. Our analysis (as many other experiments) demonstrates, however, that the second-price auction format has to be carefully chosen, as typically a large share of subjects do not easily understand the equilibrium strategy.

Appendix A: Optimal investment

Second-price auction

To find the optimal investment decision rule in the second-price auction, we solve the model backwards. Note that the expected payoff of a player 1 is given by

$$B(\delta^{SPA}) = \Pi_1 E(C_2 - C_1 | C_1 < C_2) \tag{9}$$

where E denotes the expectations operator and Π_1 denotes the probability for player 1 to win the auction.[22] Obviously both Π_1 and $E(C_2 - C_1 | C_1 < C_2)$ will depend on whether an investment was undertaken. Furthermore it is clear that the optimality of such an investment will depend on whether its cost k is higher or lower than the expected gains it promises. Evaluating (9) in the two cases $\delta^{SPA} = 1$ and $\delta^{SPA} = 1$ yields

$$B(0) = \frac{(\bar{c} - \underline{c})}{6}$$

and

$$B(1) = \frac{7(\bar{c} - \underline{c})}{12} - k,$$

respectively. Investing will be optimal whenever $B(1) > B(0)$. Consequently, the optimal investment decision is:

$$\delta^{SPA}(k) = \begin{cases} 1 & if & k < \hat{k}_{SPA} = 125/3 \\ \{0, 1\} & & if \ k = \hat{k}_{SPA} \\ 0 & & if \ k > \hat{k}_{SPA}. \end{cases}$$

First-price auction

Analogously, the optimal investment decision in the first-price auction is obtained by looking at the expected profits in the auction, which are given by

$$B(\delta^{FPA}) = \Pi_1 E(b_1(C_1) - C_1 | C_1 < C_2) \tag{10}$$

Here is the advantaged bidder's bid-function as given by (3) in the case where $\delta^{SPA} = 1$ and by (2) in the case where $\delta^{SPA} = 0$. It follows in an analogous way to the above that the optimal investment rule is given by

$$\delta^{FPA}(k) = \begin{cases} 1 & if & k < \hat{k}_{FPA} = 34 \\ \{0, 1\} & & if \ k = \hat{k}_{FPA} \\ 0 & & if \ k > \hat{k}_{FPA}. \end{cases}$$

---

[22] Obviously it is without loss of generality to assume that player 1 has the right to invest.

Appendix B: Instructions (FPA treatment)

Welcome to the experiment! This is an experiment to study behavior of people making decisions. We are only interested in observing how people act on average, not how you act personally. So do not think that we expect you to behave in any particular way. Be aware that your behavior will affect the amount of money you win in this experiment. Thus, it is profitable for you to act in the best way possible. On the following pages you find the instructions on how this experiment works and how to use the computer during the experiment. The instructions are the same for all participants in the experiment.

Please, do not disturb the other participants during the experiment. If you need any help, please raise your hand and wait silently. We will attend you as soon as possible.

How to win money. At the beginning of the experiment, you receive 1000 ptas just for participation. At the end of the experiment you are paid the amount of money you have won during the experiment in addition to these 1000 ptas.

The game

You play 44 rounds of the simple game we explain in the following. In every round you play against another player from this room. This player will change in every round. Neither you know whether you have already interacted with nor does the other player know whether he has already interacted with you. This means that your decisions are anonymous at all times.

At the beginning of each round you receive an initial endowment that can be different in different rounds. Every round of the game consists of two phases: an investment phase and a procurement auction phase. You can only win money in the procurement auction. The investment phase only enables one of the two players to achieve an advantage in the procurement auction. The rounds (remember: every round consists of two phases) are completely independent and nothing you do in one particular round will influence any of the other rounds.

In the investment phase only one of the two players has the opportunity to make an investment at a certain expenditure. The investment will lead the player that has invested to have an advantageous distribution of costs (we explain later on in detail what that means). You have the opportunity to invest every two rounds. In the other rounds the other player has the opportunity to invest.

In the procurement auction, you and the other player compete for the right to undertake a project. You have to bid in order to determine the winner of the procurement auction and the price to be paid to the winner for undertaking the project. The player who places the lower bid wins. Realization of the project is costly. This cost will change in every round. It is chosen according to a distribution. Your distribution is the initial distribution if you did not invest (or if did not have the opportunity to invest) and it is the advantageous distribution if you did invest.

If you win the procurement auction, your profit will be the price that is paid to undertake the project less the cost of undertaking it.

The investment phase: in the investment phase only one of the two players (either the other player or you) has the opportunity to invest. If the player who can invest does so, he has the *advantageous cost distribution* in the procurement auction, while the other one has the initial distribution. If the player who has the opportunity to invest decides not to do so, both players have the *initial distribution*.

Now we explain in more detail what it means to have an *advantageous distribution*.

If the player who has the possibility to invest decided not to do so, both players have the *initial distribution*. This means that each player has cost between 300 and 400 ptas, where all numbers in this interval are equally likely.

If the player who has the opportunity to invest did so, this player has the *advantageous distribution*. This means that the player has cost between 200 and 400 ptas, where again all numbers in this interval are equally likely.

Note that whenever you invest you have a higher probability to have a low cost, which may lead to a higher probability to make more profits in the competition.

In any case the player who could not invest has the *initial distribution*, i.e. cost between 300 and 400 ptas.

Investment is costly. The investment expenditure is different in every round and will only be known to the player who can undertake the investment. This is why in every round the player has to decide again whether the investment seems profitable to him or not. If he decides to invest, the investment expenditure is deducted from the initial endowment he has received at the beginning of the round.

In every round, before the procurement auction, both players will be informed about whether the investment has been undertaken or not.

The procurement auction: in the second phase of each round both players participate in a procurement auction for an imaginary project. In every round, the cost of undertaking the project is determined randomly for each of the players according to his distribution (advantageous or initial). If the player has the initial distribution his cost is between 300 and 400 ptas. Each number in this interval is equally likely. If he has the advantageous distribution his cost is between 200 and 400 ptas. Again, each number in this interval has the same probability to appear.

Before you decide about your bid, the cost you have in this round appears on your screen. It indicates the amount of money you have to spend to undertake the project (in case you win). The other player will not be able to observe your cost, nor will you be able to observe his cost. You and the other player have to decide on your bids, knowing only your own cost and the distribution of cost of the other player. Who gets the project, and how much money you win depends on your bids as follows.

The procurement auction is always won by the player who offers to undertake the project at the lower cost, i.e. the player that places the *lower bid*. The winner is paid his bid. Consequently one can interpret the bid of a player as the amount of money for which he would be willing to undertake the project. Remember that undertaking the project is costly (you observed this cost before placing your bid). The player who wins the procurement auction has to pay this cost upon undertaking the project. This means that the winner only makes a positive profit from the procurement auction if the price he receives is higher than his cost.

The losing player receives no payment in the procurement auction and incurs no cost.

What does it mean to have an "advantageous or initial distribution"?
We would like you to focus once more on what it means to have
an advantageous or initial distribution of cost in the procurement
auction. Having the initial distribution means that any number
between 300 and 400 ptas has the same probability to appear as
your cost in this round. With the advantageous distribution, every
number between 200 and 400 ptas will have the same probability to
appear.

		advantageous distribution	initial distribution
The probability	400 ptas	100%	100%
to have cost	350 ptas	75%	50%
lower than	300 ptas	50%	0%
	250 ptas	25%	0%

As you can see in the table the probability of having cost of less then 350
ptas is 50% with the *initial distribution*. While with the *advantageous
distribution* the probability of having a cost of less than 350 ptas is
higher, namely 75%.

Note that if you have the *advantageous distribution* there is a
probability of 50% to have a cost of less then 300 ptas. In this case
your cost will be lower than the other player's cost for sure (he has the
initial distribution and, thus, a cost between 300 and 400 ptas).

Observe that having the *advantageous distribution* does not
necessarily imply that you have a lower cost than the other player.
You will only have a higher probability than with the *initial distribution* that this is the case. Having a lower cost allows the player
to place a lower bid and, thus, have a higher probability of winning.
Still the identity of the winner and the profits depends on *BOTH*
bids.[23]

---

[23] The instructions were followed by a number of control questions, and, there-
after, a short summary of the rules.

Appendix C: Estimation results

Key: *, ** and *** refers to an estimate being significant at the 10, 5, and 1 per cent level respectively.

Table 11A.1 *Random effects linear regression for treatments FPA and SPA (see equation (7))*

	FPA		SPA	
Bid	firm 1	firm 2	firm 1	firm 2
a_0	126.66***	139.68***	80.63**	88.65**
	(16.66)	(12.43)	(33.95)	(35.35)
β_0	0.67***	0.64***	0.68***	0.69*
	(0.05)	(0.04)	(0.10)	(0.10)
a_1	135.14***	−32.84**	21.56	−12.62
	(19.57)	(15.04)	(38.01)	(39.69)
β_1	−0.46***	0.08*	−0.13	0.01
	(0.06)	(0.04)	(0.12)	(0.11)
a_2	−103.41***	–	35.07	–
	(18.85)	–	(30.70)	–
β_2	0.37***	–	−0.04	–
	(0.06)	–	(0.10)	–
σ_u	7.35	7.28	28.02	31.67
σ_e	23.99	18.39	41.28	43.46
ρ	0.09	0.14	0.32	0.35
R^2 *within*	0.54	0.55	0.50	0.19
R^2 *between*	0.58	0.11	0.27	0.0
R^2 *overall*	0.54	0.51	0.42	0.13

Table 11A.2 *Comparison of treatments with endogenous investment (END) and exogenous asymmetry*

	FPA		SPA	
Bid	firm 1	firm 2	firm 1	firm 2
Cons.	245.70***	86.51***	72.10**	48.28**
	(12.72)	(9.95)	(24.90)	(24.26)
Cost	0.25***	0.78***	0.70***	0.81***
	(0.05)	(0.03)	(0.09)	(0.07)
Break	−111.17***	–	−64.97	–
	(22.47)	–	(42.97)	–
	0.39***	–	0.21	–

Table 11A.2 (*cont.*)

	FPA		SPA	
Bid	firm 1	firm 2	firm 1	firm 2
Break*c	(0.07)	–	(0.14)	–
	13.72	21.70*	30.33	26.09
END	(17.40)	(13.01)	(31.51)	(30.75)
	−0.03	−0.06	−0.15	−0.11
END*c	(0.07)	(0.04)	(0.12)	(0.09)
	26.67	–	130.05**	–
Break*END	(24.60)	–	(44.88)	–
	−0.07	–	−0.40**	–
Break*END*c	(0.07)	–	(0.13)	–
σ_u	12.56	7.28	29.56	27.15
σ_e	24.60	18.39	43.95	43.80
ρ	0.21	0.14	0.31	0.28
R^2 within	0.57	0.55	0.49	0.20
R^2 between	0.27	0.11	0.02	0.06
R^2 overall	0.50	0.51	0.38	0.17

Table 11A.3 *Comparison of treatments FPA (SPA) and COMPFPA (COMPSPA)*

	FPA		SPA	
Bid	firm 1	firm 2	firm 1	firm 2
	259.46***	108.32***	101.79***	73.65***
Cons.	(12.32)	(9.36)	(18.47)	(18.74)
	0.22***	0.72***	0.55***	0.70***
Cost	(0.05)	(0.03)	(0.07)	(0.05)
	−101.43***	–	36.45	–
Break	(20.47)	–	(30.87)	–
	0.36***	–	-0.04	–
Break*c	(0.07)	–	(0.10)	–
	34.88	−24.48	−17.02	−62.38
COMP	(25.93)	(21.43)	(43.61)	(42.04)
	−0.10	0.07	0.03	0.18
COMP*c	(0.10)	(0.06)	(0.17)	(0.12)
	−11.77	–	−179.68**	–

Table 11A.3 (*cont.*)

	FPA		SPA	
Bid	firm 1	firm 2	firm 1	firm 2
Break*COMP	(41.95)	–	(59.74)	–
	0.04	–	0.49	–
Break*COMP*c	(0.11)	–	(0.17)**	–
σ_u	7.91	6.92	34.51	37.57
σ_e	25.81	20.22	41.17	42.47
ρ	0.09	0.10	0.41	0.44
R^2 *within*	0.51	0.52	0.51	0.21
R^2 *between*	0.41	0.32	0.04	0.0
R^2 *overall*	0.49	0.50	0.34	0.12

References

Arozamena, L. and E. Cantillon (2004), Investment Incentives in Procurement Auctions, *Review of Economic Studies* 71, 1–18.

Bag, P. (1997). Optimal Auction Design and R & D, *European Economic Review* 41, 1655–1674.

Cox, J. C., R. M. Isaac, P.-A. Cech and D. Conn (1996), Moral Hazard and Adverse Selection in Procurement Contracting, *Games and Economic Behavior* 17, 147–176.

De Silva, D., T. Dunne and G. Kosmopolou (2003), An Empirical Analysis of Entrant and Incumbent Bidding in Road Constructions Auctions, *Journal of Industrial Economics* 3, 295–316.

Fischbacher, U. (2007), Z-tree Zurich Toolbox for Readymade Experiments, *Experimental Economics* 10(2), 171–178.

Grimm, V. (2006), Sequential versus Bundle Auction for Recurring Procurement, *University of Cologne Working Paper*.

Güth, W., R. Ivanova–Stenzel, and E. Wolfstetter (2005), Bidding behavior in asymmetric auctions: An experimental study, *European Economic Review* 49, 1891–1913.

Kagel, J.H. (1995), Auctions: A Survey of Experimental Research, in J. Kagel and A. E. Roth (eds.) *Handbook of Experimental Economics*, Princeton, NJ.

Maskin, E. and J. Riley (2000). Asymmetric Auctions, *Review of Economic Studies* 67, 439–454.

Myerson, R. (1981), Optimal Auction Design, *Mathematics of Operations Research* 6, 58–73.

Piccone, M. and G. Tan (1996), Cost-Reducing Investment, Optimal Procurement and Implementation by Auctions, *International Economic Review* 37, 663–685.

Tan, G. (1992), Entry and R&D in Procurement Contracting, *Journal of Economic Theory* 58, 41–60.

12 | Experimental economics and the practice of competition policy enforcement

JEROEN HINLOOPEN AND
HANS-THEO NORMANN*

In this concluding chapter we discuss more specifically the use of experimental economics for the enforcement of competition policies. Broadly speaking they may serve two goals. First, to better understand the behavioral aspects of practices with which competition authorities have to deal, and, second, to be used as a pedagogical device for those involved in the day-to-day implementation of antitrust policies. Examples are discussed of both uses. Some final remarks sketch possible future developments.

1. Introduction

Enforcement of competition policies is difficult as they constitute a violation that typically remains hidden (cartels), that involves conduct that is difficult to assess (abuse of dominance) or that requires an assessment of some would-be world (merger control). Moreover, parties involved are likely to submit crucial empirical facts for the competition authorities' judgments themselves, and knowing this there is ample room for strategic behavior. Indeed, quite a large and active industry exists that specializes in supplying precisely these facts.

Experimental economics is particularly well-suited for helping competition authorities with the implementation of competition laws. For instance, the laboratory setting allows for observing practices that would remain hidden in practice. This helps to understand, for example, under which circumstances cartels form and break down. The data may also explain cartel recidivism. Is it due to market structure or rather related to the type of the individuals involved?

* Thanks are due to Adriaan Soetevent who was partly responsible for the classroom experiment conducted at the premises of the Dutch Competition Authority that is discussed in this chapter.

Experiments further allow for a direct market performance assessment of business strategies that could involve an abuse of dominance. There are business strategies, such as product bundling or predation, where the impact of the strategy on market performance is difficult to assess theoretically. Finally, rather than making an educated guess about what the world would look like after a proposed merger, this world could be simulated in the laboratory. Even if it is difficult to analyze precisely what drives the experimental findings, it would provide valuable information in itself as to the likely market development after the approval of a proposed merger.

But experimental economics can do more. It is an established practice to use experiments in graduate and undergraduate teaching. These so-called classroom experiments feature prominently in several mainstream textbooks (see e.g. Holt, 2007) and journals like *The Journal of Economic Education* have particular sections dealing with newly devised classroom experiments (see e.g. Goeree and Hinloopen, 2008). Meanwhile it has been proven quite convincingly that the use of classroom experiments enhances students' learning abilities (Emerson and Taylor, 2004). In fact, in a country like The Netherlands the use of classroom experiments is obligatory in economics teaching at high schools as of 2010 (Teulings, 2005).

A natural extension of experiments as a pedagogical device is to involve professionals from the field of competition policies (Binmore and Klemperer, 2002). These could provide suggestions as to which type of behavior should feature in a classroom experiment. More importantly, they can participate in these experiments themselves. Especially for professionals not having a formal economics training this could serve as an effective and accessible entry into the economics of competition. In this respect, a tradition is developing in The Netherlands where once every year employees of the Dutch Competition Authority (NMa) take part in a classroom experiment conducted at the premises of the NMa. The participants typically are professionals responsible for the day-to-day implementation of competition policies, but are not trained economists. Through the on-site classroom experiments, they experience the working of markets and what incentives market participants have in response to competition policies. More often than not, this experience is not documented in standard textbooks.

In this concluding chapter we first discuss an example as to how experiments can help the practical enforcement of competition policies. We then report on an experiment conducted at the NMa that served as a pedagogical device. We conclude with some observations on future prospects for experimental economics in relation to the design and enforcement of competition policies.

2. Experiments and competition policy enforcement

Experimental economics is known for revealing behavioral aspects that remain unaccounted for in traditional neo-classical economics models. As such, much research has to be done into almost all aspects of economics, the workings of competition policies in particular. Here we report on the effect of corporate leniency programs on cartel behavior.

In 1978, the US government introduced a so-called corporate leniency program whereby cartel members are granted fine reductions in exchange for providing information on their cartel activity and that of other members. In 1993, the program was revised in that much higher fine reductions are given, up to full immunity, for the first cartel member to report the cartel. The EU introduced a corporate leniency program in 1996 and revised it in 2002 much along the lines of the US revision. Since the implementation of those revisions, the number of cartels detected has increased dramatically both in Europe and the US (for more details see OECD, 2002, Hinloopen, 2003 and Spagnolo, 2006). This led the Director of Criminal Enforcement of the US Department of Justice antitrust division in 2000 to conclude that "over the last years, the Amnesty Program has been responsible for detecting and prosecuting more antitrust violations than all of our [other investigating] tools" (Hammond, 2000). Likewise, the EU Commissioner responsible for competition observed in 2005 that "the leniency program is proving to be an efficient tool to detect and punish cartels" (Kroes, 2005).

The success of the leniency programs is not that obvious, however. On the one hand they could, indeed, destroy the necessary trust among cartel members such that formerly successful cartels are reported and dismantled. On the other hand, leniency programs reduce the expected costs of cartel participation as the expected fines are reduced. Accordingly, it could be more attractive to start a cartel. Indeed, since the introduction of leniency programs the number of cartels that is detected has increased quite dramatically, but "in principle [this] could be due to an increase in cartel activity" (Spagnolo, 2004).

Hinloopen and Soetevent (2006) report on an experiment that tests the workings of a particular leniency program (see also Hinloopen and Soetevent, 2008). Indeed, as empirical information about cartels that have not been detected is in principle not available, an experiment is an obvious alternative to obtain relevant data.

Subjects anonymously interact in groups of three for at least twenty consecutive rounds in a discrete Bertrand pricing game. Each individual has to pick a number from the set {101,...,110}. The lowest number "wins" and the pay-off for the winner equals (winning number − 101)/ (number of winners). The minimum number of 101 can be interpreted as the marginal cost of production. In the one-shot Nash equilibrium, the price equals 101. Subjects have the possibility, however, to discuss the number that they submit. In particular, a cartel is established if all subjects within a group agree to discuss prices. In that case, a communication window opens that is operational for one minute (see Hinloopen and Soetevent, 2006 for specific details of this communication phase). As in practice, the agreed-upon price is not binding. If a cartel is established, members face a per-period detection probability of 15%, a fraction that is inspired by the related empirical finding of Bryant and Eckard (1991). Upon detection, all cartel members have to pay a fine equal to 10% of their gross earnings. The detection probability disappears only in case the cartel is discovered. The period of limitation is thus infinite (see also Hinloopen, 2007).

Before cartel members learn whether their cartel is detected, they are asked if they want to report the cartel or not. Upon reporting, a fine reduction is given of 100% to the first reporting member, of 50% to the second member that reports, and 0% to the cartel member that is last. This stylized leniency program resembles the current practice in both the US and the EU.

Table 12.1 contains the average pricing patterns across the different treatments. Note that in the Benchmark treatment no communication is possible. In the treatment labeled Communication, price discussions do not trigger a detection probability. Such a detection probably is present in Antitrust. Only in the final treatment, Leniency, it is possible to report the cartel.

The pricing patterns prompt a number of observations. First, as predicted by theory, some tacit collusion occurs in Benchmark. The average price of 103.2 is significantly above the one-shot Nash equilibrium price of 101. Second, introducing the option to communicate

Table 12.1 *Average prices across treatments (source*: Hinloopen and Soetevent, 2006)

	Benchmark	Communication	Antitrust	Leniency
All	103.2	103.3	103.0	101.4
Cartels	*	105.4	104.8	103.4
Non-cartels	*	101.4	102.4	101.1

Table 12.2 *Fraction of subject-decisions in favor of cartel formation (source*: Hinloopen and Soetevent, 2006)

	Communication	Antitrust	Leniency
Cartel intention	78.1	64.7	62.3
Always	30.8	20.5	23.8
Never	0.0	0.0	9.5
Cartel formation	47.3	27.3	12.9

on average does not raise price above the one obtained in Benchmark. However, those groups that do communicate are able to increase the price further while tacit collusion is absent in all other cases. Introduction of a detection probability again does not affect the average price. Yet the average cartel price is lower compared to Communication while some tacit collusion is observed again in all cases when a cartel is not formed. More importantly, introduction of the leniency programs leads to a significant reduction in the average price. It is even below the average price obtained in Benchmark.

Hinloopen and Soetevent (2006) carefully reveal what drives the result that Leniency yields the lowest price of all scenarios considered. First, in Leniency, the group of noncooperators is more persistent in their behavior than in any other of the treatments. Table 12.2 lists the fraction of decisions in favor of cartel formation and the fraction of cartels actually formed. An important finding is that, in Leniency, there is a positive and significant fraction of subjects that *never* wants to form a cartel. As this persistency precludes subjects that do not want to discuss prices to be distributed randomly over the entire population, the number of cartels actually formed is significantly

Table 12.3 *Cartel breakdown (source: Hinloopen and Soetevent, 2006)*

	Fraction of cartels			Fraction of cartel members	
	Defection	Detection	Reporting	Defection	Reporting
Communication	0.67	*	*	0.52	*
Antitrust	0.68	0.17	*	0.50	*
Leniency	0.94	0.03	0.78	0.72	0.40

below what is expected based on the fraction of subjects that do want to discuss prices (see Hinloopen and Soetevent 2006). Hence, in Leniency, the number of cartels that is being formed is significantly lower than in Antitrust, although the fraction of subjects that want to discuss price does not differ significantly between these two treatments. This is the first reason why Leniency yields low prices.

Second, the lifetime of cartels is significantly reduced by the introduction of a corporate leniency program. In fact, no cartel lasts more than one period in Leniency while in both Antitrust and Communication the average cartel life time is 1.3 periods (Hinloopen and Soetevent 2006). Table 12.3 includes the fraction of cartels and subjects that defected from the cartel and, if possible, reported the cartel as well. The fraction of cartel members that charge a lower-than-agreed price is not affected significantly by the introduction of a detection probability. But introducing a leniency program significantly increases this fraction from 52% to 72%. Indeed, the resulting reduction in cartel lifetime is the second reason why Leniency yields the lowest price.

Third, the average difference between the agreed-upon price and the market price in Leniency is 5.9. This is significantly larger than the average undercutting size in both Communication (4.7) and Antitrust (4.9). One interpretation of this result is that, in Leniency, defecting cartel members want to be "more certain" that defection yields the capturing of the entire market. As a result, average prices drop.

The leniency program considered by Hinloopen and Soetevent thus seems to be very effective in reducing cartel activity and thereby reducing market prices. Yet, in all treatments there are "repeated offenders", groups that form a cartel more than once. In Communication, on average about seven cartels are established per group. This

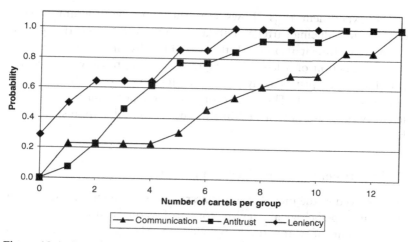

Figure 12.1 Cumulative density function of the number of cartels established per group

number drops to 4.5 in Antitrust, and reduces further to 2.6 in Leniency. These findings are not restricted to experimental studies only. Connor (2004) reports that 50 cartels out of a sample of 167 discovered international cartels have members that are involved in two or more cartels.

To examine whether the leniency program has an effect on cartel recidivism, Hinloopen and Soetevent (2006) consider the cumulative distribution function of the number of cartels established by each group for the several treatments. These density functions are replicated in Figure 12.1. The jump at zero for Leniency is caused by the fact that about one-quarter of all groups never form a cartel. In Communication and Antitrust all subjects join a cartel at least once. Except for this difference, the shape of the Leniency curve is very similar to that for Antitrust whereas the Communication curve is more flat. Estimating the concomitant slopes (with a two-sided Tobit estimator) reveals indeed that equality of these estimates for Leniency and Antitrust (0.088 and 0.093 respectively) cannot be rejected while that for Communication (0.070) is significantly lower. That is, introduction of a detection probability significantly reduces the probability of cartel recidivism; this probability is not reduced any further by the leniency program.

The experiment thus shows that the leniency program is very effective in reducing cartel activity and, ultimately, in lowering prices. At the same time it also reveals that cartel recidivism is not affected by the introduction of a leniency program. That is, those who report a cartel today are just as likely to join a cartel tomorrow as those that do not report a cartel. This might suggest a further adjustment of the leniency program in that multiple offenders should be punished more harshly.

3. Experiments as an educational device

As observed in the introduction, classroom experiments can serve as a particular pedagogical device for professionals involved in the enforcement of competition policies. In May 2007, a classroom experiment was conducted at the Dutch Competition Authority (NMa) that involved a Bertrand duopoly in which players possibly have private information about their costs. The issue was whether more market transparency leads to lower prices.

The game is an extension of the Bertrand duopoly experiment introduced by Dufwenberg and Gneezy (2000). In the Benchmark treatment subjects are asked to write down an integer number from the set $\{51, 52,\ldots,100\}$ on a note without showing their choice to anyone else. The notes contain random identity numbers that vary in each round such that individuals remain anonymous during the experiment. All notes are then collected in a bowl and the instructor subsequently draws two notes randomly. The numbers and identification numbers of these two notes are written down on a white board such that the participants involved can figure out their earnings. As in a Bertrand setting, the lowest number wins, with profits being equal to the number chosen minus 50. The latter can be interpreted as a fixed marginal cost. In the benchmark treatment this cost is identical for all subjects. The instructor then continues with the next pair of notes until the bowl is empty. The unique Nash equilibrium number for this game is 51.

A typical finding is that after several rounds there is some convergence towards the Nash equilibrium price level although the average price remains higher as there is always a possibility that someone writes down a very high "crazy" number (Dufwenberg and Gneezy, 2000, formalize this idea). Figure 12.2 contains the pricing behavior of the NMa experiment over the three rounds the several treatments were

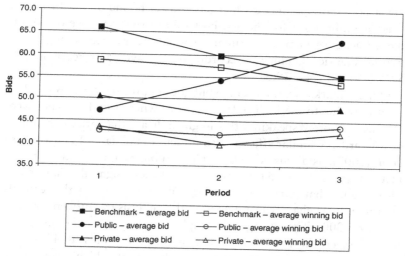

Figure 12.2 Pricing behavior of the NMa experiment

played.[1] In Benchmark the average bid starts at 66 and is down to 55.2 in round three. The average winning bid drops from 58.6 to 53.6.

In the second treatment, labelled Public, half of the participants received a note specifying a lower bound of 0 rather than 50. This lower bound allows for any integer from the set {2,3,...,100} to be chosen. Each trading round now consisted of two distinct phases. First, the matching was organized. This was established by collecting the bottom half of every note that specified the lower bound and identity numbers only. Two notes were drawn consecutively in the same way as in the Benchmark treatment. Both the respective identity numbers and concomitant lower bounds were written down on the whiteboard. Subjects then observed not only with whom they were matched, but also what the lower bound is of their rival.

Depending on the realization of the lower bounds, this game has different Nash equilibria in pure strategies. When two subjects are matched with a lower bound of 50, the Benchmark treatment is mimicked with an equilibrium price of 51. If both subjects have a lower bound of 0, the equilibrium price is 2. And if either subject has a

---

[1] Due to the time constraint when conducting the classroom experiment at the premises of the NMa, we were able to conduct three rounds per treatment only.

lower bound of 0 while the other has a lower bound of 50, the unique Nash equilibrium is for the low-cost subject to set a price of 50. On the whole, the asymmetric matching should occur twice as often as the two symmetric matchings. Accordingly, the average price would be $51/4 + 50/2 + 2/4 = 38.3$.

Quite remarkably, the average bid goes up, from 47.3 to 63.1. This is entirely due to the high bids in the case where two low-types were matched. Loosely speaking, this might indicate that prices are sticky downwards. A similar effect is also present in the data of Dufwenberg *et al.* (2007), as discussed in Chapter 4. Subjects have to adjust to the fact that prices below 51 are allowed. But they might also have some idea about what constitutes an "equilibrium" price in this case. If anything, this behavior is in line with the analysis of Dufwenberg and Gneezy (2000). The average winning bid on the other hand displays a much less erratic pattern. It starts at 42.9 and ends at 43.8. The average winning bid over the three rounds is 42.9, which is somewhat above the predicted value of 38.3.

In the final treatment, Private, the second treatment was mimicked without, however, revealing the lower bounds. All the subjects knew was their own lower bound. For subjects with a high lower bound the unique Nash equilibrium is to submit the number 51, independent of the type they are matched with. For subjects with a low lower bound no Nash equilibrium in pure strategies exists. They mix prices on the domain {25,51}, according to some discrete CDF (see Doarest *et al.* 2008). The expected price for the lower bounds is 35.4. Accordingly, the expected average winning bid is $51/4 + 136.2/4 = 39.3$. Uncertainty should thus lead to a slightly higher price. We observe the opposite however: the average winning bid in this treatment is 41.9. In the experimental data, less information leads to lower prices. This conclusion of course should not be taken too seriously as it is obtained in a classroom experiment. But for getting the point across that the relationship between market transparency and market performance is not one-to-one, the experiment was quite instrumental.

4. Conclusions

Experimental economics can be valuable for the theory and practice of competition policies. It allows for mimicking situations that competition authorities are confronted with in their day-to-day practice. A valuable feature is that all market developments can be observed in the laboratory, an issue that is particularly difficult in practices when potentially legal offenses are involved. Here we report on one example of such use of experimental economics: the assessment of the recent claimed succes of corporate leniency programs. The experiment shows that these programs can be successful indeed in diminishing cartel activity and ultimately in reducing price. At the same time, the experimental evidence reveals that cartel recidivism is not affected by a corporate leniency program.

Another important usage of experiments lies in their pedagogical value. In particular, conducting classroom experiments with the professionals that are responsible for the day-to-day implementation of competition policies helps to bring subtle notions of market competition to the very heart of competition authorities' operations. In this respect a tradition is shaping in that every year such a classrooom experiment is conducted at the premises of the Dutch Competition Authority (NMa).

Reviewing all the chapters in this volume, and our closing chapter in particular, provides ample evidence as to the added value of experimental economics for competition policies. Yet, much work needs to be done. Indeed, more experiments, and more specific experiments are needed to address the whole range of competition policies.

References

Binmore, K. and Klemperer, P. (2002), The Biggest Auction Ever: The Sale of the British 3G Telecom Licenses, *Economic Journal* 112, C74–C96.

Bryant, P. G. and Eckard, E. W. (1991), Price Fixing: The Probability of Getting Caught, *Review of Economics and Statistics*, 73: 531–536.

Connor, J. M. (2004), Extraterritoriality of the Sherman Act and Deterrence of Private International Cartels, Purdue University, unpublished manuscript.

Doarest, A., Hinloopen, J., and Soetevent, A. R. (2008), Signalling in an Experimental Bertrand Duopoly, *Tinbergen Institute Discussion Paper*.

Dufwenberg, M. and Gneezy, U. (2000), Price Competition and Market Concentration: An Experimental Study, *International Journal of Industrial Organization*, 18: 7–22.

Dufwenberg, M., Goeree, J., Gneezy, U. and Nagel, R. (2007), Price Floors and Competition, *Economic Theory*, 33(1), 207–224.

Emerson, T. L. N. and Taylor, B. A. (2004), Comparing Student Achievement across Experimental and Lecture-Oriented Sections of a Principles of Microeconomics Course, *Southern Economic Journal*, 70(3): 672–693.

Goeree, M. S. and Hinloopen, J. (2008), Cooperation in the Classroom: Experimenting with R&D Cooperatives, *Journal of Economic Education*, in press.

Hammond, S. D. (2000), *Detecting and deterring cartel activity through an effective leniency program*, speech delivered before the International Workshop on Cartels, Brighton, England, November.

Hinloopen, J. (2003), An Economic Analysis of Leniency Programs, *De Economist*, 151(4): 415–432.

(2007), The Pro-Collusive Effect of Increasing the Repose Period for Price Fixing Agreements, *The B.E. Journal of Economic Analysis & Policy*, 7, Issue 1 (Contributions), Article 17.

Hinloopen, J. and Soetevent, A. (2006), Trust and Recidivism: The Partial Success of Corporate Leniency Programs in the Laboratory, *Tinbergen Institute Working Paper*.

(2008), Laboratory Evidence on the Effectiveness of Corporate Leniency Programs, *RAND Journal of Economics*, forthcoming.

Holt, C. A. (2007), *Markets, Games, & Strategic Behavior*, Upper Saddle River, NJ: Pearson Addison Wesley.

Kroes, N. (2005), EU to beef up its cartel busters, *International Herald Tribune Business*, 11 March.

OECD (2002), Fighting Hard-Core Cartels: Harm, Effective Sanctions and Leniency Programs, Paris: OECD.

Spagnolo, G. (2004), Divide Et Impera: Optimal Leniency Programs, *CEPR Working Paper*, No. 4840.

(2006), Leniency and Whistleblowers in Antitrust, in Buccirossi, P. (Ed.), *Handbook of Antitrust Economics*, Cambridge: MIT Press.

Teulings, C. (2005), *The Wealth of Education*, Enschede: SLO.

Index

pricing
  squeeze, 117

quantity discount, 162, 173, 175

rebates
  loyalty, 112, 119, 162
  non-linear, 112, 118, 119, 161, 173
  selective, 112, 120
risk aversion, 26, 173, 259, 260
Roberts, J., 134
Roth, A. E., 1, 3, 196, 239
Ruffle, Bradley, 4, 34, 127, 128, 160,
  164, 168, 169, 170, 174, 204

Scherer, F. M., 62, 81, 82, 145, 161,
  168, 171
Schmutzler, Armin, 4, 61, 185, 194, 209
Schoonbeek, Bert, 3, 9
Selten, Reinhard, 14, 16, 20, 36, 138,
  139
Smith, Vernon, 1, 2, 17, 38, 43, 62, 63,
  64, 70, 75, 84, 126, 127, 137, 138,
  164, 166, 167
SSNIP Test, 206
Stigler, George, 14, 89, 91, 161

Sunder, S., 233
supplier switching, 172

Tirole, Jean, 10, 13, 14, 62, 140, 141,
  203, 208, 209
trade associations, 11, 22, 26, 28, 81,
  93, 96
trading institutions, 2, 16, 17, 126
transparency, 4, 35, 81, 82, 83, 84, 85,
  89, 91, 93, 94, 308, 310
Tversky, A., 193

van Damme, Eric, 4, 9, 107, 162
vertical integration, 112, 131, 140,
  141, 170, 208, 209, 210
Viianto, Lari Arthur, 5, 267

welfare, 62, 109, 110, 121, 125, 132,
  146, 173, 178, 185, 189, 194, 199,
  200, 201, 202, 205, 207, 208, 218,
  219, 225, 235
whistle-blowers *see* leniency programs
Wilson, R., 2, 62, 125, 131, 132, 138,
  139, 140, 145, 148, 168, *187*, 199,
  202, 204, 207, 237
Winkel, Barbara, 3, 9, 84

Printed in the United States
By Bookmasters